VULTURES

VULTURES

Doctors, Lawyers, Hospitals

and Insurance Companies

What's Wrong, and What to do About It

FARID A. KHAVARI, Ph.D.

ROUNDTABLE

Publishing, Inc.

 For information, address Roundtable Publishing Company, 29169 Heathercliff Road, Malibu, CA 90265.

Library of Congress Cataloging-in-Publication Data

Khavari, Farid A.

Vultures : doctors, lawyers, hospitals, and insurance companies : what's wrong, and what to do about it / by Farid A. Khavari.

p. cm.

ISBN 0-915677-52-0 : $19.95

1. Damages—United States—Popular works. 2. Personal injuries—United States—Popular works. 3. Insurance, Liability—United States—Popular works. I. Title.

KF1250.Z9K52 1990

346.7303'23—dc20 90-52811

[347.306323] CIP

CONTENTS

DEDICATION

This book is dedicated to the memory of my late wife, Louise, and to the countless other victims of the Vultures. May her senseless, tragic death, as the inspiration for this work, serve in some way to prevent the needless suffering and death of others.

ACKNOWLEDGEMENTS

Half of this book comes from my own personal experiences, and the subsequent study and research, over a period of ten years. For the rest of the information, which makes this book possible, I thank the Florida Trial Lawyers Association, the Florida Medical Association, the Florida Hospital Association, and the Insurance Information Institute. I also thank Dr. Donald Gifford, Associate Director of the Academic Task Force for Review of the Insurance and Tort System, for providing the studies made by his group. Other sources are acknowledged in the Bibliography.

This book portrays a reality that is not at all pleasant to contemplate, but which must be acknowledged if it is to be changed. There are many sincere and didicated professionals in all of these fields, who would be the first to agree that the System is overdue for change. Some of these professionals for whom I have the deepest respect and admiration are: Robert M. Sherman, M.D., Robert H. Karl, M.D., Luis E. Augsten, M.D., Victor H. Barredo, M.D., Basil M. Yates, M.D., Stephen H. Nelson, Esq., Roger L. Blackburn, Esq., and David J. White, Esq.

One group of professionals whose contribution to our nation's health is grossly underrated are the more than 30,000 Doctors of the Chiropractic. I thank one of that field's most dedicated practitioners, Chester A. Wilk, D.C., for his helpful insights.

I also salute the hundreds of thousands of good and conscientious nurses, who are truly the unsung heroes and heroines of our nation's health-care system.

I thank my loving wife, Janilla, for her patience and understanding while I was preparing this book.

This book is not a work of fiction. All of the incidents described herein are true. The names of all the participants other than Louise and myself have been changed. Any similarities that may exist between characters in this work and actual persons alive or dead is purely coincidental.

Farid A. Khavari, Ph.D.

Introduction

I wrote this book to alarm you. I also wrote this book to help you. I hope that you never need that help, but it is all too likely that you, or someone you know, will, when you least expect it. I also wrote this book to illuminate an insidious situation that is eroding our economy and threatening our way of life at this very minute to an extent that rivals the federal budget deficit, and to propose countermeasures to remedy the situation before it is too late.

This book is about a national crisis that directly affects you.

Although my background in economics may help me to recognize the broader implications of this situation, what qualifies me to tell you about it is my own experience, which I would not wish upon anyone.

Maybe you are lucky and you were not involved in one of the 33,000,000 motor vehicle accidents this year, or at least you were not one of the 5,300,000 people injured in one. Maybe you did not undergo one of the 10,000,000 or so unnecessary surgical procedures that were performed this year. Maybe you were not one of the 12 million people who turned to the legal system for redress.

If not, count your blessings, but beware: the Vultures are waiting for you.

Meanwhile, if you are lucky, this crisis is only costing you money, about $1,000 per year for every member of your family in direct costs of needless insurance, medical and legal costs. What is impossible to quantify is the overall impact on the economy as these senseless costs compound and add to the cost of every product and service we purchase.

As a nation we bravely face a new crisis every time we read the papers or watch the news. Lately we have been presented with several "crises," which individually are bad enough. What is worse is that the Liability Crisis, the Malpractice Crisis, the Lawsuit Crisis, and the Health Care Crisis are not separate and distinct issues. They are inseparably parts of a larger problem that poses a far greater threat to our nation than even the sum of its parts.

I call it our Vulture Crisis.

A vulture is a scavenger that flies around looking for something dead or helpless to feed upon, often the remains of a predator's meal. The vulture is one of nature's garbage collectors, or recycling centers. The balance of nature requires scavengers to keep it tidy. Who wants a world with rotten carrion lying all over the place? So the vulture serves a purpose under heaven and is worthy of respect. So, too, with our figurative Vultures, but there is one difference.

In the real world, the number of vultures is limited by the amount of carcasses nature serves up, and the vultures stay in their place. In the case of our metaphorical Vultures, they have transcended respectable scavenging and have become full-fledged birds of prey. They gain in numbers and voracity every day.

And they are in charge.

There are several subspecies in the World of the Vultures, including doctors, lawyers, hospitals and insurance companies. Together they form an overworld that rules us all. Their combined share of the Gross National Product eclipses the Defense budget. We already have more than enough Vultures picking at us. In every city there are tall buildings full of them. At the rate at which they are multiplying, they will eat us all alive before we know it.

We have heard from the lawyers, we have heard from the doctors, and we have heard from the insurance companies, each with their own interests, and none of them addressing the entire problem. This book looks at all of the Vultures from the same perspective: that of the victim. If it is biased, at least it is biased in favor of all of us.

The first part of the book is a grand tour through the darkest alleys of the World of the Vultures. It is a true story involving an automobile accident, medical malpractice, the senseless death of my wife, and a two-year legal ordeal. It is told to illustrate the frustrating complexity of the problem, as only a victim who has been there can know it.

Partly it is a love story, but my purpose is not to tell you a love story; it is to show that there can be no real compensation in many cases. Mostly it is a horror story, however the real horror is not my story, but the fact that it could be your story. The real horror is that similar dramas are playing thousands of times every day, starring people like you and me, in the World of the Vultures. I sincerely hope that it never happens to you or to anyone you love. But if you ever fall into the clutches of the Vultures, at least you can be prepared enough to crawl away with your life.

I followed my case day by day. I attended hearings and depositions that most victims don't see. Along the way I accumulated copies of every document, which have been used to reconstruct the story here. (The files on this routine case weigh nearly 150 pounds!) In the ten years that have passed, I have recovered my objectivity, although these events undeniably changed my life. As a human being, I see needless suffering and death. As an economist, I see senseless waste of a magnitude rivaling the federal budget deficit.

The second part of the book examines the problems that arise when doctors, lawyers, hospitals and insurance companies abdicate their proper roles in society. Doctors are supposed to heal, lawyers are supposed to work for justice, hospitals are supposed to deliver health care, insurance companies are supposed to help society function. In short, these people and institutions are supposed to serve us.

To an extent that few of us realize, if they serve us, it is for dinner. What happened?

Once you have taken the victim's-eye tour of the World of the Vultures, you will understand how far so many of society's good intentions have been perverted.

But what can we do about it? The answer begins with the realization that the blame for this situation does not belong solely to the doctors, or the lawyers, or the hospitals, or the insurance companies. Our Vulture Crisis is visited upon us by an unholy alliance of all of the Vultures.

Piecemeal approaches will not solve the problem. Capping damages to plaintiffs does nothing to prevent malpractice or negligence; in fact, it tends to have the opposite effect. Arbitrarily limiting insurance rates will only result in reduced coverage, limited availability, or bankrupt insurance companies. Limiting legal fees will reduce the quality and availability of contingency-fee lawyers, who are the only practical legal resource available to anyone who is not independently wealthy. And what can be done about skyrocketing medical costs without adverse effect on the quality and availability of health care?

At the end of the book I propose comprehensive, rational changes that would restore sanity to our system. The practical results of these changes would be safer, more affordable health care for people, improved coverage and reduced rates for health and auto insurance, better justice, and less victims. Macroeconomically, the result would be sound growth.

To your family and mine, these changes would result in immediate gains in purchasing power and simple cash savings, amounting to hundreds of dollars per person per year. However, no plan is perfect, and this one would have a side effect: it is certain to make the Vultures squawk. This would be a good indication that we were on the right track.

VULTURES

PART ONE

The Nightmare Begins

1

Dinner Is Served

The accident happened so fast that I didn't exactly experience it as much as I remembered it a minute later. It was over before it began. There was blood in my mouth, and I couldn't move.

We had walked out of the taco place. My wife, Louise, climbed into the back seat of our new burgundy Honda Accord, the first delivered to Miami, and our friend and business partner, Ed Park, got in the front seat. "Is this living or what?" he said. And we chatted on, probably about business, which was going well. I don't remember for sure; it doesn't matter now. I guess if Ed had known it was his last meal, he might have chosen something other than tacos for dinner.

I turned right onto U.S. interstate 1 to drive the few blocks to our place, where Ed's car was, in a residential neighborhood on the south side of Miami. I signaled, and moved into the center of the three southbound lanes. Ahead of me, in the left lane, a van was making a U-turn through an opening in the median. From behind the van a huge white car lunged in front of us, hitting us almost head-on at the front left corner of our car.

The sound was like a giant lightbulb exploding, and it left me deaf for a few seconds. My hearing came back to an eerie silence punctuated by bits of glass tinkling on metal. A hubcap rolled along the pavement, tipped over and spun to a stop. My hands gripped the steering wheel, which was bent back to the dash on both sides.

I don't remember my face hitting the top of the steering wheel. That must have happened as the entire front end of the car was crushed back into the firewall. I sat stunned, gaping through the shattered windshield at the folded hood of my car, and, a few inches farther, a crumpled piece of white metal, practically in my face, with gold letters: Y-S-L-E-R.

I could only move my eyes. When I tried to lift my right leg, a bolt of pain shot from my back, through my body, to where I had just been hit in the chest with a sledgehammer, which was the seatbelt. Hot, sticky blood was running down my chin and neck into my shirt. "Oh, shit, I'm paralyzed," I said to myself, although I was amazed at how calm I was.

"Louise," I half-gasped, half-moaned. "Darling, are you all right?" No answer. I couldn't turn around and look, and the rear-view mirror was gone. I tried to turn my eyes to the right. "Ed?" Nothing. They're okay, I thought to myself. They're just unconscious. The car hit on my side, and I'm alive. "Louise?" Still nothing.

I could see movement in the white car. Although my view of the car was partly obscured by the broken windshield and the bent hood of my car, I could see three young black women in the big old Chrysler. The passenger door opened and a hefty black girl in her early twenties seemed to float over to my car. She was wearing a blue football jersey with the number '69' on it in orange, partly covered by a tangle of gold chains. She put her face to the window, and I could see bits of glass sparkling in her oiled curls. She looked at us, with her mouth half open. Her lips pulled back and I could see that one of her front teeth was gold, with a heart cut out in the middle of it. Her eyes got big, and as she backed away, she screamed.

I knew my nose has been smashed, I told myself calmly, so I breathed very shallowly through my mouth, each inhalation bringing a wave of total pain, and each exhalation sputtering though the blood that was running into my mouth. I sat there, still gripping the steering wheel with both hands. The red and white lights from the first ambulance played across the windshield in front of me as it pulled up behind us from out of nowhere. It seemed like it got there ten seconds after the impact.

Doors slammed, and the back door of our car opened. A moment later I could see Louise sitting hunched over in the median in front of the car. Thank God, she was alive and seemed okay. They opened the front passenger door. "Ed?"

"Just sit tight, sir. We'll be right with you," someone said.

"I can't move," I answered, as a wave of pain turned my vision red.

"The door is too damaged. We're going to cut it out, so close your eyes." There was a terrible shrieking sound as they cut the driver's door out of my car. Somehow they got me onto a stretcher and laid me down on the median. There was a big puddle of gas around the car. They must have known that the sparks from the saw could have blown us all to bits..

"My wife..."I started.

"She'll be fine," the medic said. He had a black mustache with two gray whiskers on one side of it. He pulled off one of my shoes and tickled the bottom of my foot. "Can you feel that?" I could. "No spinal cord damage," he announced. "Thank God."

Whatever relief I felt at not being paralyzed did nothing for the pain. Thank God Louise was going to be all right, I thought. An ambulance left the scene, lights flashing and siren whooping. The medic poked around my arm, trying to find a vein. It seemed like he stabbed me twenty times before he found one. His sweat rained on me as he inserted the needle. I didn't mind much; I scarcely felt the needle over the pain that filled my body. Thank God Louise was all right.

They carried me into the ambulance, and we followed Louise to Colonial Hospital, which was less than a mile away. Louise didn't even want any tacos, I remembered. I had talked her into coming along. I guess if you knew what was going to happen, there wouldn't be any accidents. I felt that I deserved my pain for talking her into coming. I could stand it, as long as she was all right.

The next thing I knew, I was in the corridor in the emergency room at the hospital, lying on a gurney next to Louise's. I still couldn't move, but from the corner of my eye I could see her lying there, her face swollen like a purple cauliflower, with dried blood caked around her mouth. Her eyes were almost swollen shut, but I could see her breathing. The light from above was very white. I couldn't smell the hospital smell that had to be there; my nose was full of blood. I could hear people talking in hushed voices, and walking around with their soft rubber soles squeaking on the linoleum.

After a few minutes, a pleasant looking man in a white coat with a stethoscope around his neck looping up into his breast pocket, came over and stood beside me. He looked down and said, "Mr. Khavari?" I shifted my eyes to look at his face, which was surrounded by white light. "You're going to be all right now, Mr. Khavari. Do you have insurance?"

I was in shock, I suppose. I was in a hospital, and I didn't have hospitalization insurance. "No," I groaned. The pain, which had subsided for a while, was coming back. It didn't occur to me that my car insurance provided for medical payments. "Do you have any credit cards?" I had none.

"I'll pay," I said. I couldn't hear what he said as he turned and walked away.

I don't know how long we lay there, staring at the ceiling. The accident had been at about 8:30 p.m. We must have gotten to the hospital shortly after 9:00 p.m. I found out later that we were finally admitted to the hospital at 12:30 a.m. I am sure that we could have laid there and died and no one would have noticed, because no one paid us the least attention for what had to have been over two and a half hours. It was as if we didn't exist. I spoke to Louise occasionally, but she didn't answer. At least she was breathing. Finally I thought of my brother, who owned a restaurant less than two miles away. When a nurse walked by, I asked her to call him.

Before long, my brother was standing there. I was never so glad to see him. He looked at us for a second, and rushed over to the desk. He had no idea that we had not just arrived, and that is a good thing, because my brother has a temper. He signed some papers and they came and took Louise away. "She's going to be fine," my brother told me, "and you'll be okay, too. They'll get to you in a minute. Her face is pretty smashed in, but she'll be okay."

Once again I thanked God, and would have breathed a sigh of relief, but sighing would have been unimaginably painful. Then I remembered Ed. Funny, I hadn't thought of him for a long time. The doctor came over. "Ed," I asked.

"Mr. Park was killed instantly." Just like that, a punch in the stomach. In spite of the pain, my mind was instantly numb. I closed my eyes as they wheeled me down the hall. Ed hadn't been wearing his seatbelt.

As it turned out, Ed was the lucky one.

When I had been at the University of Hamburg in West Germany, I had worked for one day at one of the nearby hospitals. I couldn't take it. Ever since, I had had nightmares of having my nose broken, and of having a tube forced into my penis. I would cry out and wake up covered in sweat. How's this for a Saturday night? December 2, 1978, my worst nightmares came true. Maybe I blacked out when they did it, or maybe it was just so horrible that I have suppressed the memory for all these years. I know I couldn't move, and somehow they got that tube into me. It felt like a firehose.

The ceiling flowed by as they rolled me to room 217, my brother walking alongside. They had just gotten me into bed when they brought Louise in. Naturally, through her broken face and swollen lips, she asked how I was. Talking must have been incredibly painful for her, but her first concern was for me. Tears came to my eyes when I heard her muffled voice. Nothing could keep my Louise down.

And then she started to cry. It was hard to understand her, but finally I gathered that the X-ray technician, a man from India or Pakistan, had been impatient when she couldn't move her head, and had slapped her face to roll her head to the proper position. My brother and I didn't know what to do. We were at the mercy of these people and needed their help. We decided to let the incident pass. Anyway, I was so glad that Louise was alive, and I wasn't paralyzed, and the horror was over, I said, "Let's sleep now, darling, and the pain will be better in the morning." Her last question was about Ed. I couldn't say anything. My brother told her he didn't know for sure how Ed was, but would let us know. Thankfully, I fell asleep at once.

Little did I know that a simple automobile accident was about to turn into a major medical fiasco, and that in the days ahead I would envy Ed a lot.

The next morning, Louise asked about Ed again. I told her that Ed was dead, and she got very quiet. The stillness was broken by the arrival of the first of the parade of doctors, each of whom breezed through, I discovered, to pick at the carnage. The first was Dr. Wiesel, the partner of the good Dr. Ebner who had let us rot for nearly three hours the previous night and then had cordially welcomed us to the establishment when my brother had signed the payment guarantee. We should have gotten the hell out of there right then.

Dr. Wiesel announced that there was no blood in my urine, which meant no internal bleeding, as if he himself had caused this miracle. With that, the fire hose was yanked out of my penis. During the night it had gotten covered with broken glass, I noticed. Dr. Wiesel vanished with a wave of his healing hand and cheerful assurances that we were under the best care available. I guess maybe he had a right to be cheerful, walking around smiling at people and getting paid about fifty bucks a minute for it.

Next came Dr. Garagozlu, the neurosurgeon. He came on December 3, the day after the accident, and again on December 4. He peered at Louise, and looked in her eyes a few times, and told us that there was no brain damage. He didn't seem especially pleased. I must commend his efficiency, though; his bill arrived in the mail on December 8.

Within the first two days we were visited by Dr. Koss, the plastic surgeon, Dr. Grossinger, the dentist, Dr. Miller, the orthopedist, and the good Dr. Ebner whose title was general surgeon. When I inquired of Dr. Ebner why we had been left alone for so long in the emergency room, he replied, "I needed to know how to run your bill."

By now everyone concurred that Louise had broken her nose, cheeks, palate, jaw, chin, and various other facial bones, and was missing a few teeth. There appeared to be no further damage to her body. Drs. Koss and Grossinger were elected to fix her up. Actually, Dr. Koss warmed up on me. On December 4, he performed surgery to repair my nose, with a Dr. Walters as anesthesiologist.

I was returned to my room from the surgery just as Louise was leaving for another X-ray. I begged the nurse to take special care of her since the X-ray technician had been so rough with her, and then I fell asleep. When I woke up, Louise was laughing with my brother. She told me that I had been talking nonsense, first in English, then in German, then in my native Persian, and then mixing up the three. My brother said the same thing. It was so good to hear her laugh, and to see the sparkle in her swollen eyes.

That afternoon a different kind of vulture descended upon the carnage, in the person of Howard Bellman, Attorney-at-Law. I had been acquainted with him socially, and imagined that he was a friend. I had a great deal of respect for Mr. Bellman, as we regular people tend to have for attorneys. Mr. Bellman was a stocky guy, about five feet six, with wavy dark hair combed back from a high forehead.

He said he was sorry about our accident. Actually, he looked about as sorry as a body shop manager when they tow in a crumpled Ferrari. Later I discovered that the analogy wasn't quite accurate: at least the body shop man hopes the Ferrari isn't totaled. The lawyer's job is so much easier when the client is dead, preferably horribly, needlessly dead. I didn't realize then that in the World of the Vultures, this guy was just a little hatchling, handling real estate closings, petty lawsuits, and the like. Well, all we needed was someone to collect on the insurance for us, so I signed the contract he happened to have in his pocket, agreeing to give him a third of the money received from the insurance company. Our insurance company. And, of course, forty percent if he had to sue to get it.

It was around this time that Dr. Gozar, an Iranian doctor, came to visit us. He had nothing to do with our treatment; he had seen our name on the roster and found out that I was Iranian, and had just come on a social call. We chattered away happily in Persian until I told him Louise was Dutch, so we switched back to English. He told us he was sorry about our accident, wished us a speedy recovery, and invited us to his home as soon as we got out of there. Dr. Gozar was very intrigued by our solar energy business, and seemed to be interested in investing in the company.

On the evening of December 7, Dr. Leonard Cooley, an anesthesiologist, came to see Louise. He talked with her for a few minutes and described the surgery that was to be performed on her the next morning. Dr. Koss also came by to reassure us.

At 7:30 on the morning of December 8, Dr. Koss performed the first surgery on Louise. He worked on her chin and jaw, and cut under her eyes to work on her cheek bones. The surgery lasted about two and a half hours, and Louise returned to our room at about one o'clock in the afternoon, after spending over two hours in the recovery room. The surgery was successful, but Louise's cheeks were so swollen that her eyes were closed, and remained so for four days. We had not been told to expect this, and when we asked Dr. Koss about it, he said, "I am sorry."

Gradually, I was regaining my ability to move, and the pain was subsiding. By the time of Louise's first surgery, I was able to make it to the bathroom by myself, thus ending my adventures with the bedpan, and not a minute too soon. An annoying thing about Colonial Hospital, with all of its nurses, was the fact that whenever you pushed the call button, no one came. After a few minutes, a voice would come on the intercom asking, "Can I help you?" Now, when a person's face is smashed in and her jaw wired, it is pretty difficult for them to talk, especially loudly enough for the intercom. So, we were left alone a great deal of the time. Fortunately, I was able to help Louise with the bedpan, day and night, and I stayed awake, watching over her, for almost the entire four days while her eyes were swollen shut.

Another thing that annoyed us very much was Louise's diet. Hospital food is not known as haute cuisine, but I managed on the bland food they brought me. Louise, on the other hand, couldn't chew, so her diet consisted of tea and a chemical brew euphemistically referred to as soup. After several complaints to Dr. Wiesel, a nurse and a nutritionist came to see us. The nutritionist changed Louise's diet to one heavy on milk and ice cream. This had to be an improvement over the witches' brew of before, but certainly did nothing to help build up Louise's tired blood.

On December 9, Louise's parents, the van Bussels, called from Holland to tell us they would be coming to Miami on the 12th. Louise was very pleased and looked forward to their visit. Although her eyes were swollen shut, Louise was beginning to talk better, and her spirits were high. We laughed and joked about our pathetic situation, and dreamed of going home.

On the morning of the 12th, I was ready to be discharged from the hospital. While Louise slept, I gathered up all of the flowers our friends had sent us and placed them on the two rolling tables that they used to feed us. I arranged the tables so that when Louise woke up she would be surrounded by flowers. When she woke up, however, she was startled and got a funny look on her face that made me forget to breathe for a moment. "Darling," she said slowly, "I feel like I am at my own funeral. Please take them away."

At least her eyes were open again. As I left, promising to return later in the day, Valerie Russo, a nurse's aide, came to clean Louise's eyes. These two talked together often, and I was sure that they would be good friends as soon as Louise was released. I was happy about this, because Louise didn't have any real girl friends here yet. How the performance of this one nurse's aide contrasted with that of the entire rest of the nursing staff!

On my way out of the hospital, I was delivered into the office of a Mr. Smith, the hospital administrator, for a friendly chat about our monumental hospital bill. I assured him that the bill would be covered by our car insurance, and signed papers authorizing the insurance company to pay the hospital directly. When I looked over the bill, I noticed that the partnership of Wiesel and Ebner was billing each of us for a consultation each day. I flashed back to Ebner saying, "I needed to know how to run your bill."

"One or the other of these guys breezes by each morning, and says, 'Hi, how are you?' and waves, without even coming into the room, and they charge fifty dollars each time, for each of us?" I was outraged.

"Relax, your insurance will cover it," Mr. Smith said gently.

"That doesn't make it right," I said. "These two doctors aren't doing a thing for us. They're general surgeons, and now the case is being handled by Dr. Koss and Dr. Grossinger. Please take these guys off the case at once."

Louise called Wiesel and Ebner the "sunny boys" because of the way they would fly by smiling. Now I knew why they were smiling. What I did not know was what a big mistake I was making.

Later that afternoon, Donna Lang, the head nurse, told me that no one had ever discharged a doctor in this hospital before, and that it could "cause some inconvenience." I didn't realize yet just how dangerous stepping on their majesties' egos could be.

My brother and I went to Miami International Airport to pick up Louise's parents. As soon as we met them, we called the hospital so they could talk with Louise, and then we drove directly to the hospital. When we arrived, our friends, Sally and Donald Meyer and Patricia Sachs were visiting Louise. They left shortly after being introduced to Louise's parents.

Louise and her parents talked non-stop in Dutch until eleven that night. I don't speak Dutch, but it is similar enough to German that I could understand that she was telling them all about what had happened to us since we had returned to America on October 16. Seeing her parents seemed to bring Louise the rest of the way back to her old self. Although I took little part in the conversation, and sat on the sidelines with my brother, I was relieved and delighted to see Louise in such excellent spirits. She asked her parents to bring her some handicrafts to occupy her during the time she was alone in the hospital.

On the 13th and 14th we came to the hospital at 9:30 in the morning and stayed with Louise until one o'clock in the afternoon, when we went out for lunch. We came back each afternoon and stayed with Louise until eleven or so at night. On the afternoon of the 14th, Dr. Ebner dropped by, looking a little forlorn. He told us that he and his wife had lost a child the previous year, and that one of his other children was mongoloid. Louise and I felt very sorry for Dr. Ebner, but in the days to come he didn't seem to need our compassion. I guess that his and Dr. Wiesel's real concerns were for their reputations.

That evening the woman in room 217 was the girl I had fallen in love with ten years earlier. She laughed and talked, and spent a lot of the evening catching up on paperwork for our business, which had gotten behind while we were in the hospital. She visited with her parents and our friend Rod Sachs who dropped by. She wrote a letter to my parents in Iran. Later in the evening, Dr. Koss, the plastic surgeon, and Dr. Forstmann, an anesthesiologist, came to see her.

After they left, Louise told us that when she returned from surgery the next day, we were not to be alarmed. "Darling, if there is a tube in my mouth, that is only for breathing. The doctors told me that I will need it." Dr. Forstmann had also told her that there was not enough hemoglobin in her blood, which could cause problems with the anesthesia, but that there was nothing to worry about, as he would have fresh blood standing by for a transfusion if needed.

Then Louise got out of her bed, embraced and kissed her parents, and they left us alone together. She put her arms around me and said, "My parents are very diplomatic, to leave us alone." We laughed about that. I told her how much I loved her and that she meant the world to me. A careful kiss, "bye-bye," and that was it. I did not imagine that I would never talk with her again.

They had told us that Louise would be back from surgery at 1:30 p.m. the next day, December 15. My parents-in-law and I paced around the townhouse all morning, and finally went out to lunch to fill the time. On the way, we each got a big long-stem red rose for Louise. We went to the same taco place where we had gone that fateful Saturday night. As we were sitting there, a feeling of foreboding came over me and I couldn't eat any more. "Come on," I said, "we have to get to the hospital right away." I rushed out, with my worried in-laws at my heels. We arrived on the second floor of the hospital at exactly 1:30 p.m.

As we got out of the elevator, I saw the head nurse, Donna Lang. I asked her whether Louise was back from surgery yet, and was told that she had been in her room since 12:40. I rushed into room 217. Louise was alone. The silence in the room was broken only by her struggle to breathe. She was almost panting, as if she had just run a fast mile. I went over to her and called her name, but she seemed to be in a deep sleep. I shook her, but got no response. I went back into the hall and asked Donna Lang to come right away and see how Louise was breathing.

Donna was filling out some reports, and scarcely glanced up. She said I would have to wait for a couple of minutes, and went on with her paperwork. Finally she came, looked at Louise, and told us that everything was normal, and not to worry, and she left.

As she left, she moved the rolling tray-table next to the bed. On it I saw two napkins, each with a happy face and a message in Louise's handwriting. The first was in Dutch and said, "Mom and Dad, I am glad you are here, Love, Loes," which was her nickname. The other was in German, for me: "My Treasure, I love you so much! Love from your Jewel," which was one of my pet names for her.

My in-laws and I sat for a while, watching Louise struggle for every breath. We didn't take our eyes off her. Finally, I couldn't stand it anymore and went out to call for another nurse. This time Mary Knopfloch came. She moved the pillows around and said the same thing: everything is normal, don't worry. How could we not worry? The nurse disappeared and left us watching our Louise fight for each little breath of air. Worry? Hell, I had never felt so helpless in my life.

Again I went looking for a nurse, and this time I came up with Valerie Masters. I approached her with dread; from my stay in the hospital I knew that this woman got upset whenever you asked her for anything. I guess she could see the concern in my face, because although she looked annoyed and put-upon, she didn't say anything, but followed me back to Louise. Valerie rearranged the pillows, took a suction tube and ran it around inside Louise's mouth. She told us everything was normal, and not to worry.

By 3:30, Louise's breathing had become dangerousely shallow. I ran out of the room to find a nurse. Pressing the buzzer would do no good. I spotted Donna Lang and asked her to come see Louise. She replied that her duty was over and she had to go home. My mouth fell open in astonishment. After a moment of hesitation, she came to Louise's bedside and repeated the familiar refrain: everything is normal, don't worry. Donna Lang hurried on home.

This time I simply could not believe it. I immediately went back to the nurses' station. This time I found Barbara MacMillan. Dr. Wiesel was standing nearby. He kept looking at his clip board and pretended not to notice me. I said to Barbara, loudly enough for anyone on the floor to hear, "My wife is having trouble breathing. Could you come quickly, please?" Dr. Wiesel kept on reading his charts, and Barbara followed me back into Louise's room, which was perhaps twenty feet away. She checked Louise's pulse and said that she was going to call for a doctor. She returned to the nurses' station and picked up the phone.

Whether Dr. Wiesel heard her call for a doctor, or whether she ever reached any doctor, I will never know. Certainly no one came. After a few eternal minutes, a young nurse's aide named Louise King came in, checked Louise's pulse, and ran out like a rocket to sound a Code Blue (patient in acute respiratory distress). Dr. Wiesel continued to stand in the hall, twenty feet away. Why he did not respond to a Code Blue, least of all twenty feet away from him, I don't know. There must have been something pretty interesting on that chart. Perhaps he didn't want to save a patient who had had the cheek to fire him.

More time passed. Six minutes, seven minutes, ten. With the telephone calls for the doctors and the Code Blue, someone had to come any second, I kept telling myself. I was frantic, pacing and praying. I went back into the hall to see why the hell no one was coming. And along came Dr. Walters, the anesthesiologist from my own nose surgery, strolling along, completely unaware of the crisis. He just happened to be there. I thanked God and rushed Walters into the room.

Dr. Walters took one look at Louise, called for a nurse and "the cart", and immediately ordered us to wait in the lounge at the end of the hall.

For the next few minutes we paced the floor of the lounge. We were scared out of our minds that something terrible had happened to Louise; had been happening all the time we were watching her, but we told ourselves that now a doctor was finally paying attention to her and she would be all right.

After the longest few minutes of my life, the nurse came out and told us that Louise had had a cardiac arrest, but that Dr. Walters had revived her. They quickly moved Louise to Intensive Care, where Dr. Forstmann, the anesthesiologist from that morning's surgery, was on duty. He had finally made it to Louise's room in time to help Dr. Walters. Apparently Barbara MacMillan had reached him, but had not described the situation as "urgent."

Dr. Walters came out of Intensive Care and told us of Louise's critical condition and that there could be some brain damage due to the cardiac arrest. I asked what would happen, whether she would be all right, all of the pathetic questions someone in my helpless position would ask. He looked grim and said we would just have to wait and see.

After Dr. Walters left, Barbara MacMillan appeared and started to explain the situation to me. When I asked why she didn't react faster when she saw Louise's condition, she said that she had immediately gotten on the phone and called Dr. Forstmann. I still couldn't understand why she had not sounded the Code Blue herself. Anyway, we went back down the hall to wait for more news.

Dr. Gozar, the Iranian, came by after a few minutes. I told him what had happened, and he was appalled. He asked me who the anesthesiologist was, and I told him Dr. Forstmann. He said, "I just don't understand him leaving her alone in her room like that right after surgery. He always baby-sits his patients. It doesn't make any sense." He was further astonished by Donna Lang's telling us that her duty was over and she had to go home, when we had asked her to help Louise. Dr. Gozar told Barbara MacMillan that this was an outrage.

Presently a Dr. Manson came and introduced himself as a pulmonary specialist. He told us Louise was on the heart and lung machine. At this very moment, Howard A. Bellman, Attorney-at-Law, walked in. I had had an appointment with him at my place that afternoon, which I had not kept. He had the instinctive sense of timing that makes vultures such viable life forms, I'll say that for him.

When Dr. Manson went on to say that Louise was in a coma, and that we had to be prepared for the strong possibility of brain damage, Howard Bellman, Attorney-at-Law, just about tinkled in his wingtips. I was numb, but not so numb as to miss the feeling that my world was coming to an end.

I made it into Louise's room. I walked toward her bed, somehow certain that she would turn to me and smile, but already knowing she could not. Dr. Forstmann came in and expressed his sympathies to my parents-in-law and me, I told him what had happened that day, about the carelessness of the nurses. I was careful not to say anything that would reflect badly on a doctor, though. I felt that the good will of the doctors was my only hope of getting Louise back.

Meanwhile, Howard Bellman was talking with my brother. This was an obvious case of medical malpractice here, said Howard, and we should be compensated for it, very much. He said that he would personally see to it that justice was done for the same percentages previously agreed upon. When my brother explained this, I nodded dumbly, my mind not really on the conversation. Howard made some sympathetic sound, and left.

The next day, the 16th of December, there was no change in Louise's condition. Dr. Garagozlu, the neurosurgeon, and Dr. Martin, a neurologist, visited Louise. They told us that there was indeed brain damage, but they couldn't say how much. If Louise were to wake up within three days, there would be some hope. If not, then they didn't know.

An odd thing happened that afternoon. Dr. Forstmann came to see me. He started by telling me how sorry he felt, and how we had his sympathy. Then he told me that in order to prevent anything like this from ever happening again, he had hired an investigator. He wanted me to repeat what I had told him the day before. I told him that I would not mind repeating the facts, and that he should talk to my lawyer. I didn't want to tell him that, as far as I was concerned, the greatest part of the responsibility for Louise's predicament was his. Then again, perhaps he had hired the investigator to try and cover his own ass. I don't know.

We wanted further opinions, and Dr. Martin, who was by now somehow in charge of the case, obliged by calling in Drs. Glenn Muezzin and Basil Gates, both neurosurgeons, to examine Louise. Dr. Muezzin seemed optimistic. He told my brother and me that it was not a question of whether Louise would wake up, but of when, and of how great the extent of the brain damage would be. Dr. Gates was less enthusiastic, but suggested some particular medicine. No one paid attention to him. Dr. Martin told me that Dr. Gates belonged to the old generation, and that his old-fashioned medicine worked in theory but not in practice.

Over the next couple of days, Louise began to improve. She could breathe on her own, her eyes were moving, and she even opened her eyes completely three different times. She moved her hands and her body, and responded to pain. She also responded to our talking. When I would say something emotional, like telling her I loved her, she seemed to respond even more. Her lips would move, and I was sure that she was trying to say something. Within four days she would squeeze a hand that squeezed hers.

One evening, I went to see Louise as usual, and I ran into Dr. Grossinger, the dental surgeon, in the Intensive Care Unit. I asked him several questions about Louise's condition. When I asked him what time Louise's surgery had been finished on December 15, he looked at her records for a moment and said, "12:30."

"Then how in the hell did she get through the recovery room and back to her room by 12:40, which is the time Donna Lang says she got there?" I demanded. Dr. Grossinger looked somewhat disturbed.

"I can't read anywhere exactly," he said carefully, "but I think it was 12:15. I really don't know." Was he really baffled, or was he trying to smooth over the obvious negligence that had taken place?

On the fourth day of Louise's stay in Intensive Care, Dr. Koss said that in order to protect Louise's larynx from damage that would result from leaving the breathing tube in her mouth and throat, he was going to remove the tube and perform a tracheotomy, opening a hole in Louise's throat that would allow her to breathe somewhat normally. He said that Dr. Forstmann was coming to handle the anesthesia. At first I told him that I didn't want Forstmann anywhere near Louise, but then I figured that Forstmann's conscience might make him extra careful, so I said go ahead. The operation was a success.

Dr. Koss looked a little pale, and there were dark circles under his eyes. I asked him if he was feeling all right, and he said that he had not slept the night before. He had had a dream about Louise. Dr. Koss had been visibly upset about Louise since her difficulties had begun.

Each day Louise seemed to improve a little bit. Dr. Koss and Dr. Martin started to act somewhat optimistic, telling us that her reactions now seemed to be with purpose, and not just reflexes. Dr. Koss said that when he tried to insert a tube through her nose to feed her liquids, she rejected the tube by turning her head. We began to be hopeful that Louise, even with a little brain damage, would come back to us. To celebrate, my brother and his family, my parents-in-law and I went out for dinner at a fancy restaurant on Biscayne Bay in Coconut Grove.

One afternoon when my in-laws, my brother and I were walking across the hospital parking lot on the way to visit Louise, we ran into Frank Cunnings, the business office manager of the hospital. We exchanged greetings, and he asked about Louise's condition. I told him that there were signs of improvement.

He said, "Great. And I want you to know that you can be sure everyone will do their best. The administration of the hospital is strongly involved in this case." He gave a cheery wave and we parted. As I walked into the hospital, I asked myself what he had meant by that. Were they beginning to recognize their responsibility?

All of us visited Louise four or five times every day. Our lives revolved around trips to the hospital, where we would eagerly look for even the slightest sign of improvement, and encourage each other. Each time we came to the Intensive Care Unit and announced ourselves, we were told to wait for fifteen or twenty minutes. It was as if we had dropped in on a neighbor unexpectedly and they rushed around picking up the living room before letting us in. Each time we found Louise freshly cleaned up, sometimes with her skin still damp. One nurse, not too sharp, told us we would have to wait while they cleaned Louise up before we could come in!

Anyway, the care given in I.C.U. was not always as intensive as I would have expected. Whenever the shift changed, the nurses from both shifts would go into the coffee room for fifteen to thirty minutes while the departing shift reported to the incoming one. More than once my brother and I walked right into the Unit after having rung the phone for minutes on end without an answer. Obviously, no one was watching the monitors, either. What if something happened to one of the patients and no one noticed for fifteen minutes?

The Intensive Care Unit was the domain of one particularly brutal nurse, Trudi Berns, a chunky blonde in her mid-thirties. The first night that Louise was in Intensive Care, I saw Trudi telling one patient to stretch his leg. This was obviously very difficult for the old man. Finally, she grabbed his leg and jerked it to where she wanted it, while the man cried out in pain.

Each time Trudi was on duty as I sat by Louise's bed, Trudi would come in and tell me matter-of-factly that I shouldn't have too much hope for Louise's recovery, and that Louise didn't respond when Trudi called her name. Now you hear all the time that the sense of hearing is the last sense a person loses, and that many people have recovered from comas and reported that they had heard the doctors and nurses give them up for dead, so talking like this in Louise's room didn't make any sense to me at all.

Realizing that Louise was at the mercy of this woman bothered me a great deal. Finally I couldn't stand it anymore. One evening Trudi came in with her gloom and doom routine. I held my tongue, and took my brother home with me. We were supposed to have dinner out with my in-laws. I made up some excuse about waiting for a phone call from my brother in Germany, and the three of them went out without me.

I immediately got in the car and returned to the hospital. I went straight to the Intensive Care Unit and stood in front of Trudi Berns. I glared at her, but I spoke very quietly and evenly. I told her that her attitude was brutal, and that even if Louise was not progressing well-and even if there was no hope at all, the fact was that Louise was alive and could quite possibly hear the negative things she said. I told her she should keep her comments well away from Louise.

Trudi could see how serious I was, and wisely kept still until my quiet tirade was over. I am sure that if she had given me the least excuse I would have torn her head off.

Early on the morning of Saturday, December 23, I was standing at Louise's bedside, talking softly to her, when Dr. Martin appeared beside me. He asked whether I noticed any change in Louise, and I had to admit that I did not. He told me that this morning Louise's eyes had stopped moving, and the pupils did not respond to light. He said there was danger of extensive brain-stem damage, and that he wanted to send her immediately to Baptist Hospital for some tests. It had to be right away, he said, because tomorrow was a Sunday, Monday was Christmas, and Tuesday would be far too late. I did not have to be convinced. I followed her to Baptist Hospital, where Dr. Martin's suspicions were confirmed: extensive brain-stem damage had occurred. Louise was returned to Colonial Hospital.

Dr. Martin said that he wanted to take "precautionary measures" to prevent any further damage. What these measures might have been, he did not say. Perhaps he changed her medication; I don't know. He did not, however, place her on a respirator.

At 2:40 a.m. on December 25, a nurse called to tell me that Louise had had another cardiac arrest, and that I should come immediately because it looked like the end. I called my brother, and he and our friend Donald Meyer met my parents-in-law and me at the hospital less than half an hour later. Dr. Martin was there, and told us that Louise's brain was completely damaged, that there was no brain wave activity at all. Prior to this there had been as much as half of normal activity, he explained. Dr. Martin wanted me to decide to stop all support measures. I refused, numbly and stubbornly clinging to my torturing hopes.

My brother asked Dr. Martin how Louise could have been allowed to have a second cardiac arrest, especially since it was known that there was brain-stem damage. Dr. Martin shook his head and said, "I don't know. I am baffled." A wave of anger washed over me. I told him that if he was baffled, he should get another doctor to help him, not just stand around and let my wife die. My reaction cornered him, and when I demanded to know why he had not taken these so-called precautions before, he replied that doctors and nurses are overworked. That stopped me for a second. His answer was shameless and arrogant.

I told Dr. Martin that if he or anybody else was too tired to do his job properly, he should turn over his responsibility to someone else. I told him that there were thousands of jobs where one could make good money without fooling around with other people's lives, and that if he wasn't capable of being a doctor, he should get out of that line of work. I told him that at one time I had wanted to become a physician, and had quickly learned that I was not cut out for it, and had become an economist. At least in my field, I could only mess up with money, and I couldn't kill anyone. I guess I made it clear that I was very upset with him and his stupid answer. Finally I calmed down a little, and Dr. Martin mumbled something and left quietly.

Slowly I was beginning to get the feeling—a feeling I cannot get rid of even today, that a "strongly involved" hospital administration had made the decision that keeping Louise alive was pointless. It is said that doctors bury their mistakes, and having made an irreversible mistake in Louise's treatment, what else could they do? Painlessly dead, she would soon be forgotten. Alive, she would be a helpless, damning reminder, and infinitely more expensive to the hospital, doctors, and their insurance companies.

Another test the next day reaffirmed the diagnosis: no brain waves. I left the decision to Dr. Martin. I don't know who stopped the life-supports on December 27, but it happened, and a part of me died, too.

My parents-in-law, my brother and I started to gather around Louise's bed for a final prayer. In stormed Trudi Berns, primly informing us that we were not all allowed in there together. My brother began to turn purple, and even in my numbness my temper began to boil. I don't know what would have happened if the head nurse had not called Trudi away and apologized to us.

I went home very late that night. As I went to sleep, I prayed that I would never wake up.

In 1971, Louise and I had made a trip to visit my parents, in Yazd, Iran. There we visited the large stone block, surrounded by high stone walls, where the Zoroastrians leave their dead—to be eaten by the vultures. As I mustered the strength to deal with the funeral arrangements, it suddenly struck me that things weren't all that different here in America.

My brother, who had attended Ed's funeral on our behalf, said that the Everest Funeral Home was beautiful and tasteful, so we went there. I was impressed by the understanding and courtesy of the somber man who explained their services and took me into the showroom to select a casket. I had no idea there were so many kinds of caskets. He showed me the basic, bottom-of-the-line models, and spoke warmly of the deluxe features of the high-priced ones. When he started to talk about how much more comfortable a silk-lined casket was, I quickly settled on a "mid-priced" job, at nearly $2,000.

We arranged to have the ceremony on December 29, with burial to follow at the Everest Memorial Park.

I must admit that the funeral home was most accommodating in signing me up for a convenient payment schedule. With the numbness from Louise's death to anesthetize me, these Vultures extracted their piece of flesh most painlessly.

The next stop was at the cemetery. Even in my grief I could not help but observe that this was some pricey real estate. Once again, I was at least treated with dignity. The black-suited gentleman explained that the Park was divided into different sections, according to what type of monument would be installed on the final resting place of the departed. He was certain that I would want something better than a plain, flat marker set into the ground, and I agreed. This, of course, meant that the departed would rest in one of the better parts of the Park. That is where the prices were just about double. To keep out the riffraff, I suppose.

This was of no concern to me. I loved Louise and would have built a cathedral in her memory if I could have. I could have made a sizable down-payment on one, by the time it developed that you had to get two resting places side by side to place a respectable monument. And there were not two available. Would I prefer three, or five?

Once again, with the utmost of dignity and courtesy, a convenient payment plan was arrived at, and I gave instructions for Louise to be buried in the center of my three gravesites.

Through it all, I functioned as if I were participating in a movie. I was insulated by my grief. My brother never left my side, and for that I will always be grateful to him.

Louise had always favored organ donations, and I authorized the donation of her eyes and kidneys. At least part of her lives on, having saved a life and given sight to two blind people. The autopsy named the primary cause of death as, "...right lower lobe pneumonia due to hypoxic encephalopathy." The autopsy also revealed that Louise's jaw had been wired after the second surgery, which the doctors had told us was not the case, when she was sent to her room alone immediately following the surgery with her nose full of gauze and no breathing tube.

Whatever the real name of Louise's primary cause of death, it didn't matter. But whatever the case, her life ended in a physcian's care. Looking back, I am sure that my anger is what kept me alive.

When I went to see Louise at the funeral home, I didn't recognize her. The surgery had made a mockery of her beautiful face, and with the make-up she looked like a little Mongol girl, with a round flat face and flat nose. In a way, I suppose this helped me maintain my composure. But when I saw her hands—Louise's hands and wrists crossed on her breast, I cried.

The funeral home was filled with flowers and wreathes sent by our family and friends. One arrangement of roses had a little card that said, "With our sympathy, from your lawyer." Once a friend, now a Vulture. I guess that if he had signed the card as a friend, he could not have deducted the flowers from his taxes.

On the afternoon of the funeral, as our friends and family were assembling for the service, Howard A. Bellman, Attorney-at-Law, walked in excitedly and went straight to my brother, waving a piece of paper. I could see that he was overcome with joy, and I was amazed at the complete inappropriateness of his manner. Later, my brother told me why Howard was so elated. The piece of paper was a letter from Stanley Rosenbloom, one of America's most famous malpractice attorneys, right here in Miami. Stanley Rosenbloom agreed to handle our case. As part of his standard attorney agreement, Howard had the right to employ whatever trial counsel he chose. As part of the normal arrangement in such matters, Howard would receive one-third of Mr. Rosenbloom's forty percent share of whatever glorious verdict—and Howard was sure it would be exemplary—that Mr. Rosenbloom would win for us.

No wonder Howard was happy. My tragedy was his ticket to the "big time." I guess every cloud does have a silver lining.

The guests at the funeral filed past me, murmuring their condolences. My parents-in-law were in shock, and sat woodenly between spells of weeping. I retreated into myself, and took little solace from friends or family. My real comfort on that terrible day was my little nephew, Jason, who was not quite four years old. He quietly came over to me, climbed up into my lap, and put his arms around my neck without a word.

After Louise's casket was lowered into the ground, I stood at the head of the open grave with a red rose in my hand. I closed my eyes and remembered Louise, alive and well and in my arms, smiling at me, kissing me. I looked at the red rose in my hand, and remembered the single red rose I had brought for her on the day of her second surgery. I dropped the rose onto the casket and slowly walked away. To this day, red roses are no longer tokens of love; to me, they symbolize death.

And that is how I said good-bye to the woman who had been everything to me for the ten years I had known her. I buried her on our sixth wedding anniversary.

2

Table Manners

I was destroyed. I had no drive, no ambition, no desire, no will to live. My family and friends came to help me, bringing food and sympathy. Always the conversation turned to, "You ought to sue" or "You've got to get the bastards. Sue them!" And so on. I needed their sympathy, and their sincere feelings that a terrible thing had been done. I naively imagined that I could bring the murderers to justice, that these doctors could be arrested, imprisoned, fined, or at least lose their licenses before some other poor patient lost her life, or some other husband lost his wife, or some child his mother.

After a few days I went to see Howard Bellman, Attorney-at-Law. Mr. Bellman expressed his condolences, and assured me that a grievous wrong had been done. At least a million dollars worth, he said. He was having a hard time staying seated. He was eager to call Stanley Rosenbloom, the big-time malpractice lawyer who had accepted my case, and arrange an appointment to get the wheels of justice turning. I guess that I should not have been surprised when I got the feeling that Howard's motives were a little less than altruistic.

"Meanwhile, Howard," I said, "about the insurance money. There are hospital bills to pay, and I'm in no condition to be working right now. Since we are going to win a million dollars, and since Stanley Rosenbloom is going to get four hundred thousand of it, and since you are going to get about a hundred and thirty-some thousand of that, couldn't you please just fill out the paperwork to collect from the insurance company, my insurance company, and waive your fee for that?"

Howard Bellman, Attorney-at-Law, looked at me like I had just peed on his carpet. "I couldn't do that," he said indignantly. "That wouldn't be right." I guess his idea of what was right involved getting paid twenty or thirty thousand dollars to collect the money that was mine under the terms of my insurance policy. I was to find out later that getting what is yours from your own insurance company is not quite that easy. I asked Howard to please reconsider. By now his attitude was beginning to upset me. He wouldn't budge, and I went home. At least his greed and callousness were starting to wake me from my empty stupor.

As I was driving home, I remembered visiting an attorney with a friend recently, concerning my friend's business. The attorney's name was Joseph Black and when I got home I rummaged around on my desk and found his card. I called and made an appointment for the next afternoon.

Joseph Black listened to my story with an attentive gaze that nearly showed sympathy. He asked a few questions, and advised me to fire Howard Bellman if I wanted him to handle the case. He then told me the first concrete, sensible thing I had heard from an attorney. He told me to write down the entire story, complete in every detail, however insignificant it might seem. I should start with the accident and continue through the entire experience with the hospital, doctors and nurses. I wondered why Howard Bellman had not told me to do that.

Mr. Black told me that when I was finished, we would meet with a highly successful trial lawyer about my case. Joseph Black said that it sure looked like a million-dollar situation to him. He was smiling as he shook my hand.

Now I had a purpose, and something meaningful to do about it. I wrote a letter to Howard Bellman, expressing my regrets at his uncompromising attitude concerning fees, and, well, firing him. As Joseph Black had explained to me, any time you have a lawyer working on a contingency contract (that is, an agreement whereby the lawyer gets paid a percentage of what he collects) you can fire him any time before a settlement or verdict is reached, and only have to pay him for actual time and expenses spent on your case. Actually, what I was doing was pushing a small vulture away from the carrion to make room for a larger one. Vultures' rules of order.

I set to the task of writing a detailed account of the accident and the events at the hospital with single-minded zeal. It was painful reliving every moment of that horrible time, but it was a step on the road to justice, I believed, and I owed it to Louise to see that justice was done. Perhaps my expectations of justice were a little naive, but I was new in America and took things like "justice for all" at face value then.

Another thing I took at face value was lawyers. To me, the law was the law, and therefore, since they were trained to know the law, a lawyer was a lawyer. This simply is not true; there are lawyers for every type of case, and just because a lawyer is successful in landlord-tenant disputes or immigration matters does not mean he is qualified to handle a business merger or a malpractice case any more than a proctologist is qualified to perform brain surgery.

And, as I was to learn, there are also some lawyers who are just plain incompetent, just as some doctors are.

For two days and nights I worked feverishly on my report, barely sleeping and scarcely eating. I finally took a break and went to my brother's restaurant for dinner. There I got into a conversation with Jerry the bartender, who was familiar with the situation. "I'll tell you who you need," Jerry said. "You need Peter Fox. This guy is just about the biggest malpractice lawyer in the country, I guess, and his office is right downtown. When I was tending bar on Key Biscayne he came in all the time, and told me stories you would not believe. This guy wins million-dollar verdicts like you or I go to the bathroom." I thanked Jerry for his advice, and made a mental note to ask Joseph Black about this champion of justice.

On the third day, I finished my report and took it to Joseph Black's office for his secretary to type it. When I got home, there was a letter from Howard Bellman, Attorney-at-Law. It was two pages long, and explained in fine detail why I should not fire him, and so on, although he did not point to one single thing he had done to even begin getting the insurance money. He did point out that he had spoken to Stanley

Rosenbloom's office "on more than one occasion."

The paragraph that caught my eye stated that "...there are cases in the State of Florida that say before the case is settled or a settlement offer is made a contingency fee contract cannot be enforced. Clearly I have achieved no settlement offer for you and I am entitled to no percentage of the fees collected, unless your attorneys and yourself choose to settle my lien against your case in this matter (sic)." I was truly amazed that Howard Bellman knew all along what thin ice he was standing on, yet had stood by his fees until he sank.

A couple of days later, I signed a contingency contract with Joseph Black and learned that he had made an appointment with none other than Peter Fox.

When we entered the hushed office of Fox and Altman, P.A., we were surrounded by framed newspaper clippings, each attesting to some million-dollar, or $800,000, or other massive verdict awarded to Peter Fox's fortunate clients. After a few minutes we were shown into a conference room, whose floor-to-ceiling windows looked out over downtown Miami twenty stories below.

A moment later, two men came in. The first, a slight, sixty-ish man who looked exactly like a cross between David Brinkley and Richard Nixon, introduced himself as Peter Fox and shook hands with me and Joseph Black. Joseph acted like a village priest who had just met the Pope. He couldn't help looking at his hand out of the corner of his eye, as if in disbelief. Peter Fox introduced the other man, of medium build, perhaps thirty-two, with dark curly hair and a beard, as James B. Altman, one of his junior partners.

The famous Peter Fox, champion of the underdog and slayer of giants, looked about as awe-inspiring as a wet newspaper. Surely all of his victories had taken a lot out of him to reduce him to such a mild-mannered gentleman. I was to learn later that the crack of his tongue could silence a room full of high-priced defense lawyers.

Mr. Fox told me that he was sorry about what had happened. He commended me for my thorough report on the matter, which he had read, and said that his firm would handle my case if I wished. I felt pretty good about that, and I really liked this guy, and felt an affinity for James Altman as well.

Then Peter Fox got down to what was going to happen. To my surprise, none of what I hoped for in the way of justice was even remotely possible. At the worst, the doctors would be inconvenienced by having to give a few depositions, and their insurance premiums might go up. Naturally their insurance companies would provide them with the finest legal talent that money could buy.

Mr. Fox was not interested in going after the driver of the other car in the accident, who had no driver's license and no insurance. That, he said, would be a complete waste of money and time.

"What we are going to do," he said, "is sue absolutely everybody in that hospital, sue them all, and let them point fingers at each other. We'll sit back and pick out the guilty ones."

Now that made a lot of sense to me. I signed papers requiring the hospital to turn over copies of Louise's and my medical records to Fox's firm, and a contract giving one-third of the proceeds of my case to Fox's firm if it could be settled without trial or mediation, or forty percent if the case required that much work. And I agreed to pay the expenses. Mr. Fox explained that if we did not prevail, there would be no attorney fees, but that I would still have to pay for the expenses incurred. When I asked how much that might be, he said, "In a case like this I'd say, oh, seven, eight, maybe ten thousand dollars. I can't see it being over that."

Joseph Black already had the standard agreement with Fox that gave him a third of whatever Fox got out of the case.

"Your report will be turned over to our in-house private investigator this afternoon, and he will go get the hospital records," Fox continued. "We will be in touch with you in person." After handshakes all around, we left. Joseph Black was beaming as we stood waiting for the elevator.

Although I was aware that Black would be getting a sizable sum for doing essentially nothing but taking me to Peter Fox, I comforted myself with the idea that somehow Black would be overseeing the case, keeping an eye on things for me, and so on. But this was not to be. A few days later, when I went to see Black to ask him some questions about how the case was to proceed, he literally threw me out of the office, saying, "Fox is handling the case now. Talk to him about it." I was outraged, I was hurt, and then I smiled. Joseph Black himself had shown me what to do when an attorney pisses you off.

"Fire him," said James Altman. "Absolutely. Pay him for the time he has spent on your case and fire him." This was a situation where serving the client's needs also did not hurt the lawyer. Altman's firm would get an extra $133,000 or so if there was a million-dollar verdict, by taking Black out of the picture. This was a couple of days later, but I was still angry about Black's attitude. I was in James's office and we were chatting before getting down to business.

James told me how he had started out as a young lawyer, washing Fox's car for him on weekends, and how he had worked his way up in the firm for six years to become a junior partner. He would be working closely with me on my case, he said. That was fine with me; I liked the guy.

The case was moving right along, too. The investigator had gotten the medical records and had verified my story as much as he could. James presented me with a copy of the lawsuit he had filed, which seemed to accuse everybody on earth of just about every conceivable malfeasance and failure of duty imaginable.

This was a hefty document, running twenty-three typed sheets on legal sized paper, with the double pink stripes down each side and the name of the law firm in little letters across the bottom. It named fifteen people and corporations as defendants. "And every one of them will have lawyers fighting us all the way," said James. He seemed almost exhilarated by the thought of it. "By the way, I was talking with a few of their lawyers, and one of their defenses is going to be that you killed her."

"What?" It was as if he had punched me in my nearly-healed nose. "Oh, now, don't take it so hard. These guys are just doing their job," he continued. Their job was to obfuscate, tie things up, delay at every step of the way, and generally make the plaintiff, me, wish he had never been born, or at least had never dared to challenge a doctor.

The lawsuit was filed in the Circuit Court of the 11th Judicial Circuit in and for Dade County, Florida, General Jurisdiction Division. I was shown as the Claimant, "as personal representative of the Estate of Louise Khavari, deceased, individually and on behalf of the Estate of Louise Khavari" verses Miami Colonial General Hospital, Inc., a Florida corporation doing business as Colonial General Hospital; Firth Wiesel, M.D.; Howard Ebner, M.D.; (the "sunny boys") Wiesel and Ebner, M.D.'s, P.A.(their business entity); Charles Koss, M.D. (the plastic surgeon); Fred A. Forstmann, M.D. (the anesthesiologist); Bernard Walters, M.D. (my anesthesiologist and the one who stepped in and revived Louise after her first cardiac arrest. We were suing him to gain information we hoped to use against the others, and because he was the head of the anesthesiology department of the hospital and thus Forstmann's superior); Donna Lang, Mary Knopfloch, Valerie Masters, Barbara MacMillan and Trudi Berns (the all-star cast of nurses); Michael Martin, M.D. (the neurologist) and Robert J. Manson, M.D. (the pulmonary specialist).

The claim went on to say that the Claimant (I, as personal representative, etc.) demanded mediation of this claim for wrongful death against the Defendants, who were then listed all over again. Then each of the parties was identified, myself as before, the hospital as themselves, and each doctor was described, such as "The Defendant, Firth Wiesel, M.D., is a general surgeon who treated the decedent, Louise Khavari, in Dade County, Florida, out of which case this action arose. Furthermore, said Defendant is an officer, agent, servant, and/or employee of Wiesel and Ebner, M.D.s, P.A." The nurses were identified as "The Defendant, Mary Knopfloch, was and is a nurse providing nursing services to the decedent and is a resident of Dade County, Florida. Said Defendant is an agent, servant or employee of the Defendant, Colonial Hospital."

Then came the Statement of Facts Giving Rise to This Claim, which explained about the accident and what doctors and nurses took care of Louise. Then it told how Louise had undergone the second surgery, performed by Dr. so-and-so, and how she had developed breathing difficulty "as a direct and proximate result of the negligence of the Defendants, so-and-so, and their agents, servants, officers and/or employees." Furthermore the nurses had not recognized the respiratory crisis, the hospital failed to monitor it, and then along came a couple of more doctors whose negligent medical care "jointly and severally, in conjunction with the negligent acts of any or all of the other Defendants, resulted in her death on December 27, 1978."

Then came the individual claims against each defendant, one after another. In each claim, the suit started by adopting and realleging all of the claims previously mentioned, and further alleged that this new defendant was whoever they were, was involved with Louise's case, and then it would go on to list fifteen or twenty acts, "all of which were deviations from accepted standards of care."

For example, the claim against Dr. Koss said:

34. The Claimant adopts and realleges paragraphs 1 through 33 and further alleges:

35. At all times material to this Statement of Claim, the Defendant, Charles Koss M.D., was and is a plastic surgeon who undertook to care for and operate on the decedent, Louise Khavari, and thus had the duty to do so in accordance with the accepted standards of care for like specialists in Dade County, Florida, or some similar medical community.

36. Notwithstanding said duty, the Defendant, Charles Koss, M.D., breached said duties in that he did or failed to do one or more of the following acts of omission or commission, any or all of which were a deviation from the accepted standards of care for such a specialist in said medical community:

a.failed to familiarize himself with the decedent's underlying medical condition prior to and/or during surgery; and/or

b. failed to properly perform surgery on said decedent; and/or

c. failed to properly maintain an airway in said decedent; and/or

d. failed to properly consult with other co-defendants; and/or

e. failed to properly monitor his patient's post-operative care; and/or

f. failed to properly instruct nurses and/or other co-defendants in proper operative and post-operative care; and/or

g. failed to properly order that said decedent remain in the recovery room for a sufficient amount of time; and/or

h. failed to issue appropriate operative and post-operative orders; and/or

i. failed to advise the co-defendants, including the nurses, as to appropriate care for said patient in the event of a respiratory emergency;

and/or

j. failed to respond promptly to a respiratory emergency code or another distress code called for said decedent; and/or

k. abandoned his patient; and/or

l. caused or allowed the nostrils of said patient to be improperly packed during surgery; and/or

m. caused or allowed said decedent's mouth to be wired shut along with her nostrils packed thereby cutting off her airway; and/or

n. improperly and prematurely extubated (removed the breathing tube from) the decedent; and/or

o. improperly and prematurely allowed said decedent to be extubated; and/or

p. improperly failed to re-intubate said patient after surgery; and/or

q. failed to properly re-intubate said patient timely when a medical emergency arose; and/or

r. ordered improper medications for said patient; and/or

s. failed to order appropriate medications for said patient; and/or

t. was otherwise negligent.

37. As a direct and proximate result of the negligence of the Defendant, Charles Koss, M.D., as aforesaid, jointly or severally, in conjunction with the negligence of the other co-defendants, said decedent died on December 27, 1978.

Whew! And just when you might suppose that the "aforesaid Defendant" had failed at so many things that he must be the biggest failure in the world, along would come the next defendant who would get an alphabetical litany of scorn and derision. Doctors pretty much all got up to "t," while the nurses didn't get off too lightly, either, although they only got up to "k," except for Trudi Berns, who made it to "m." Each of the nurses was accused of doing or failing to do one or more of the following acts:

a. failed to provide proper pre-operative, recovery room, and post-operative nursing care for said decedent; and/or

b. failed to promptly notify qualified physicians and/or other skilled medical help when said decedent developed an emergency respiratory condition during or after surgery on December 15, 1978;

and/or

c. failed to carry out the orders of the various physicians attending said decedent; and/or

d. failed to properly maintain an airway for the decedent; and/or

e. failed to recognize that the decedent needed emergency medical attention; and/or

f. delayed unnecessarily in sounding an emergency code for said decedent; and/or

g. failed to monitor the patient commensurate with the standard of care required; and/or

h. failed to have wire cutter in place at bedside for said decedent; and/or

i. failed to have the emergency medical cart available at the time of said emergency medical condition; and/or

j. failed to intubate and/or re-intubate said decedent and/or failed to have said decedent re-intubated by a physician; and/or

k. was otherwise negligent in the care and treatment of said decedent.

Trudi Berns got a couple of bonus letters, because she "negligently inflicted emotional distress upon the decedent by insisting that said decedent was going to die in the decedent's presence" and "negligently and carelessly caused the decedent to lose her will to live by stating in the presence of said decedent that she was going to die."

Then came two lesser doctors: Martin, who only rated up to a "j" and Manson who got up to "o." It was plain to see that Peter Fox did not miss a single opportunity to call attention to every shortcoming, however minor or even imaginary, of every player, however minor, in the entire black comedy of errors. All of this led up to my claim, and that of Louise's estate:

75. The Claimant reserves the right to demand full damages available for the subject estate and for himself individually under the Florida Wrongful Death Act at the termination of the jurisdiction of this medical mediation panel.

76. Furthermore, the Claimant respectfully insists that the entire Medical Malpractice Act including Florida Statute 768.44 et seq. is unconstitutional and said claimant specifically does not waive his

right to a jury trial on all issues of this matter or to challenge the constitutionality of said Act at any time before, during or after these proceedings.

The filing date was March 2, 1979, and this masterpiece of legalese was signed with a flourish by Peter Fox himself, as attorney for the claimant.

On the 26th of March the first barrage of paper was launched by Peter Fox. This was the beginning of what he called the "discovery phase" of the case, where we set out to establish the facts, and see what we were up against. This involved serving Interrogatories served upon the defendants.

These were a series of questions that, by law, the defendants were required to answer "under oath, in writing, and within the time allowed by the Rules of Procedure." Each interrogatory had a cover sheet that announced the name and number of the case (the case "styling") and certified that a copy had been mailed to the defendant's attorney.

The doctors each got three separate interrogatories. The first was a standard form of thirty-three questions, actually preprinted, which is presented to every doctor in a malpractice case. This requires the doctor to tell his life story from his school days, getting his licenses, certifications, every job he ever had, whether he ever had his license suspended, and whether he had ever been charged with malpractice, professional neglect, lack of professional skill or breach of professional ethics by any claim, suit, grievance proceeding or investigation. It asked whether he had ever been convicted of a crime, what articles and books, etc., the doctor had ever published, and what awards he had ever won.

Each question demanded explicit, multipart answers. For example, if the doctor had ever had any medical experience or training as a member of the military, he also had to tell us what branch of the service, dates of service, each station of service, and complete description of the training or experience he had.

Question 18 finally got around to the business at hand, demanding a written account of each and every professional contact he had ever had with Louise, including dates and times, detailed descriptions of each examination, test or procedure performed, his diagnosis or impression of the patient's condition on each occasion, etc., etc. Question 21 asked whether the doctor contended that a person other than himself was responsible in whole or in part for the patient's complications, and, if so, who, and why he thought so. The doctor was required to list every doctor with whom he had ever consulted regarding Louise, why, and what was learned, each time.

The doctor was required (and here even I felt almost sorry for him) to list every single medical book or article he owned that referred to the conditions or complications of the nature of this patient's, and to state which ones he found to be authoritative. Because this question could conceivably take hours to answer, and would be sure to outrage the lucky respondent, Fox placed in parentheses a case reference wherein this question had been ruled proper. This gave us the opportunity to possibly use his own authorities against him, or perhaps show that he wasn't up-to-date.

Then he had to list every time he had offered an explanation of the patient's condition or complications, to whom, what, and when. Then he had to say whether, in his opinion, given what he knew about the patient, whether the complications could have been avoided, and how. Did he ever get any statement from anyone concerning the case? Who, when, and where is the statement now?

To wrap things up, he had to tell us the names and addresses of any witnesses who knew of the case, anyone who had knowledge of it, any expert witnesses and any just plain ordinary witnesses he was going to call for his defense.

All of this would give us a lot of useful information, and clues to where to look for more. I derived a great deal of satisfaction from the sheer amount of grueling paperwork forced upon the enemy. I knew that the enemy attorneys would be neither surprised nor the least bit displeased. They worked by the hour. They are paid by the doctors' insurance companies.

And, of course, all of that was only the first interrogatory. To further clarify the defendant's position, he also had to respond to an interrogatory concerning his expert witnesses. Who were they, what were their credentials, what were they going to testify about, what would they say, and what would be the basis of their arguments?

The third interrogatory served upon each doctor concerned his insurance coverage. At the time of the relevant incident, was he covered by liability insurance? For each policy of primary or excess liability coverage, he had to tell us the carrier, amount of the policy, where the policy was, policy number, whether he had notified the insurance company, and so forth.

We also fired off a few interrogatories to the hospital and to each of the nurses, to find out what their stories were going to be, and who their experts would be.

In spite of the incredible amount of work that would be entailed in responding to these interrogatories, the answers were due by the end of April. Meanwhile, we would continue to investigate, and wait for the defendants to help us build our case against them.

On April 9, Peter Fox filed an amended claim in our case, which was essentially the same as the original claim, but added the Professional Associations (these were the doctors'corporate entities) which employed Drs. Manson and Martin. At the same time we received interrogatories from Dr. Martin, which asked us what we were going to claim who did, and who our expert witnesses were going to be. Copies of the interrogatories and my answers were furnished to every attorney involved in the case. We could have fielded a baseball team with all the attorneys who were involved by now.

The next part of the discovery phase involved the taking of depositions. A deposition is the testimony of Claimant, Defendant, or other witness, taken under oath in front of a certified court reporter, generally at an attorney's office. There is no judge present, and the proceedings are conducted by the attorney who represents the party calling for the deposition. In our case, every deposition would be quite an affair, because usually all of the defendants' lawyers would be present, as well as one or two of mine.

The first deposition in the case was taken on behalf of Forstmann and Walters, by their attorneys, Benito Gonzalez and Paul Sparks. The witness was a nurse named Gail Geraldo, who was the "PAR" (Post Anesthesia Recovery) room nurse on both occasions when

Louise came out of surgery. Since there was nothing in any of the records which could possibly exonerate Forstmann, apparently they were trying to start things off by shifting some of the blame onto someone else. James Altman appeared on my behalf at the four-hour proceedings on May 11, 1979.

He reported that we learned some "pretty interesting stuff" and found out about a couple of more people whose depositions we would take, and who may end up joining our growing list of defendants. We would have the transcripts of the deposition in a week or two. Our investigator had discovered that on the day Louise returned from her second surgery, Gail

Geraldo had left work early to get her hair done for the hospital Christmas party, which was held that night at the Doral Country Club. I decided that deposition might be interesting reading.

The next deposition in the case was mine. We received a notice that my deposition would be taken on May 23 at the office of Daniel Weiss' law firm, which represented the hospital and the nurses. James spent a few hours preparing me for the deposition, asking me every question that he would have asked if he were the defense lawyers. He advised me to make a full, frank and honest disclosure of whatever I was asked about, but never to volunteer anything. He said never to explain myself, but that he would ask questions at the end to see to it that anything requiring explanation would be brought out.

I was advised to dress conservatively, but not to overdress. I was to be polite and respectful, answering "Yes, sir" and "No, sir" whenever possible, no matter how sarcastic the other attorneys might get. If they tried to ask an improper question or twist one of my answers, I could disagree with them. James said that he and Peter Fox would be right at my side through the whole thing, but that I shouldn't look at them every time I gave an answer. If the question was improper or tricky, they would stand up for me. He explained that every aspect of my life would be called into question during the deposition, and that the nature of these cases was that there were few secrets by the time they were over. He reminded me that we would be probing the defendants just as deeply. I would likely be asked all kinds of questions about Louise's and my lives, our health, marriage, and so on, and that I should not get offended, but answer truthfully and as briefly as possible.

He said I would be asked about how the accident happened, what happened at the hospital and so on. He also said that I should freely admit that I had conferred with him and Peter Fox prior to the deposition, concerning my testimony. "They all know that you have; everyone does. It's almost a trick question," James said. "No jury in the world would ever believe that you hadn't planned your testimony with your attorney."

He also told me that I should expect a private detective to watch me from a distance, any time at all. There was big money at stake here, and the insurance companies would love to find any evidence that I was less than totally bereaved at the loss of Louise. Specifically, they would like to get pictures of me with another woman. Of course I was nervous when we entered the conference room on the 24th floor of a downtown office building. There was a view of Biscayne Bay, but it was to my back. This was the first gathering of a group of lawyers who would spend a great deal of time together on this case. Each of them was paid by the hour to represent his client (actually his client's insurance company), for all of the countless hours of depositions to come. None of them seemed at all unhappy to be there at 10 a.m., even though each of them would receive a complete transcript later (which they would, no doubt, bill their clients for reviewing) and could have called for another deposition any time they felt something was left out. This one small event generated thousands of dollars in attorney's fees. As an economist, I was suddenly fascinated by the implications of the story that was unfolding.

3

The Vultures Squawk

Just before the deposition began, as I sat there surrounded by navy blue pinstripe suits, horn rim glasses and manicures, was the first time I ever became interested in the financial aspects of the case. It was plain to me that nobody was going to lose his license, or be arrested, or even chastised one little bit. Now, confronted with the smug forces against me, I vowed that they would never have the satisfaction of beating me. If justice was to be measured out in dollars, then I was going to get everything they were willing to fight so hard to protect.

I knew that plaintiffs' lawyers take a big bite out of some big settlements, but for the first time I was really beginning to see that they weren't going to get that money handed to them. And how else could most people even hope to get any kind of justice at all? Who could afford to pay for the hundreds and thousands of hours of legal work it takes to plow through a routine case, especially where significant amounts of money are at risk—and will be defended commensurately.

Now this is not to say that there are not bad plaintiff lawyers, who hurt us all by prosecuting and winning ridiculous, trumped-up cases. Still, what is the alternative? I was plenty glad to have a couple of heavyweights on my side as I saw the six Vultures preening around the table.

But the defense lawyers get paid by the hour. It doesn't matter to them if their client is guilty as sin. It is their job to use every trick they can to prolong the process, and the process opportunities to drag a case out for a long time running up thousands of hours on the meter. And, it is a fact that they often succeed at preventing the insurance companies from paying out large sums, justly or not. At the very least they see to it that the insurance companies don't have to pay for a long, long time. An insurance company can earn a hundred-thousand dollars or more by holding onto a million for a year. And a year is nothing in the legal system.

My nervousness gave way to disgust and contempt as the six Vultures licked their chops and the deposition began. The people who had as much as murdered Louise were nowhere around, and these guys were going to get fat trying to help them get away with it entirely. And the longer it took them to do it, the better; they were getting paid by the hour.

I was sworn in, and Dan Weiss, attorney for the hospital and the nurses got started on me. Half a dozen gold pens poised over a half a dozen yellow pads, and the young woman court reporter poked at her machine. Mr. Weiss started by asking me my name, address, and so on, about when Louise and I had come to America, and a lot of questions about Louise's involvement in our business. Then he asked about Louise's medical history, whether she had ever been depressed, whether she had taken drugs like tranquilizers or alcohol. Finally he began to discuss the accident, and then the situation at the hospital. Through all this Peter Fox and James Altman sat diffidently beside me, and I scarcely noticed them. Then we got around to the part where I found Louise alone after the second surgery.

Q. Now after the surgery on December 15th, what is the first thing you remember about any conversations you had with anyone, a doctor, a nurse, or anyone?

A. As I came—it was about 1:30 I think—to the hospital after the surgery, I saw Donna Lang, the nurse. I asked when she (Louise) came back, and she told me about 12:40.

Q. Excuse me?

A. 12:40. Forty minutes past twelve o' clock. Then I went to her room, and I called to her, but she was deep in sleep. She was unconscious. The night before, she told me, exactly in these words, that if I came there and saw some tube in her mouth or throat, I should not worry, this is for breathing. But it was not there.

Q. Who told you this now?

A. Louise.

Q. The night before the surgery she told you what?

A. She told me that there would be a tracheotomy—is that the word?

Q. Okay.

A. (continuing)--and that that had been told to her by Dr. Forstmann or Dr. Koss. One of those two.

Q. What was the first doctor you said?

A. Koss and Forstmann.

Q. So she told you to expect a tube in her throat, and there was no tube when you arrived? Did you bring that to anyone's attention at that time?

A. At that time, I was trying to get somebody to get her to be able to breathe, and to get her to wake up. (By this point in the proceedings I would have gladly sent this guy to the hospital so that he could get a taste of it.)

Q. You said she was unconscious? Can you tell the difference, or can you describe the difference to me, at this point, between her being asleep and being unconscious?

A. You see, I had—a few days before that, I had surgery on my nose. I also had anesthesia, and when I came back to the room, I was talking nonsense, but I was aware of everything that was going on. Everything I said, I knew what I was saying. I remember it. But as I came in I shook her, I called her. No response.

Q. Because she was reacting differently than you reacted, you assumed she was unconscious?

Peter Fox snapped, "Objection to that," nearly blowing me into the wall. "That is an improper question and I object to that!" Every defense lawyer in the room froze. Their reaction was quite satisfactory to me.

MR. WEISS: Go ahead.

MR. FOX: Do not answer it. If you want him to tell what

happened, fine, but we are not going to put words in his mouth.

We continued through the aftermath of the second surgery, and then got down to my specific complaints concerning each of the nurses. In spite of my coaching, I did get in some editorializing on the subject of the nursing profession. Then he asked me what doctors I had spoken with since then, and what they had said, and whether they had had any comments about the nursing staff.

All in all, I told just about the entire story, and then there was an intermission while the Vultures decided who would get the next bite, who had to be where when, and so on. Finally, Dr. Koss' lawyer, Charles K. Wilson, Esquire, began to delve into Louise's and my personal relationship, and he asked a lot of questions about whether Louise had been getting any kind of medication. He asked whether Louise had been concerned that she would not be beautiful anymore. These questions, I understood, were aimed at bolstering the defense's contention that I had poisoned Louise by giving her barbiturates, because she was no longer beautiful. They got nothing from me to remotely substantiate that absurd and despicable notion.

When he led up to the time after the second surgery, I told about the little notes Louise had written to me and her parents on the napkins:

Q. Do you have both of those napkins?

MR. ALTMAN: I would like him to have them for old times' sake.

MR. WILSON: What is the basis of that?

MR. ALTMAN: I just want him to have them because evidently he is inspiring you to ask some questions about his marriage. I assume you would not know anything, so I guess your clients must have asked you to ask him some questions.

MR. GONZALEZ (Forstmann and Walters' attorney): Come on.

MR. WILSON: I am asking routine questions and I think appropriate.

MR. ALTMAN: I am not faulting you at all for asking questions, Charles.

James never passed up an opportunity to put a defense attorney on the defensive, personally.

Next I was questioned by Joel Swimmer, Esquire, for Drs. Wiesel and Ebner. This guy I had to respect, because he went straight to the business of proving his contention that his two clients had nothing whatsoever to do with Louise's death. He immediately had me state that I had fired Wiesel and Ebner prior to the second surgery, and repeated in several ways the facts that clearly showed that Louise was just fine up to the second surgery. This became the liveliest few minutes of the day.

Q. So at the time you were joking and talking and laughing with your wife in anticipation of taking her home, by that time you had already discharged Drs. Wiesel and Ebner?

A. That is true.

Q. So you are fully aware of the fact that Dr. Wiesel and Dr. Ebner in no way participated in the surgery that your wife underwent on December 15, 1978?

James leapt up.

MR. ALTMAN: He is not going to answer that question. I will tell you why. We have not taken their depositions and I do not know what they did, if anything.

MR. SWIMMER: I have talked to Mr. Fox on this case, and I can put on the record that Mr. Fox is fully aware that my clients played no part in that surgery and, in fact, has indicated to me on numerous occasions that they are going to be eventually dropped from this lawsuit and I think I have got every right to ask this man, as far as his own personal knowledge, since he fired them and discharged them from her care, whether he understood that they participated in any way or anybody represented to him that they participated in the surgery. (Here the guy was making sense. And crocodile tears, too. Now he could point to the record, but you could bet that he would have no reason to be sorry if the case dragged on.)

MR. ALTMAN: That is a much different question. Would you want to ask him whether or not he knows if they participated in the surgery or not, that is different, but we do not know what decisions they made because we have not taken their depositions.

MR. SWIMMER: I am not going to argue with you, James. I will just ask the question.

MR. ALTMAN: I want you to ask the question.

MR. SWIMMER: Sir, was it your understanding that Dr. Wiesel and Dr. Ebner in no way participated in the December 15, 1978, surgery of your wife?

A. You know, please let me finish my—just listen to my answer and don't be too quick to cut me off until I give my—

Q. If you can, answer my question yes or no.

MR. ALTMAN: Why do you not want him to answer your question for you?

THE WITNESS: I cannot give that question a yes or no answer.

I went on to tell of Donna Lang's warning when I told her I had discharged the "sunny boys," of Ebner's tales of woe to win our sympathy, and of Wiesel's smug, "It seems that you have some problems" when I met him in the hall soon after Louise's cardiac arrest.

Then Mr. Gonzalez, attorney for Forstmann and Walters, took over, and after a few questions Mr. Weiss started to object to something or other. James cut in, "What about us taking a lunch break?"

MR. GONZALEZ: I do not have very much longer. We all want to get out of here. I know I am at the tail end of it...

MR. ALTMAN: If you tell me that you are at the tail end, I believe you. (Good old James)

A few minutes later, the party was over. It had lasted nearly four hours. I was hungry. Peter and James were pleased with my performance, and I was satisfied that these Vultures were only human, after all. None of them had shown any evidence of cleverness or even conviction. But I had figured out why they were smug.

Defense attorneys win as soon as there is a case, and for as long as there is a case.

Gail Geraldo's deposition transcripts arrived, neatly bound. Its 179 typed pages became the first volume in the encyclopedic mass of testimony that was to come. (My deposition produced a 159-page volume when we received it a couple of weeks later.) During lunch, and on our way to the 3:30 p.m. deposition of our next defendant, I read through Gail Geraldo's testimony. Fresh from my own experience, I could imagine myself being there and hearing her and seeing the Vultures and their gold pens, although I had never seen Gail Geraldo before.

Then I learned that Gail Geraldo was the Post Anesthesia Recovery nurse, with some five years' experience in that specialty. We also learned that she had been assisted on December 15 by another nurse, Sharon Todd, whom James had already signed up as more grist for the deposition mill. Gail Geraldo said that, according to her records, Louise had come into the recovery room from surgery at 12:10 p.m. on December 15. Louise was the only patient in the recovery room that day. Her records further indicated that she had deemed Louise sufficiently revived to return to her room by 12:40, a scant thirty minutes later.

The record after that, "Discharge from PAR/Forstmann," was in Gail Geraldo's handwriting, with a check mark and someone else's writing beside it. This turned out to be that of one Nurse Nancy Roberts, who had relieved Gail Geraldo that day (another deposition to take). Gail Geraldo had written the note in "anticipation" of Forstmann's order, which she had expected to receive by telephone, but did not. She left early that day, at 12:40, and by that time Forstmann had not seen Louise, nor had Gail talked with him. She herself had, as was the norm if not the policy, declared Louise sufficiently recovered from four and a half hours of anesthesia that she had tidied up Louise's file to send her back to her room.

To questions concerning where she had been going, well, no, she hadn't gone home, but no, she couldn't say where she had gone. To get her hair done? She could not say. (Our investigator had told us that Gail Geraldo had left to get her hair done for the big hospital Christmas party that had been held at a posh local country club that evening.)

Then who had released Louise from the recovery room? It must have been Nancy Roberts, acting on a telephone conversation relaying Gail's comments to Forstmann, who then had said to send Louise back to her room.

James had really gotten into her about where she got her hair done. Various places. Where? This place and that place. Had she had her hair done in December? She didn't remember. And so on. Then he had gotten her talking about how long patients normally take to recover from anesthesia, especially, say, four and a half hours of anesthesia if they had serious surgery to, say, the head area. Well, there wasn't really any set amount of time. He had tried that question several different ways, but hadn't gotten anywhere.

Then he had gotten her to say that yes, sometimes patients did seem awake and aware soon after surgery, only to lapse back into an anesthetized state. Yes, that happened frequently, she had grudgingly admitted. But, yes, in her opinion, a woman whom she had seen—just a week earlier—take over two hours to come around, and whom she had kept in the recovery room for nearly three hours at that time (December 8, Louise's first surgery), that same woman had been ready to go after less than half an hour this time. After all, she had made "short sounds for yes and no" when responding to Gail Geraldo a few minutes after coming out of the operating room.

James had wrapped up by exploring the extent to which doctors, who by policy are required to see and discharge a patient from the PAR personally, relied on Gail Geraldo's assessment by telephone and never came back to see their patients at all. It had turned out that this was quite usual.

All in all, the hospital wasn't looking too good, for allowing this sort of thing to go on, in clear violation of their own policies. Forstmann looked pretty irresponsible here, too.

At 3:30 that afternoon we were in another conference room, high above Miami in another downtown office building. Paul Sparks, attorney for Forstmann and Walters, was wasting no time trying to clear his clients. As he had with Gail Geraldo, he had called for the deposition of Mary Knopfloch so that he could be in charge of it and work things around to show that Forstmann and Walters had had nothing to do with Louise's death. Several of the Vultures I recognized from earlier in the day, although there were a couple of new faces, and a couple of the old ones were missing. It was amazing how alike they all were.

Mr. Sparks started out with the usual formalities: name, rank, serial number, work history, and so on, leading up to the fact that Mary Knopfloch had had charge of Louise most of the days between December 3 and December 15, and had been the nurse who had sent Louise to surgery at 7:30 a.m. and received her back from the recovery room at 12:40 p.m. on December 15.

Her records showed receiving Louise at 12:40 p.m., at which time she wrote, "Returned from O.R. Appears sleeping soundly. Complains of not being able to breathe. Explained nasal packing, encouraged mouth breathing." Her next note said, "1:20 p.m., vital signs stable."

It was beginning to look like Louise had not even spent half an hour in the recovery room. Then it developed that Mary had been at lunch that day until 1:15, and had written the first note after that time, on the instructions of Donna Lang, the head nurse. Mary herself had checked the vital signs at 1:20. No mention had been made of Louise's respiration count. Mary stated that she had been back to see Louise several times, and then she read the next record. "3:00 p.m. Suctioned to establish better airway. Unable to awaken or get response."

Q. (MR. SPARKS) When you write the words, "Unable to awaken or get response," I would take it that that was something of an alarming finding, was it not?

A. For a post-op patient at that time, that was—at that time I had gone to—I had asked Donna Lang to— you know, when I had seen this and thought that this was the way it was, I went to Donna Lang and asked her to come look at the patient along with another nurse who was coming on duty at that time, Valerie Masters.

Q. The question I am asking you, Miss Knopfloch, is that you went in to suction Mrs. Khavari, you found that she was unable to awaken or give response, so is it not true that you immediately went out to talk to Donna Lang and some of the other nurses? You wouldn't start writing notes in the face of such a finding?

A. No.

MR. WEISS (defending hospital and the nurses): Objection. There has been no predicate as to when this note was written.

MR. SPARKS: I am sort of backing into it.

Q. (MR. SPARKS) This note which appears here on the chart, "3:00 p.m. Suction, unable to awaken or get response," when was that written?

A. That was written after she had been coded (i.e., after the nurse's aide had finally sounded the Code Blue).

Mr. Sparks went on through the chart, where several notes indicated that a supervisor had been notified, vital signs taken (although there was no record of them), through "Code Blue called" and its sequel, "CPR initiated immediately with response."

The key words here, I remembered, were "with response." Dr. Walters had accidentally been there to save the day.

Mr. Sparks got Mary to explain that all of these notes were written at the same time as the last one, "3:45, transferred to CCU" (Cardiac Care Unit), and that therefore all of the times shown were at best guesses after the fact. The implication was that they might also have been ass-covering after the fact.

He went over and over the events of the afternoon of December 15, and she painted a picture of such a flurry of nurses, doctors, "crash carts" (emergency resuscitation equipment carts), telephone calls and other goings-on that the whole scene was blurred by the confusion. Then, as it was getting late, Mr. Swimmer asked if he might interrupt to ask his two questions so that he wouldn't have to come back the next day. Did she know Wiesel and Ebner? Of course. Did they have anything to do with Louise's care at that point in time? No.

The only other thing established that day was that Mary and Valerie Masters had made a joint decision to call in Barbara MacMillan the head nurse who had come on duty when Donna Lang had gone home. Shortly after that, the proceedings were adjourned, to be continued the next afternoon at 3:30, so as not to interfere with Mary Knopfloch's job.

Taking depositions was none too dramatic, but I resolved after this first day to see the entire case through personally. The list of depositions to be taken was growing faster than we were taking them. I realized that it was now nearly five months since Louise's death, and that the case was just getting started. James reassured me that this was, in fact, whirlwind speed for such matters and that with any luck we would finish the case before either of us died of old age. We were still at the finger-pointing stage, where we sat back and let the defendants squabble about who had done what.

The next day, when the deposition continued, there was some finger-pointing that made me mad as hell. We started with James cross-examining Mary Knopfloch about a lot of little details concerning her record-keeping and such. Then, after determining that Mary had experienced six or seven "Code Blue" situations in her career, James changed the subject.

Q. Have you ever heard anything about this lady with respect to taking medication not prescribed by any physician or not given to her by any nurse at the hospital? Have you personally heard anything about it?

A. Have I heard anything about her—

Q. Taking any medications that were not prescribed for her by a physician.

A. No.

Q. Have you heard anything about her marriage, the nature of her marriage?

A. No.

Q. Why did she die, as you understand it?

MR. WEISS: Objection.

MR. SPARKS: Objection.

MR. WEISS: Calls for a medical conclusion.

Q. (MR. ALTMAN) Have you heard?

A. From whom?

Q. From any source.

A. About why she died?

Q. Yes.

A. No.

Q. Have you heard from any source as to why she had a cardiac arrest or why the Code Blue was called?

A. No.

Q. Do you have an opinion of your own?

A. Certainly.

Q. What is it?

THE WITNESS TO MR. WEISS: Should I just tell him my opinion?

MR. WEISS: What is the question? MR. SWIMMER (Wiesel and Ebner's attorney, back with us after all, apparently having nothing better to do): Objection. No predicate for being asked why—

MR. ALTMAN: Other than the fact that her heart stopped. As to why she had the code, I asked, and you didn't object quite properly.

MR. WEISS TO THE WITNESS: You didn't call the code. Do you know why some doctor or other person called the code?

MR. ALTMAN: What happened to her that required all this, in your opinion? That's what I'm trying to find out.

A. She became unresponsive.

Q. But do you know why?

A. Do I know why?

Q. Yes.

A. No, I don't know why.

Q. So then you don't know anything about what occurred with respect to this lady that caused her to be unresponsive that in turn caused the code to be called that in turn called for CPR to be instituted and her transfer down to the Unit and her ultimate demise; you don't know anything about why all of this chain of events happened?

A. I don't know why.

Q. You have no opinion as to why?

MR. SPARKS: Objection.

MR. WEISS: She doesn't know why. Any opinion would be speculation. I won't let her answer that.

But James was just warming up.

Q. Do you have any opinion in your own mind, based upon the

review of the records today?

MR. WEISS: You are dealing with a Licensed Practical Nurse and asking for a medical opinion. Don't answer the question.

MR. ALTMAN: She won't have any opinions later, then?

MR. WEISS: She won't have any opinions.

He would know; he was her lawyer. But James was not going to change course now.

Q. With respect to anything you might have heard from other persons, do you have any recollection of having heard anything as to why this chain of events took place? And the chain of events I'm talking about are, very simply, her failure to respond post-operatively as recorded in your notes, and then all of the things that took place after that.

MR. WEISS: In answering this, I don't want you to indicate anything that may have come up in my conversations with you about opinions that I may hold about the case.

Q. I'm not asking you to be a judge. What have you heard?

MR. WEISS: Have you heard anything specifically from any specific source about what happened and why it happened, other than what I have told you about?

MR. SPARKS: Object to the form of the question as being too broad and inviting any kind of scuttlebutt without the time, date, and place.

Q. (MR. ALTMAN) I want to hear the scuttlebutt.

A. Gossip?

Q. Yes.

MR. SPARKS: I object to giving gossip.

Q. (MR. ALTMAN) Go ahead.

A. I do, too.

MR. WEISS: Unless you can say specifically—she is not required to do that. Under what rule is she required to do that? Unless you know something and it's not something you just generally heard in the air and you can't name time or place—

THE WITNESS: That's really what I—

MR. ALTMAN: Do you instruct her not to answer this question? She's a defendant in this lawsuit. That's not what I'm asking her. (to the witness) I am asking you. What have you heard?

MR. SPARKS: I object to the form.

MR. ALTMAN: He objects to the form. You object. Just tell me what you have heard.

A. And I don't remember who this was from, but I have heard that she could have been receiving medication from her husband, like under the table type of thing.

This contradicted her earlier answer completely. And infuriated me. I sat quietly, but my hands practically crushed the arms of the chair.

Q. Under the table type of things. Did you hear that at a point in time when you were in this hospital?

A. I can't remember.

Charles Wilson, attorney for Dr. Koss, asked a few questions to confirm that Mary had, and had heard, no criticism of Dr. Koss' treatment of Louise. The other Vultures took halfhearted nips at her for a little while, and then it was done. Score for Mary Knopfloch: five and a half hours, 176 pages, a few facts.

I was thoroughly disgusted that anyone could imagine that I had killed Louise. James said, "I had to keep hammering at her about that, so that we could get on the record that it's just gossip. I'll tell you who told her that: it was Dan Weiss. I'd bet my ass on it. Anyway, they certainly don't seem to have any other defense, do they?" And he laughed.

The next morning our little deposition club set up shop at Colonial Hospital, in a conference room near the hospital offices. This time it was our party, and Valerie Masters was the guest of honor for the morning session. James led her through her education and career, and then began to ask her about what had happened on December 15.

Valerie said that she had come to work a little early, at perhaps quarter to three, and had been standing at the nurses' station talking with Mary Knopfloch when I had come to them to ask for help for Louise. She said that she went straight to Louise and decided that

Louise needed to be watched very closely. She went to Donna Lang, the head nurse, who told Valerie to suction Louise.

When the suction yielded nothing, and Louise still would not wake up, Valerie went looking for Donna Lang.

Q. How long did you look for Donna Lang?

A. No, I didn't. I just walked to the desk and she wasn't in the realm of my view, and I went immediately to the phone.

Q. Who did you call?

A. The nursing supervisor.

Q. Do you remember what you told her?

A. Basically, yes.

Q. First of all, who was it, MacMillan?

A. Yes.

Q. Did you ever deal with her before?

A. Yes.

Q. So you recognized her voice?

A. Oh, yes. Once I knew I was talking to the supervisor, I told her I needed help up here, I needed the patient watched at all times.

Q. During the time you were on the phone making this conversation with Nurse MacMillan, did you see Donna Lang?

A. No, she had left.

Q. Where did she go?

A. Home.

Later, James asked her whether she had called a doctor to see Louise. She replied, "I didn't call a doctor until Louise coded."

Q. To your knowledge, was a doctor called before she coded, and if so, who?

A. Any doctor?

Q. Yes.

A. Aren't anesthesiologists doctors?

Pretty good question from a nurse, I thought.

Q. Yes.

A. Yes.

Q. So someone was called before she coded?

A. Yes, most definitely.

Q. Who was that?

A. A combination of Forstmann and Walters. I'm so tired I can't even think of the names anymore.

Q. Forstmann?

A. Forstmann and Walters, but that is all MacMillan's department. I didn't call anybody there, see. As far as I can go is to call the supervisor, okay? That is my chain of command. When I walked out of the room, I told you on my mind was call anesthesia stat ("stat" is the emergency term for "immediately") and then get a bunch of things up here, but I didn't do that. I paused, called the supervisor, told her what was going on, and she did everything else.

Q. Why didn't you call anesthesia?

A. Why didn't I? Because it is not my position. I don't know what anesthesia is up to. They may be in OR, and here I am paging them to come to the floor.

Q. But you thought about doing it?

A. Yes, I did.

Q. You would never know where they were, would you?

A. No.

Q. Why didn't you call?

A. Because it is my chain of command, that my job is to call the supervisor and inform her. I can get more in trouble for jumping the line. You know, supposing Louise turned out to be absolutely fine, and here I've got three-thousand anesthesiologists up to the floor. You know, it is like calling a code before a code. You know, if the patient was alive and stable you don't get the whole team up there.

Q. So the reason you didn't call the anesthesiologists, if I understand it, is because you might get in trouble?

MR. SWIMMER: I object to the form.

MR. GONZALEZ: I object also.

MR. WEISS: That is not what she said at all. She said in her judgment she didn't feel it was warranted at the time.

Well, to me it sounded like she had said she didn't want to get in trouble. Dan Weiss was using an old attorney trick, the objection which also tells the client what to say.

A. I made a judgment about Louise, that there was more care that needed to be done to help her, okay? There was something evidently going wrong or not getting any better or she was going off deeper or there was something there. I couldn't figure out what it was. Was it too much anesthesia or was it too much pain medication? I don't know what it was. She was almost in a deep sleep. I didn't know what the problem was. I called the supervisor, told her about it, told her I wanted help now and hung up the phone.

Barbara MacMillan had come and Valerie had gone on to look after other patients until Louise had coded, at which time Valerie had tried to call for a doctor. Buck passed, very neatly.

James asked a lot more questions to try to establish the exact time everything had happened. Joel Swimmer asked his usual questions to further isolate Wiesel and Ebner from any possible implication of involvement. Then Charles Wilson, attorney for Koss, asked her whether anyone had talked with her about the situation, and when she had first been contacted concerning this case.

A. That is a tough one. Let me think. When was I first contacted? It was a while after it happened.

Q. Was it within a day or two?

A. After it happened?

Q. Yes.

A. You mean contacted by people like him (Weiss)? Well, I was contacted by my supervisors immediately to act accordingly and respect what happened and "keep it to yourself." Okay. And any doctors that wanted information, I was told to hush up, and, you know, that is the way it went. Okay. They didn't want me giving any information to anybody about anything. I was told it was none of anybody's business but my own, and I don't remember the first time I saw him (Weiss), no idea.

Then, she said that Koss had come to see her.

Q. Do you recall what you said to him and he said to you?

A. Well, it was in strictest confidence. At the time he was very emotionally upset, and this was way after the code, and very late that evening he came up to the floor and just hung with me for a little while.We were both pretty upset about the whole thing.

Q. Were there any discussions about the care and treatment that he rendered?

A. Not care and treatment, no, just about what had happened and how upset he was and how upset I was and, you know, he was just really, really upset, and I told him at that point that I was not supposed to discuss anything with anybody at it was just a little conversation between us.

Just before we finished with Valerie's enlightening testimony, James asked her, "Have you heard any suggestion by any source that this lady's husband had given her some drugs or some medication?

A. That is not what I heard.

Q. What did you hear?

A. I heard that her autopsy showed that she had elevated substances in her blood.

Q. Do you have any idea how that would be?

A. Yes, sir.

Q. How?

A. It would have to be administered. Somebody would have to have given it to her.

Q. Do you know who did?

A. Do I know?

Q. Yes.

A. No, sir.

Q. Have you heard who did?

A. No, sir.

Q. What was the reason you were told to keep this thing quiet? What was the reason given to you?

A. There was no reason given to me.

A few more questions revealed that two supervisors had come at different times that afternoon to tell her to keep her mouth shut about it.

4

The Squawking Continues

Valerie went back to her post, and we broke for lunch. Her two and a half hours of testimony added another 112 pages to our collection, and some interesting pieces to the puzzle. James was delighted.

An hour later, we reconvened at the hospital conference room to hear Donna Lang's story. James reviewed her education, licensing, and professional experience, up to her becoming the head nurse on the 7:00 a.m. to 3:00 p.m. shift on Louise's floor. He established that she had provided care to both Louise and myself during most of our stay in room 217. He then had her read just about the entirety of Louise's chart, most of the notes on which had been written by Donna herself, and then she explained that the notes of December 15 beginning with the one designated "12:40 p.m.," were actually written after 1:15 p.m. by Mary Knopfloch, at Donna's direction.

Donna had been filling in on Mary's patients while Mary had been at lunch, returning at 1:15. Donna had received Louise back from the recovery room at 12:40 or shortly before. Now she read the post-operative orders from the chart.

Suddenly I was thrown back into the horror of five months ago, that afternoon in December. I sat transfixed as the feelings of helplessness I had felt that day washed over me.

Q. Now when did you sign that order off?

A. It was approximately two o'clock. I was standing there at the nurses' station with Mr. Khavari. I had gone to get the chart to review it with him.

Q. Okay. At about two o'clock. Would you tell us why it was that at two o'clock you were standing there with him?

A. I had gone into the room and he had asked me some questions.

Q. What questions?

A. Did I speak with Louise after the surgery.

Q. What did you tell him?

A. I told him I did.

Q. What did you tell him you said to her?

A. I told him that—what I told him was I asked her if she had any discomfort. Then I related to him the conversation I had with her.

Q. Tell me about the conversation.

A. She came back from surgery on the stretcher.

Q. Yes?

A. Which was being transported by Ernie Moran. I walked into the room with my vital sign sheet and—

Q. Do you need the notes?

A. No, I don't. I remember. I walked into the room with my vital sign sheet and Ernie said, "We are going to need more help. This lady is very sleepy."

Q. Ernie told you that?

A. The transporter. So I went to the stretcher—

Q. Ernie Moran?

A. Yes.

Q. Go ahead, I'm sorry.

A. And spoke her name, Louise. I said, "Louise, wake up, your operation is over. We are going to put you in bed now."

Q. Did you agree with Ernie Moran that the patient was very sleepy?

MR. SPARKS: I object on the grounds that it calls for speculation.

A. This patient was a fresh post-operative patient still under the effects of anesthesia.

Q. Is this type of sleepiness that you described something you saw frequently, or not?

A. I would not speculate on the amount of times. I cannot give you a numerical ratio, but we do see very sleepy patients.

Q. And you suspected in your own mind, whether or not it was the true reason, but in your own mind, you suspected she might still be under the effects of anesthesia?

A. Yes.

Q. And yet you had a conversation with her?

A. I aroused her.

Q. Aroused her?

A. Yes.

Q. You said, "Louise." How many times did you say "Louise"?

A. I cannot recall exactly. I would say twice.

Q. Did you yell her name?

A. No.

Q. Did you touch her?

A. Yes.

Q. Did you shake her?

A. Yes.

Q. How hard did you shake her?

A. That is purely—I cannot tell you how hard I shake somebody.

Q. Did you shake her?

A. I touched her face and shook her shoulder.

Q. Did you touch her face where she had just been operated on?

A. No, I touched her very lightly here with my hands.

Q. So you would not touch her hard on the face?

A. No, no. I put my hand on her shoulder.

Q. Then what? Did you shake her on the shoulder?

A. No, I touched her.

Q. Where did you shake her?

A. Well, shaking—all right, I can see where you are trying to establish a method or a degree, say.

Q. I want to know where you shook her, forget the degree.

A. Okay, I touched her on the face, and I also touched her on the shoulder to hopefully arouse her with my cold hands.

Q. Your hands were cold that day?

A. Yes, my hands are always cold.

Q. Touch my hand. Tell me, if you would, what it was that happened when you did that. Anything?

A. Yes.

Q. What?

A. She shook her head.

Q. She shook her head?

A. Yes, she moaned. And I said, "Louise, are you in discomfort?" and she said, "No."

Q. She said no? Then what happened?

A. She said, "I am having difficulty breathing through my nose."

Q. She told you that?

A. Yes.

Q. And then what happened?

A. I said, "You have packing in your nose. That might make you feel stuffy. Will you breathe through your mouth?"

Q. You suggested that she do that?

A. Yes, and I repeated my command, "Louise, breathe through your mouth."

Q. What did she say when you told her that?

A. She didn't, but I said, "Take deep breaths through your mouth," and she complied.

Q. How long did you stay there?

A. I told her to take five deep breaths.

Q. Yes?

A. And she took—I just kept saying, "Deep breathe, deep breathe," and she complied.

Q. Were her eyes open or closed.

A. Closed. I said, "Louise, come on, now, I want you to be very careful and take a deep breath."

Q. Why did you tell her to be careful?

A. Well, I wanted her to listen to me. I wanted her to talk as much as she could to bring her out to the point of arousal.

Q. Why?

A. Because I wanted her to wake up, to be more alert.

Shortly after 1:15, when Mary Knopfloch had returned from lunch, Donna told her that Louise was still very sleepy, and needed to be aroused, and that Mary should keep an eye on Louise's vital signs.

Then Donna went off to meet with Mr. Jenkins, the director of nursing, to discuss a new soap-dispensing system for the hospital and the fact that one of her nurses was quitting the following month. James jumped on this for a while, just to make it clear that neither of these situations was an emergency. She returned to the floor at about 1:50 p.m., and was planning on leaving early that day, by two o'clock.

This was when I had encountered her and Mary. Donna had made a tour of the floor to make sure everything was quiet, and then had gotten involved with Mary and me. She was still on the floor when Valerie Masters arrived, probably about 2:45.

A. I know when I was getting ready to leave I was telling everybody I was leaving. Valerie was on the floor, and Valerie and Mary and I were standing at the desk. And Farid came and said something to them and they both went down to the room. Then Farid looked at me and—I don't recall. But there was a cue there that I thought, "Well, let me go see what this is." I think Mary turned around and motioned for them.

Q. So the three of them went back to the room and you followed?

A. Yes. And I stood in the door and I must have—I do recall I said, "Is everything all right?" And Mary said or Valerie said, Mary or Valerie said, "Farid said Louise is breathing funny." I looked at her, and I said, "Yes, she is breathing more shallowly." At that time I believe Valerie was taking a pulse. I said, "Why don't you check her position and suction?" She was breathing more shallowly than I had seen before. I then said to Mary or Valerie, I believe Valerie was taking her pulse, I said, "Will you two be able to handle this? Is everything okay?" And they said yes, or whoever said it, I'm not sure who, I think it was probably Mary, that things were okay. And I said, "Okay," and I left.

Q. You did what?

A. I left.

Donna Lang had turned the situation over to "competent" hands. They were doing what they should be doing. The situation was in capable hands. They were doing exactly what I would have done."

And she had left early that day. First stop: a department store, to buy Christmas paper.

Q. When was the next time you had any knowledge about the condition of this lady?

A. Later that evening.

Q. How did it come to pass that you had some knowledge of that?

A. The first knowledge was, I think, Mary called me at home.

And, of course later that evening, at the Christmas party, when Mr. Jenkins, the nursing supervisor, had come and asked her all about the case, he then told her to keep her mouth shut about it.

James let that go, and turned to ask whether she had heard rumors to the effect that Louise had been given or had taken some drugs that had not been prescribed by a physician or given by a nurse.

A. I was made aware of those rumors.

Q. You were made aware of them? You heard them?

A. No.

Q. How did they get into your mind, through what orifice?

MR. WEISS (the hospital's attorney): I don't want you discussing anything that came from any conversation with me.

Q. This has another purpose. I want to know the name of the person who told you that.

A. I can't discuss it.

Q. Why?

A. Because I was just—I was made aware in conversations with Mr. Weiss that people had heard this, and he wanted to know if I had heard it. And I told him no.

James flashed me a look that said, "I told you so."

A couple of other Vultures took their shots at making Donna Lang look irresponsible, to deflect guilt away from their clients. Mr. Sparks got a lot of mileage out of Donna's mission to pick up Christmas paper.

Joel Swimmer piped his usual chorus to get it on the record that his clients' Wiesel and Ebner, had not been on the case for days at that point, and thus were not involved at all. And that was about it. Everyone was getting a little cranky from being cooped up all day, but the defense lawyers were good-natured about it. They were getting paid by the hour.

In exactly three hours, we had added another 125 pages to an already impressive stack of testimony. The next scheduled meeting of the inquisition was two weeks away.

Somehow during these five months, the company that Louise and I had started two months before her death, and which had taken off from the first day, continued to make me a good living without requiring very much attention from me. That is a good thing, too, because I certainly didn't give it much.

I had bought a new four-bedroom house in a nice neighborhood not far from the cemetery (James had wanted me to buy the house next door to his), and had bought myself a new BMW automobile.

It is also good that the business did well, because I was not in any condition to concentrate on work, and not one cent had come in from the insurance company, either, in the six months since the accident. Our policy had included a $50,000 per person/$100,000 per accident uninsured motorist bodily injury provision. Although Louise and I could have been allocated most or all of that, I had agreed to give Ed Park's widow $50,000 of it. The paperwork was still dragging on, and James had amassed a considerable file of correspondence concerning simply getting paid by our own insurance company.

Ed Park's widow, Dorothy, could have sued me for whatever more she wanted to. Although the accident was not my fault, the other driver certainly wasn't worth going after. But in a way the accident was serendipitous for her. I do not mean the fact that his half-million dollar life insurance policy paid double for accidental death. I mean that a week later their divorce would have been final. Ed had been scheduled to marry a stewardess in Los Angeles the next month. I guess Dorothy didn't hold it against me.

For the first two and a half months there were flowers on Ed's grave when I visited it, but then no more.

I spent a lot of time at the cemetery, and I spent a lot of time driving aimlessly in my BMW. I loved that car, and I recognized that a lot of my love for it was possible because no one could kill the car and take it away from me. I could always get a new one. I drove from Miami down to the Keys and then turned around and drove back. I drove out to the Everglades, and then drove back. I enjoyed driving around, forgetting everything and concentrating on the road, but I was lonely.

I had always been a person who loved life, but now Miami, which had always seemed full of life to me, was empty and deserted. I enjoyed the material things, but I longed for something more. I was lonely, dead lonely.

One evening, I went to the movies with my teenaged niece, Lisa, and her younger brother, Robert. I don't recall what the movie was, but it had something to do with life after death, a subject which dominated my reading and thinking in those dark days. Standing some ways back in a ticket line parallel to ours was Daniel Weiss, Esquire, attorney for the hospital and the nurses, with a woman I supposed was his wife. Seeing me with a young woman, Dan Weiss rushed right over to catch me in the act of being less than bereaved.

This was the guy who had spread the rumors about me killing Louise with pills, and under other circumstances I would have gladly smashed his face in. However, I remained polite. When I introduced my niece and nephew, he looked a little sheepish. He stammered for a minute, and then attempted to extricate himself gracefully by saying how sorry he was about what had happened, and that, well, he just did what he did to make his living. Dan Weiss would have been scandalized if he had known what was really going on.

Although I went to the cemetery nearly every day, I placed fresh flowers on Louise's grave every Saturday. I stopped at the same flower shop every week, and gradually became acquainted with the lovely young woman who sold me the flowers each week, whose name was Phyllis. Finally, in late May, Phyllis said that she knew what a terrible time I had been through, but maybe I ought to get out a little bit. I took the hint and asked her out.

We went driving that afternoon to a park in the Keys. We talked about little things, and walked around quietly by the water and in the cool shade of the mangroves. Her dark blonde hair and bright blue eyes reminded me of Louise, and reminded me how lonely I had been. We stopped at the Tiki Bar around sunset and drank pina coladas with little umbrellas and slices of orange and a cherry.

We talked on into the evening, and suddenly I found myself doing something I realized I had missed for all of these months. I was laughing. We both got a big laugh out of the fact that not only was her father an attorney, but, as it developed, he was the Senior Partner in the firm that was representing Drs. Ebner and Wiesel!

In the next couple of weeks we spent almost every evening together, and we both enjoyed the time we spent together, and desperately needed to hold another human being. Phyllis was a very comfortable person for me to be with.

One evening Phyllis told me that she had been to see her father that afternoon, and he had asked her why she seemed so radiant. She told him that she was seeing a wonderful guy, and her father then said: "Wonderful. Bring him home for dinner, and tell him that if he needs some good legal advice I'll help him for free."

"I told him, 'Oh, I don't think you'd want to be his lawyer,' and just about burst to keep myself from laughing!" she said. "I couldn't stand not telling my sister, and do you know she was shocked? I couldn't believe she said, 'How can you do this to dad?' Seriously, though, I want you to know that if he did find out, and tried to use it against you, I'd testify against him, and tell what a terrible time you've been going through."

I told her I appreciated that, and hugged her.

The next time I went to Fox's office, I told James about Phyllis, and the funny coincidence. James didn't think it was funny. James smashed his fists against his forehead so hard I was sure he had given himself a concussion.

"Jesus Christ, Farid," he screamed. "What in the hell are you doing here?

Jesus, I can see it all now. Here we are in the trial, and the defense lawyer says, 'Well, the plaintiff isn't doing too badly these days,' and the judge says, 'What do you mean, counselor?' and the guy says, 'Well, your honor, this asshole is fucking my daughter!' Oh, Jesus!"

Phyllis ended up going away to school in Arizona, and that was that anyway.

I was sad to see her go. Tiger Terry tried to cheer me up. Tiger Terry was a stout grandmother in her sixties, who had enjoyed some notoriety as a professional wrestler a few years back. Now she worked in my brother's restaurant as a sort of manager. One time I saw her dressing down one of the waitresses who was not filling the saltshakers or something. Tiger Terry grabbed the girl, who was no lightweight herself, by both arms and picked her right up off the floor. I thought for sure she was going to body-slam her. Anyway, Tiger Terry told me that I was going to die of loneliness, and for no good purpose, unless I did something about it. She recommended getting as many women as I could as the cure. I had to admit that the times I had been with Phyllis, I hadn't been lonely.

As time passed, I began to spend a lot of time with James. We had lunch together almost every day, and I dropped by the office frequently. We would go out and look at new cars, Porsches, BMWs and Mercedes. James was attached to his big tank of a Lincoln, but after riding in my BMW he got the lust for a German car, preferably a very fast one. Together, we annoyed a lot of car salesmen.

We also did the grand tour of Miami's finest haberdashers, restaurants and bars. Often I would go out in the evening with James and his girlfriend, a pleasant blonde named Melody. James thought she looked like Brigitte Bardot; I could detect no resemblance, but kept my opinion to myself. She was nice enough to me, but very dominating over James.

As part of what I later realized was James's campaign to keep me out of mischief, he used to call me late every evening to wish me good night (and to make sure I was at home). He did this religiously, except during the times when he was fighting with Melody. Then I didn't get a good-night call until they had made up.

Melody wanted to marry James, but later they broke up. James fell in love with a nurse who had given an honest deposition in another case involving another hospital. Her honesty paid off; it was love at first sight, and that was the end of Melody. Within a year they were married.

At three o'clock in the afternoon of June 7, 1979, the inquisition reconvened, this time in the conference room at James' office, to take the first deposition from a doctor. Dr. Manson was the pulmonary specialist who had cared for Louise beginning immediately upon her arrival in the Intensive Care Unit at approximately 4:00 p.m. December 15, shortly after her cardiac arrest and resuscitation.

We didn't think we really had any gripe with Dr. Manson and in fact, I rather liked him. He was accompanied by his attorney, Howard Barton. James got right into the Arterial Blood Gas tests that had been performed on Louise, the first at about 3:05 p.m. on December 15, and what those tests had indicated.

It seemed to take hours to get through the nit-pickings and technicalities to the bottom line, which was that Louise had had too much carbon dioxide and not enough oxygen in her blood at that time. Whether this was due to a blocked airway causing her to slowly suffocate, or whether she had stopped breathing for some other reason, Dr. Manson could not say with certainty.

Dr. Manson also described responding to the Code Blue, and arriving to find Drs. Walters and Forstmann already at work on Louise, some minutes after he had first heard the code.

Forstmann?

Well, maybe not. Maybe it was just Walters. Anyway, he, Manson, had only observed, and had taken charge of the patient about an hour later. There he did the appropriate things to keep her breathing and to correct her blood chemistry, using the mechanical ventilator up until the 22nd of December or so. The records appeared to have several mistakes in them.

The next part of James's questioning worked around whether Manson would say that he should have been called earlier, and whether one would have to be a pulmonary specialist to have detected Louise's emergency condition, as indicated by the analysis of the blood gases.

No, he said, anyone should have been able top notice her condition; it was very unusual. No, it was not likely that Forstmann and Koss would have had him standing by right after the surgery, just in case of such a problem.

It was getting late in the afternoon. James had told me that as the depositions were taken, we would be saving the best ones for last. Manson really hadn't had any responsibility for Louise's death, but we were hoping that he would point a finger or two for us. I was getting bored, and I guess the Vultures were, too.

Q. What is the nature of the problems for which you will be called, doctor, immediately post-operatively?

A. Usually when I am called in immediately post-operatively, it is for a patient who has either poor respiratory function post-operatively and who is felt to be a significant operative risk with possible post-operative morbidity or mortality and they might want to place the patient in the Intensive Care Unit for close monitoring and possible mechanical ventilation, at least overnight. To my recollection I have not been called in as a pulmonary consultant on a patient with facial or nasal surgery.

Q. As a pulmonary specialist, are you involved in the study of how patients get air? By that, I am saying through what orifice?

A. Yes.

Q. Does swelling accompany surgery as a general rule?

A. Yes.

MR. BARTON: You are talking about swelling of the surgical site?

MR. ALTMAN: Yes, swelling of the surgical site. I am sorry, Howard.

MR. WILSON: Let me object to the form of the questions as too general and too broad.

MR. ALTMAN: Go ahead.

A. The swelling is seen many times at the site of the incision.

Q. Have you ever seen that type of Vaseline-encased gauze that they place in the nose following a nasal operation?

A. Yes.

Q. Does that impair one's ability to breathe through the nose?

A. Yes.

Q. At what level of training were you when you learned that, Doctor? Is that something pretty fundamental?

A. You don't have to be a doctor to realize that.

Q. With respect to a fractured mandible, do you know what the mandible is?

A. Yes, I know.

Q. Do you know what the arch bars are?

A. No. I don't know what the arch bars are.

Q. This area of the jaw (indicating) when fractured and requiring work or when teeth are replaced by an oral surgeon—

MR. BARTON: Is that a question?

MR. ALTMAN: I am describing this.

MR. BARTON: Are you finished?

MR. ALTMAN: How could I be finished?

MR. BARTON: There was a long pause.

Q. Doctor, let us assume that the patient had the kind of nasal surgery for which she was packed following and she had her jaw repaired and she had some work done on her teeth. Have you seen the operative?

A. Yes, I have seen it.

Q. Would you expect that a patient that has this kind of surgery in the area of the jaw and has had the nose packed with gauze to have a higher risk of an airway obstruction than another patient? If they have surgical sites in here, in the area of the jaw, would you expect that they would have a higher risk of airway obstruction than other patients who have surgery in other areas of the body?

MR. WILSON: Let me object to the form.

MR. GONZALEZ: I would join in the objection.

MR. BARTON: Yes. That is getting a little too far afield, I think.

MR. ALTMAN: How about letting him answer it, Howard?

MR. WILSON: About what areas of the body are you talking?

Q. If it were arm or leg surgery would you expect it to be higher?

MR. BARTON: Are you asking the question?

MR. ALTMAN: Do you want me to go down the anatomy?

MR. WILSON: Tonsillectomy?

MR. ALTMAN: That may be a higher risk, too. Let's talk about facial surgery.

MR. WILSON: We will be here all night.

Q. Let us talk about facial surgery. Let us talk about patients who have facial surgery, specifically this type of surgery, Doctor—

MR. BARTON: You are really asking him—

MR. ALTMAN: Can I finish?

MR. BARTON: You are rambling on too much. What you want to ask is, if I may help, if a patient has surgery on the nose and has the nose packed, do they have a higher risk of developing some kind of a breathing problem post-op than patients who do not have any surgery affecting any of their airways. Is that what you are saying?

MR. ALTMAN: That is it. (To Manson) Answer his question.

MR. WILSON: I will disagree and object.

MR. GONZALEZ: I will join in the objection.

MR. ALTMAN: I adopt his question.

Q. Doctor, please answer Mr. Barton's question.

A. If they breathe through their mouth, then they really should be able to maintain an airway and maintain ventilation. If there is something obstructing the oral airway, then they would be at increased risk.

You can see why this was a long afternoon.

A young lady Vulture, a Ms. Cook, was there from the firm representing Wiesel and Ebner. She spoke for the first time, and asked Dr. Manson the standard chorus of questions to establish that Wiesel and Ebner had no more to do with Louise's death than did a juxtaposition of the planets.

Four hours three minutes and 125 pages later, we adjourned and went home to dinner.

The next morning we went back to James's office to take the deposition of Dr. Grossinger, the oral surgeon who had worked on Louise's teeth during the surgery of December 15.

Dr. Grossinger confirmed what we already knew from the autopsy, that he had wired Louise's jaw after the surgery, which was the normal way of dealing with such situations. He expressed no opinion as to whether Louise should have had a breathing tube after combining this procedure with the nose surgery and packing performed by Dr. Koss. He, Grossinger, was an oral surgeon, a dentist. He had not been the surgeon in charge, that was Dr. Koss. Or we might take a look at Dr. Forstmann. He, Grossinger, was just an innocent bystander. At least that was his position.

For some reason it was especially painful for me that day. I was coming to realize that sitting through all of the depositions, in fact the very existence of the lawsuit at all, was preventing me from putting the whole terrible affair of Louise's death behind me and getting on with my life. It was just like reopening a wound, picking the scabs off it before it can heal properly, every day, and keeping a suppurating sore where there should be a scar. But I was determined to see every step of the process through. I owed it to Louise.

The Vultures, however, made sure that they gave their clients their money's worth of objections and pointed inquiries into all sorts of theoretical minutiae. They got paid by the hour.

During the last break of the afternoon, while the court reporter was out of the room, James called down the table to Charles Wilson, Koss' attorney. It happened that Koss' deposition was next, a couple of days later. "Charlie," James said, "can you come over here and help me for a minute?"

Charles Wilson was a very large guy in his fifties. He had been a professional football player in his youth, and hadn't lost any weight since. His six-foot six inch frame lumbered over to James.

James looked up at him, and very coolly said, "Charlie, would you hold this pen for me? I have to think for a couple of minutes." The other Vultures got a real hoot out of Charlie, who stopped just short of taking the pen out of James's hand. James had executed a maneuver calculated to clip Charlie's wings. Charlie was plenty pissed, but tried to act good-natured about it.

After the final chorus from Wiesel and Ebner's attorney, we gave up on Grossinger. Three hours, 108 pages, nothing new.

When I got home that afternoon, I found a letter from a collection agency representing Dr. Cooley, who had been the anesthesiologist for Louise's first surgery. He was threatening to sue me for $1,650, his fee for that episode. I called James immediately, and he was as outraged as I was. Here I sat, grieving and wondering what had happened that my wife was dead, and this Vulture was sending the J.V.s (Junior Vultures, a team composed of collection agents, inter alia) to nip at me.

We had already explained several times to Dr. Cooley that we did not care whether his ministrations to Louise had been worthy of a Nobel Prize, we were not paying anyone until it was determined who had been responsible for Louise's death. For all we knew at that point, the whole thing had been caused by something wrong in the first surgery. Anyway, we were not going to pay anyone upon whom we might later lay blame, because they might come back and say, "How could they have been dissatisfied with me? They paid me." At the rate things were going, Cooley would have a long wait before he got his money, if he ever did. And he knew it.

It was just his Vulture instincts that made him pursue me anyway.

The deposition club met at Peter Fox's office on the morning of June 12 to hear from Dr. Koss. When everyone had arrived, Charles Wilson ushered the good doctor into the seat of honor, and James began his questioning shortly after 9:30.

James reviewed Koss' education and career, including ten years as a reconstructive or plastic surgeon. James then turned the questioning to the matter at hand, and reviewed the nature of Louise's injuries. Koss referred to his notes on the hospital chart and described them, and described the surgical procedures he had performed.

Q. And you have seen such injuries before?

A. Yes.

Q. How many times?

A. I really can't say. Dozens? Hundreds? Injuries of that nature are particularly common in automobile accident cases. Really very common.

Q. And as a surgeon you have repaired such injuries before?

A. Yes.

Q. How many times have you operated on a patient with similar injuries to those in this case?

A. Again, I really can't say exactly. I am a plastic surgeon, and when people get facial injuries I operate on them and repair the damage. That is what I do. I have done so for ten years.

Q. All right, Doctor. And when you operate on these people, are they provided with breathing tubes?

A. Of course.

Q. And who installs that breathing tube?

A. The anesthesiologist.

Q. And in the case of Louise, did she have a breathing tube?

A. Yes.

Q. And who placed that tube in her?

A. The anesthesiologist, Dr. Forstmann.

Q. You were the surgeon in charge of the case, correct?

A. Yes.

Q. Did you order Dr. Forstmann to insert a breathing tube?

A. No.

Q. Why not?

A. Because that is part of his routine, his job.

Q. I see. So when you first encountered Louise on the morning of December 15, what was her condition?

A. She was anesthetized.

Q. Was she intubated?

A. Yes.

Q. Was that a nasal tube, an oral tube, what?

A. It was a nasal tube.

Q. Could you perform the surgery with a nasal tube in place?

A. It would have been difficult.

Q. So what did you do?

A. I, after I consulted with Dr. Grossinger, I, we, asked Dr. Forstmann to re-intubate the patient, through her mouth.

Q. Was this done?

A. Yes.

Q. By whom?

A. I inserted the tube.

Q. And was this tube in place at the end of the operation?

A. Yes.

Q. Did you remove it?

A. No.

Q. Did you order anyone to remove it?

A. No.

Q. Who removed it?

A. I don't know. I assume it was Dr. Forstmann.

Q. Why do you assume that?

A. Because it is the anesthesiologist's responsibility to determine when the patient is ready to be extubated.

Q. So when you were finished with the operation, you simply walked away?

MR. WILSON: I object to the form of the question.

A. I—

MR. WILSON: Don't answer that.

Q. What did you do at the end of the operation?

A. I left the patient in the care of Dr. Forstmann and the nurses.

Q. I see. And what was the status of the patient at that time?

A. She was anesthetized.

Q. Yes. Did she have her nose packed?

A. Yes.

Q. With what was her nose packed?

A. Vaseline-coated gauze.

Q. Why was that?

A. To stanch the bleeding. The Vaseline makes it easier to insert and remove.

Q. And she had a breathing tube in her mouth?

A. Yes.

James then turned the conversation to the Post Anesthesia Recovery room procedures, and whether there was any minimum time for a patient to remain in PAR. Dr. Koss was not familiar with any such requirement.

Q. How long should a patient stay in the Post Anesthesia Recovery room?

A. Until he or she has recovered from the anesthesia. I don't see how there can be any set amount of time, any prescribed time period.

Q. And who makes that decision?

A. The anesthesiologist.

Q. Not the PAR nurse on duty?

A. Well, I suppose the nurse is observing the patient, that's her job, that's what she's there for.

Q. So the nurse would decide when to release the patient from PAR?

A. That is for the anesthesiologist to decide.

Q. Doctor, what, in your opinion, within reasonable medical probability, was the cause of this young woman's cardiopulmonary arrest on the afternoon of December 15?

A. I cannot say with certainty. She—

Q. Do you have an opinion?

A. Yes.

Q. What is that opinion?

A. When I last saw the patient, she was anesthetized, breathing normally, and in good condition. She was a completely normal post-operative patient.

Q. Go on.

A. The patient was awake at the time of discharge from PAR. She complained of not being able to breathe through her nose. The nurse told her to breathe through her mouth. I believe that the patient was having trouble breathing for a period of two and a half hours, and that she fell asleep and was not breathing well. The nurses on the floor observed her several times, and did not notify a physician. I feel that the nurse who is in charge of the patient in a hospital room should call a physician if the patient has trouble breathing. Obviously this was not done until it was too late. The nurse should have contacted the anesthesiologist, or some physician. She should have started with the anesthesiologist. In my opinion, inadequate nursing care is the key factor in this patient's complications.

It was to be expected that Koss would try to place blame on Forstmann and the nurses. What amazed me was how calmly he rationalized away any responsibility on his own part, while he was the surgeon in charge of the case! James ran him through each part of his opinion several times, to make sure, I suppose, that Koss was certain in his mind that the nurses were responsible for Louise's death. Then it was time for lunch. Score for Koss: two hours and forty minutes, 89 pages of predictable testimony.

June 19 was a banner day. Our deposition troupe had a double bill, featuring the "sunny boys," Wiesel and Ebner. Joel Swimmer came into the conference room at Peter Fox's office with Dr. Wiesel at nine o'clock. I could tell that Swimmer, who was fairly short and scrappy anyway, was really wound up.

The very first question that James asked the good doctor, after the usual background questions, got Swimmer started. After Swimmer objected to six questions in a row, for being irrelevant, or improper form, or immaterial, and instructed his client not to answer, Joel suddenly found James towering over him. James said evenly, "Let the record show that Mr. Swimmer objects to all of my questions, for the rest of this deposition. Now, Joel, if you don't shut up, if I hear another peep out of you, I will take you out in the parking lot and kick the shit out of you." Joel paled, and hrummphed, and became very quiet.

That sure brightened my morning.

James couldn't get Wiesel to tell us about the two prior malpractice cases that had been brought against him in the past three years, and for some reason James couldn't just outright ask him if he had been sued for malpractice before. We knew all about it from our investigator, and they knew we knew. So James turned the conversation to the event that most angered me about Wiesel.

Q. And that afternoon of December 15, between, oh, 2:50 and 3:10 p.m., you were standing at or near the nurses' station on floor 2-West?

A. Yes.

Q. Was anyone there with you?

A. There were one or two nurses there. I couldn't say who.

Q. And did Mr. Khavari come to the nurses' station during that time?

A. Yes.

Q. What did he say at that time?

A. I didn't hear him. He said something to one of the nurses, and she followed him back to the room.

Q. And when the code blue sounded, were you at the nurses' station on Floor 2-West?

A. Yes.

Q. Did you hear it?

A. Yes.

Q. Did you respond to the code?

A. No.

Q. Why not?

A. When someone has discharged you, you think they wouldn't want your services.

Q. Someone could be dying, a code—someone could very well be dying—and you didn't think they would want your services?

A. No one asked me for anything.

I was stunned. Even now, ten years later, I cannot believe that a physician could blatantly ignore his Hippocratic Oath, denying the very thing he professed himself to be, in the face of such a situation. It was absolutely incredible to me.

That was certainly the high point of the morning, casewise. We broke for lunch shortly after noon. I didn't have any appetite.

Promptly at 1:15 we got back to business, with Howard Ebner, M.D., the very first doctor that Louise and I had seen on the night of the accident, in the seat of honor. Joel Swimmer had regained his pluck to some extent. After James had run through Ebner's credentials and hospital affiliations, he asked, "Are you presently under suspension, or have you had your privileges lifted?"

A. No.

Q. Have your partner's privileges been lifted from any hospital?

MR. SWIMMER: I object to the question and instruct him not to answer.

MR. ALTMAN: Why?

MR. SWIMMER: Because it is not relevant or material to this case.

MR. ALTMAN: How would you know that?

MR. SWIMMER: Because whether or not his partner, or him for that matter, have had their privileges removed, is not relevant and will not lead to admissible evidence in this case, unless at the time they were practicing on the patient, they were practicing without privileges. Then possibly it might be relevant.

MR. ALTMAN: This is a hypothetical situation. Let us assume that one evaluates the surgeon's performance by looking at the records after the surgery has been performed, and assuming that the credentials committee meets to determine whether or not somebody should have privileges, they would look at a bunch of charts and records of a surgery that may have already taken place at some previous time—now can you say, Joel, that that may not lead to discoverable evidence? How can you make that statement?

MR. SWIMMER: I am making it. I do not think it is relevant to this case. I do not think it will lead to admissible evidence.

MR. ALTMAN: I am not going to argue with you. I would like for the record a yes or no answer to my original question. We do not have to get into any details, but he can give me a yes or no, so we can see whether or not it is worthwhile. If the answer is no, I will not continue with it.

MR. SWIMMER: I do not him want to tell you that.

MR. ALTMAN: As to his partner?

MR. SWIMMER: Do not answer that.

MR. ALTMAN: Do you know whether or not any credentials committee at any hospital is discussing your privileges?

A. Not to my knowledge.

And so on. We hardly heard a hundred words from the actual witness. James turned the conversation through the fact that I had discharged Wiesel and Ebner on or about the 12th of December, and that Ebner felt that the timing was ironic because they were ready to turn the case over to Koss anyway.

Q. Specifically, Doctor, did anybody ever tell you that they were unhappy with the care and treatment you personally rendered to his wife?

A. No.

Q. The complaint was about your partner, Dr. Wiesel?

A. Yes.

Q. What were the conversations that you recall, if any, with her husband following the time she was transferred to the Intensive Care Unit after the second surgery?

A. I believe they were just general sorts of philosophical questions or discussions. I believe I offered him my personal sympathies and commiserations. That would be the extent of it. There was no detailed physiology discussed. More or less I felt very bad that the situation had arisen for his wife.

Q. Did you have a conversation with Dr. Grossinger about this lady after the night of the Christmas party at the Doral Country Club?

A. Yes.

Q. When did that conversation take place?

A. I have no idea.

Q. What was discussed?

A. He said to me that the circumstances of her respiratory arrest were very, very perplexing to everybody involved; that they were doing everything possible at that time, of a retrospective nature, to check into why this happened, that one of the things he was doing was to discuss it, I believe, with a pharmacologist professor at the university, discussing the interaction of drugs, specifically the names of which I can't remember. He never got a follow-up on that. I know he was going to discuss certain aspects of this further with someone at the university.

Q. Did you have any further conversations about the case with Dr. Forstmann? Do you recall a conversation with him?

A. A Conversation, no.

Q. Do you recall having any conversations with him.

A. As I say, it has been a topic of intermittent and multiple discussions between concerned individuals. I do not remember any specific incidents.

Q. That is not necessary. I want you to tell me about these conversations you have had with Dr. Forstmann about this lady.

A. Again they related to similar type things that I mentioned with Dr. Grossinger, concerning the university, anesthetics and drugs, and how they may be related. That is not my field of expertise. I know he was looking into that situation just as anyone would do if they had been concerned.

Q. Where did he suggest that the drugs she was given came from?

MR. GONZALEZ (Forstmann and Walters' attorney): I object to the form of the question. He has not said that she was given drugs.

A. He didn't mention that at all.

Q. So when you say you were talking about drugs, he was talking about the drugs and anesthetic agents that had been given to the patient in the normal course of the hospital?

MR. GONZALEZ: I object to the form of the question. It calls for speculation.

A. To the best of my knowledge, I believe it related to the anesthetics and drugs used in the operating suite at the operation on the 15th.

Well, out of the mouths of babes and "sunny boys!" I said to myself, and sat up to pay more attention.

Q. That would be the same opinion for Dr. Grossinger?

A. Yes, sir.

Q. Did anyone ever approach the subject with you, Doctor, that drugs were brought in from some other source and administered to this lady by any other individual?

A. I was thinking about this. I can't remember the source or the timing of it. I heard of a possible urine or blood sample that may have shown a substance that had not been prescribed by any physician handling her case.

Q. Was this subsequent to the conversation with Dr. Grossinger?

A. Yes.

Q. And subsequent to your conversation with Dr. Forstmann?

A. To my knowledge, yes.

Q. Did Dr. Forstmann indicate to you, or did Dr. Grossinger

indicate to you that they suspected that the lady's respiratory arrest may have been related to the drugs and the anesthetic agents?

A. Well, I believe the feeling of the conversation was that.

MR. SWIMMER: Do not tell him your feeling, but what he said to you.

A. He said that they were—

MR. GONZALEZ: Who said this?

A. Both physicians related to me that they were evaluating that as a possibility at that time.

Q. Did they mention to you the fact that she might have been overmedicated?

A. No.

Q. Did they mention anything to you about the administration of the anesthetics?

A. No.

Q. Did they mention anything to you about the length of time the lady was in the recovery room?

A. No.

Q. Did they mention anything to you about the nursing care on the floor?

A. No.

Q. Did you raise any of these questions?

A. We all do when a reaction occurs.

Q. Who is we?

A. Any concerned physician would.

Q. When you say you raised it, who did you raise it to?

A. I would raise it to me, to myself.

Q. Did you seek to find an answer?

A. On that point, I have not done so.

Q. Why?

A. Because, as I mentioned, I was not on the case and the case is now being evaluated under a legal climate.

Ebner's deposition took only an hour, but it was the most productive hour, as well as the most entertaining in terms of inter-Vulture squabbles, of the season to date. Total time for the double feature: four hours. We got 164 pages of transcripts and some pretty interesting questions to ask Forstmann, whose deposition was scheduled for the next morning, June 20.

Forstmann was present with Paul Sparks and Benito Gonzalez as counsel. Everyone else arrived at James's office early, and we began promptly at 9:00 a.m.

5

Finding Prey

James reviewed Dr. Forstmann's training, professional qualifications, and business relationship with the hospital.Then he went directly to the night of December 14, the night before Louise's second surgery. Forstmann referred to his notes and described Louise as having been in good health, although slightly anemic. He had decided that in light of the anemia, he would have two units of whole blood standing by during the operation; the anemia could possibly reduce the amount of oxygen getting into her blood under anesthesia. He had planned to insert a nasal tube for breathing during the surgery, apparently unaware that she was having nose surgery. Later, during the surgery, Drs. Koss and Grossinger had asked him to remove the nasal tube and place one in her mouth.

On the evening of the 14th, he had talked with Louise, and had ordered her preoperative drugs for 7:00 a.m.: ten milligrams of Valium, ten milligrams of Morphine Sulfate, and two-tenths milligram of Glycopyrrolate. These were to provide sedation and relief of anxiety, and the Glycopyrrolate was a "drying agent." The next time he had seen Louise was outside the operating room the next morning, where he had carefully placed an oxygen mask on her face, and had administered two and a half milligrams of Droperridol, intravenously, for further sedation, he said. (He later said that Droperridol is an antibiotic.)

This he had followed with Pavulon, a muscle relaxant. The

purpose of this, he explained, had been to prevent muscle fasiculation that would be caused by the upcoming Succinyl Choline, which could cause the patient some post-operative muscle pain. He had begun with one milligram of Pavulon, although during the operation he had injected seven milligrams more, at least some of it required to change the breathing tube from nose to mouth. Then, in the next five minutes, he had given her 100 milligrams of Succinyl Choline.

Then had come 350 mg. intravenous Thiopental, also known as Pentothal. The Pentothal had been to render her unconscious, which it had done. Then had come the Fentanyl, 800 micrograms (eight-tenths of a milligram). Each tenthmilligram of Fentanyl was equivalent in analgesic potency to ten milligrams of Morphine, Forstmann explained. He described Fentanyl as a short-acting narcotic agent. The Fentanyl, along with the 66% nitrous oxide being fed through her breathing tube, had been the actual anesthetic agent. Fentanyl and nitrous oxide enhanced each other's effects, he said.

After the surgery, he had administered ten milligrams of Regonol, a reversing agent to counteract the effects of the muscle relaxants Pavulon, so that Louise could breathe for herself again. He then had tested her nerve responses with a "nerve blockade monitor" and had verified that the muscle relaxant effects had been reversed. Her temperature at that time had been recorded as ninety-three degrees.

After this exposition, James inquired about a phenomenon called "re-curization," whereby when such a patient warms up, the muscle relaxant effects can come back. Forstmann said he knew about re-curization, but did not believe that it existed.

"There is much more to it concerning these drugs and the reversal of them than was present when this concept was first propounded, which goes way back," Forstmann explained. "I am saying that patient reversal can be more difficult when they are hypothermic (body temperature is low). If the reversal is not adequate at the time, they may go on to exhibit muscle paralysis later on. However, I am stating to you that I assured myself that this patient was fully reversed at the end of the anesthesia by performing two separate tests on her. It was through the use of a nerve stimulator, which assures me that I have, to the best of my knowledge and current concepts, fully reversed the patient. Once fully reversed, even though hypothermic, when warming they will not reparalyze. I have never been involved in a case that this had so happened." He wasn't reticent, I would say that for Forstmann.

Forstmann went on to say that Louise had been conscious at 12:05 p.m. or so, when he had removed the breathing tube. He had accompanied her to the Post Anesthesia Recovery room at 12:10, placing her in Gail Geraldo's care. He had planned to visit Louise again at 4:30 or 5:00 that afternoon.

Q. Did you ever tell this man you were going to hire a detective or investigator to find out what happened?

A. No.

Q. Did you ever conduct an investigation? Did you ever hire an investigator to find out what happened?

A. No.

Q. Did you ever ask him to make a statement to your investigator?

A. Yes.

Q. Who was your investigator?

A. It was provided by my insurance company.

Q. You were going to make the investigation yourself?

A. That is correct.

Q. You asked him if he would make a statement to your insurance company?

A. I asked if he would speak to him.

Q. So you had contacted your insurance company that day. Was that because you felt that there was a likelihood that legal action would result from the events of that day?

A. Yes.

Q. Based on your review of the chart, was she breathing adequately?

MR. SPARKS: At what point in time?

Q. Ultimately, before she had a respiratory arrest.

A. Yes.

Q. Do you think she was breathing and ventilating adequately prior to that time?

A. No, I don't.

Q. Why?

A. We have a blood gas (test) that was done during the arrest, which demonstrates a problem with respiration that probably existed before the arrest.

Q. What caused it?

This question brought down a flurry of objections from Dan Weiss, the attorney for the hospital. He may have just been bored. Finally, we got back to the question at hand. Obviously, no one had commented when Forstmann had just given two contradictory answers back to back. This happened quite often in the deposition arena, and when James didn't get the answer he wanted, he would just repeat the question until he did.

A. I can tell you what was not the cause of her respiratory difficulty.

Q. Try to tell me what was the cause, in your opinion, Doctor.

A. If you are looking for a simple answer, I can't give it to you. That is my opinion.

Q. I would like to know what you think was the cause, and what your opinion is.

A. It appears that the patient developed respiratory difficulty at some time during her stay in the room, approximately 2:00 p.m. The blood gas that was done at the time of the arrest (about 3:00 p.m.) showed severe respiratory acidosis. Since she was resuscitated shortly after the circulatory arrest, we can only presume that there was a respiratory insufficiency existing prior to the actual arrest itself. I feel that was the cause of the patient's problems, and I feel that the anesthetic agents were probably long since dissipated in their major effect by the time the patient got into trouble. Based upon observations that were made by myself and others who were present at the arrest, we can tell quite certainly that there was no obstruction, either high or low in the airway of this patient. We have a chest X-ray following the arrest, which is basically a clear chest film. So that we know that there was no major pathology that had occurred involving the lungs during this period of time. Since it does not appear to be an anatomical problem—since it really does not appear to be one of a major physiological problem, because the patient was well oxygenated during the resuscitation, because of the ease of the resuscitation. It leads me to believe that there was perhaps an additional pharmacologic agent present that got her into difficulty during the patient's stay in the room. It would take very little drug superimposed upon the recovery from the anesthetic and the surgery to cause a patient to have severe difficulty from a respiratory standpoint, post-operatively. So my best guess or opinion is that there is another drug present, drug or drugs present, that we simply do not have exhibited on the patient's chart.

I had a brief flash of Forstmann practicing that soliloquy in front of a mirror as he tied his tie.

Q. Where would she get the drugs from?

A. There are several possibilities.

Q. Tell me.

A. Nurses give patients drugs for pain, post-operatively, following doctors' orders, which is routine. Sometimes nurses give drugs to patients that are given accidentally, or a wrong drug is given, or a dose that is too large, and perhaps one can assume that this does not always get reported on the chart. Sometimes patients have drugs within the hospital.

Q. Did you have any evidence that this lady was habituated to drugs?

A. No.

Q. Did any of the nurses up on the floor have a history of giving drugs to patients that you knew of at the hospital? Did any of the nurses up on her floor have a history of giving drugs to patients who had just been anesthetized and were just coming out of anesthesia?

A. Patients get post-operative pain medication all of the time.

Q. Did any of the nurses upstairs on the floor do that incorrectly in the past, which would cause this kind of result?

A. Patients have been given medications that have produced respiratory problems for patients.

MR. WEISS: I object to the response and move to strike the answer. It is not responsive as to any of the nurses on 2-West. He cannot say whether they have ever given pain medication that would cause respiratory problems.

Q. You have no evidence, whatever, that she was given anything, or that she took a drug herself?

A. There is a toxicological report.

Q. Does that say she took the drug herself? What does that have to do with respect to her taking the drug herself?

A. The drug may have been given to her.

Q. Could it have been given to her by one of the attending physicians? Is that possible, Doctor?

A. Not to my knowledge.

Q. Is it possible, Doctor?

A. It would be in the hospital records if it were.

Q. I see. Did you find any evidence of these drugs being in the hospital records?

A. No.

Q. So let us assume that the doctor knows he is going to get sued because something happened to a patient, and would it be possible for him to give her a drug that might later show up in her blood?

MR. SPARKS: I instruct you not to answer that question. I do not know that the time period we are talking about is when he knows he is going to get sued.

Q. (MR. ALTMAN:) Sometimes they have an indication, when they come back and the patient is in Intensive Care, and in a coma, that is usually when a red flag goes up.

James' tongue was so far in his cheek I wondered why he didn't choke.

The toxicological report, which Forstmann said was performed by Dr. Grossinger, of all people, was dated the 18th and apparently referred to the 15th or 16th, when the blood and urine samples were taken. No one could say why the test was made, or if that was normal in post-operative circumstances. Evidently it was not. We never did learn exactly why it had been done. Forstmann said that it was unlikely that she got this medication on the 16th, because she was in Intensive Care, with a tube in her mouth, and that the medication would have been taken orally.

Q. What was the medication that you say was oral medication?
A. The particular combination of drugs that I am referring to are Amobarbital and Secobarbital, which are the constituents of a drug known as Tuinal.

This was followed by a lot of testimony about the laboratory, and what sort of tests had been performed.

Q. Then you do not know, do you, Doctor, whether or not Tuinal was the drug?
A. No, I don't.

Then James addressed the curious matter of Louise's release from the Post Anesthesia Recovery room in only half an hour.

Q. Did you approve her transfer to the floor?
A. Yes, I did.
Q. What was the basis for your approving her transfer?
A. The basis was a report given to me by the recovery room nurse at the time.
Q. How was that report given to you?
A. Verbally.
Q. Was it given to you by some means of transmission other than a face-to-face conversation?
A. By telephone.
Q. Where were you when the report was given?
A. I was in the cafeteria.
Q. Could you see into the recovery room from the cafeteria?
A. No.
Q. Did you confirm in any way what the telephone caller had said to you? Did you come and see the patient to confirm the report?
A. Not at that time.

Q. When did you see her next?

A. At the time of her arrest.

Q. Is it the anesthesiologist's responsibility, under the circumstances upon which this lady was operated on, to see a patient in the Post Anesthesia Recovery room?

A. I did see her in the recovery room. I initially saw her when she was transferred, and at least one other time.

Q. When?

A. Perhaps ten minutes after she returned to the recovery room.

Q. About ten minutes after she was brought to the recovery room, you came back in there?

A. Yes.

Q. You were there when she was brought in, and ten minutes later?

A. Yes.

Q. At that time she was making grunting noises?

A. No.

Q. Was she able to say yes or no?

A. I can't recall.

Q. You do not recall one way or the other?

A. I don't recall.

Q. My question is, Doctor, at the time of discharge from the recovery room, does the anesthesiologist assume responsibility for the patient's transfer and her ability to be transferred safely to the floor?

A. Yes.

Q. That is not Nurse Geraldo's responsibility, but that would be yours?

A. It is a joint responsibility.

Q. It was your responsibility, and she was discharged by what she told you on the telephone? Is that the idea?

MR. SPARKS: I object to the form of the question when you say is that the idea.

Q. Strike those words. She called you on the phone, and said what?

A. Nurse Geraldo did not call me on the phone.

Q. Who did?
A. Miss Roberts.
Q. What did she say?
A. She said that the patient is awake and has reached a score of 10. (This refers to the Bernetti Scoring System for post-operative patients.) I can't remember the exact words, but it was to the effect that she was awake and doing fine without any difficulty, and had reached a score of 10.
Q. Is it your testimony, Doctor, that prior to approving this lady's transfer, that you considered the type of anesthetic agents, the use of paralyzing drugs and/or narcotics during surgery, the type of surgery that she had and the duration of the surgery, and that is when you approved the transfer?
A. Yes.

Then James asked whether it would have been expected that Louise should have a tracheotomy tube placed in her after the surgery.

Q. Did you hear any consideration given to that?
A. The only point which I recall, is that I brought to their attention that they would not be able to wire the arch bars shut at the end of the procedure unless a tracheotomy was performed, since she had her nose packed with gauze.
Q. Were they going to wire the mouth when you told them that?
A. They were considering what to do concerning the fixation of the mandible.
Q. Did your conversation, from what you could see, alter their plan?
A. Yes.
Q. Was that because you were concerned about the maintenance of an airway?
A. You have to have a mouth, a nose, or a tracheotomy to breathe through.
Q. From whatever you could see or hear that day, you say you were by the head of the patient?
A. Yes.

Then James got back to the short stay in the recovery room. Forstmann said that there was no minimum required stay.

Q. In other words, if she reached the initial Bernetti score of 10 in seven minutes, in five minutes, or in eight minutes or in ninety minutes—take the minimum of five, eight, or ten minutes. Would that have been ample?

A. I didn't say that.

Forstmann, however, repeated that "there is no minimum time."

Q. On the 16th day of December, 1978, did you have a conversation with Mr. Khavari concerning him making a statement to an investigator, and I am talking about the day after the incident?

A. Yes.

Q. Then you were aware of the fact that something could happen, litigation-wise; is that correct?

A. Yes.

Q. Were you not aware of that on the 15th, the day it happened?

A. Perhaps.

Q. Is that not the day you reported this to your insurance company?

A. Yes.

Q. So as of the 15th, you were aware of the potential for a lawsuit arising out of the situation?

A. Yes.

At noon, we adjourned until the next morning. Forstmann was our most talkative guest by far, and James was very pleased with the way the case was shaping up. I was still puzzled. From all of the testimony we had gotten, how could we identify the guilty party when everyone involved seemed so inept? Was it Forstmann's fault for neglecting Louise or over-medicating her? Or was it Koss' and Grossinger's for wiring her jaw shut when her nose was packed and not providing an airway? Or the nurses' fault for not recognizing that Louise was slowly suffocating? Did anyone know what the hell they were doing?

The next morning, the main event was Mr. Weiss' cross-examination of Forstmann, the thrust of which was to point out that there were rules and policies in this hospital concerning doctors' being required to give written orders to discharge patients from recovery rooms, and to try to make it appear that it wasn't the hospital's fault if doctors didn't follow policy.

Joel Swimmer performed the "Wiesel and Ebner Had Nothing To Do With It Polka," and we got out in just under an hour and a half. Forstmann's prolific contribution: 150 pages in just under four and a half hours. The man could talk. With over an hour to kill before lunchtime, we walked down the hall to James'office, and found in the day's mail a little thirty-two page deposition, taken by Weiss and Gonzalez, of a Dr. Harold Pollock. We had not attended, because this was a routine matter of a "record custodian deposition" where a representative of the medical laboratory which had performed the toxicological tests delivered the records concerning those tests to the court record, as represented by the deposition ceremony.

Weiss and Gonzalez were not about to forget that they were paid by the hour, so they made sure to ask the doctor, who was the president of the laboratory, about every aspect of who had filled in which blanks, and so forth. The facts were as follows: the toxicological report was prepared on December 18, and consisted of analysis of blood and urine samples. No one knows when the samples had been taken. No one knew who had ordered the test. Subtherapeutic amounts of barbiturates, specifically Amytal and Secobarbital, had been detected. In fat, the levels of barbiturates in Louise had been "extremely low, if at all present....The result from this is very uncertain..." And so on. There could have been a small amount of barbiturates ingested twelve to forty-eight hours prior to the samples being taken. Whenever that was. For whatever reason. He didn't know.

When the defense's plans to accuse me of killing my own wife were first mentioned, James had told me not to worry about that in the least. Somehow, shortly after that, his investigator, Jack Daws, had gotten a copy of the toxicology report. Jack had forwarded the report, with a brief description of the case, to a Dr. Roger Player, a pharmacologist, for evaluation. As he filed the deposition with the report, James showed me a memorandum from Jack relating his conversation with Dr. Player on June 5. Player said that the Thiopental given preoperatively on December 15 explained the barbiturate readings in the toxicology report.

He also said that the 800 micrograms of Fentanyl, a respiratory depressant, was equal to 80 milligrams of Morphine, an almost lethal dose. When the surgery was finished, they should have given her Narcan, a drug that reverses the effects of narcotics almost instantly, Player said. She had been given Narcan after the first surgery, but not after the second. Player stated that the combination of drugs given to Louise by Forstmann was too heavy a dose, and nothing was given to her to reverse it. He felt that if Louise had been given Narcan after surgery, or at 12:40 p.m. when she couldn't breathe properly, or even at 3:08 p.m. at the time of her arrest, she could well have survived. As it was, by the time the Narcan was administered, two doses at 3:23 p.m., during the code, it was simply too late.

"We still don't know who requested that report, or when the blood and urine specimens were taken," James said as he closed the file. "I bet it was Forstmann. He knew he had given her a lot of drugs, and he is the one who called the insurance company on the 15th. It had to be Forstmann, or someone out to pin it on Forstmann. Maybe Grossinger did request it, like Forstmann says. It doesn't matter, because it doesn't prove anything. Maybe Grossinger was hoping to find evidence that Forstmann had overdosed her so that he wouldn't be looked at for failing to put in a tube after he wired her jaw. They're all guilty as hell, anyway. Let's have lunch."

Early in July, I began to get concerned that expenses in the case might be getting out of hand. There were expert witness reports, depositions, reams and reams of paperwork, and, of course, no results yet. We hadn't even collected a dime from the insurance company.

I asked James Altman and Peter Fox about the expenses, which were my responsibility. Both professed not to be concerned with such mundane matters, and said that they were just doing what had to be done. I persisted, and James said he would have a statement made up so we could all see where things stood.

On July 18, Kathy the secretary handed me a two-page itemized list of "Costs Incurred to Date" and I got a little bit faint. The total was $17,336.62, including such items as court reporters' fees for our depositions ($2,262.15) and a staggering $3,247.49 for over 20,000 photocopies! The experts had gotten most of the rest, including one Dr. Powder ($3,525), a Dr. Jeffries ($1,500) and various others for a grand here and a grand there.

I told Peter that this was quite a bit more than the "seven or eight, maybe ten thousand" he had estimated in the beginning, and he said something about what it takes to get the job done, er, ah, um, and so on. I thought it pretty curious that an experienced attorney who had handled a hundred cases like mine couldn't have estimated the probable expenses in my case any better than Peter had done. After all, he had worked with all of these experts before, and certainly knew how much they charged.

But I kept my thoughts to myself. I guess what impressed me the most was that Peter and James's firm had actually paid all of these expenses out of pocket. These weren't just bills that would have to be paid when we won the case.

I figured that meant that Peter and James were confident of our ultimate victory, and considered the case a good investment. On the other hand, they knew I'd be getting $50,000 or so from my car insurance company one fine day...

What with all the Vultures' schedules, and vacations and so on, the next time the deposition club could meet was July 9. We were to hear from two nurses that morning, neither of whom I had met. We convened at the conference room at Colonial Hospital. Our first witness was Nancy Roberts, who had relieved Gail Geraldo in the recovery room at 12:25 p.m. on December 15, about fifteen minutes after Louise had come out of the operating room.

James ran through her training and career, underscoring the fact that Nancy had had no special training as a Post Anesthesia Recovery nurse, other than a part of her basic training ten years earlier and some "orientation" by Gail Geraldo. Nancy was a "circulating nurse" and occasionally filled in for Gail in the recovery room, perhaps one day a month. The fact that she had relieved Gail so that Gail could leave early on December 15th was due to her assignment there by one Sharon Todd, who, as luck would have it, was our next guest this morning.

As a circulating nurse, Nancy happened to have been present during Louise's surgery on the 15th, and had helped Forstmann with the anesthesia prior to the operation.

Q. (MR. ALTMAN:) Did you hear any discussions take place between Dr. Koss and Dr. Grossinger concerning whether or not the patient should have a tracheal tube in place?
A. No.
Q. I take it that as circulating nurse you were close to the patient during the procedure?
A. Yes.
Q. Were you at tableside?
A. I have to remain about four feet away.
Q. When you say "have to remain," you mean that literally, that the circulating nurse's job is to stay there throughout the duration of the procedure; is that correct?
MR. WEISS: Objection to that. There is no predicate, she is not scrubbed-
THE WITNESS: You can only get so close.
Q. But apart from getting only so close, it's your job to be there?
A. Yes.

Later, when she went to relieve Gail Geraldo in the recovery room:

Q. What did Mrs. Geraldo say to you about the patient?
A. Mrs. Geraldo said that she was doing very, very well.
Q. Very, very well?
A. Very, very well and would be ready to go shortly.
Q. And did she tell you that she had written an order transferring the patient?
A. I don't remember her telling me that.

Q. Do you remember whether or not you wrote an order transferring the patient?

A. I believe I co-signed the order she had written, but I don't recall her telling me she had written it.

Q. Did she write an order?

A. I believe she did.

Q. And you say you co-signed it?

A. Well, since I was discharging a patient—

Q. This is something written on the physician's order sheet, correct?

A. Correct.

Q. And it was not written by the physician?

A. No.

Q. And is that something that is customary when it's time to discharge a patient, according to the rules of the hospital, that the nurse writes in the discharge from PAR order—

MR. GONZALEZ: Object to the form of the question.

A. Am I supposed to answer?

MR. WEISS: Yes.

MR. ALTMAN: Is it customary here that the nurses write the orders?

MR. GONZALEZ: Same objection.

THE WITNESS: Yes, if she—yes.

Q. If she what?

A. Well, if the physician isn't right there to write it himself.

Q. Let me show you this order, and this is the 15th of December, 1978, "Discharge from PAR," and the letter `F.' Did you write that sentence?

A. No, Gail did.

Q. What, if anything, did you write?

A. I wrote, "Dr. F. Forstmann, per N. Roberts" and my signature up here with the check mark.

Q. Did you rate this patient?

A. I don't believe I did.

Q. So she had already been rated a 10 prior to the time you got there?

A. I believe so.

Q. Well, how long did you spend with her, ma'am?

A. I believe about ten minutes.

Q. What did you do in this ten minutes?

A. I took her blood pressure, I talked to her, and I just observed her.

Q. What did you say to her?

A. I said, "Are you awake? Are you awake?" I think I said to her, "Are you awake? Are you all right?"

Q. Now, according to this note, she was admitted to the PAR at 12:10: "Patient awake and aware. Verbalizes appropriately in short sounds yes or no." Did you agree with that?

A. Yes.

Q. She was either nodding or saying yes or no?

A. Yes.

Q. Did you converse with her?

A. No, but she did say a sentence. I said, "How are you doing?" and she said, "I don't like to breathe through my mouth." And I said, "Well, you have to breathe through your mouth because you have something in your nose."

Q. Mrs. Roberts, was anything else said by you or her when she said "I don't like to breathe through my mouth."

A. I don't recall.

Q. Was she complaining of difficulty?

A. No.

James then led the conversation around to whether there was any minimum amount of time that a patient should stay in the recovery room after anesthesia, and about the rating system for scoring the patient's recovery.

Q. Is there anything at all with respect to the kind of surgery, the length of time of the surgery, say, oh, the amount of intubation time, how many times the patient was intubated or extubated with respect to the amount of time in the OR, or is it just conditional based on the patient?

MR. GONZALEZ: Object to the form of the question.

A. It is all based on the condition of the patient.

Q. So would it be fair to say, then, if she was brought in at 12:10, if at 12:25 she had rated out a 10, under this system of discharge, it would be fine for you to transfer the patient if you go through the telephone procedure with the anesthesiologist?

MR. GONZALEZ: Object to the form of the question.

MR. WEISS: Also object on the basis that it's not factual. It's not talking about this case. In this case she was in for thirty minutes, and it is not relevant and material in this case what would have happened to some patient that may have been in there for five minutes.

A. We would never keep a patient in the recovery room for five minutes.

Q. Why?

A. Because we usually keep them for half an hour.

Q. You just told me it's based on the condition of the patient.

A. I said based on the condition of the patient, but I didn't understand—we usually keep them for at least half an hour, at least two vital signs.

Q. Is there a minimum time that you keep patients at this institution, regardless of how they rate out under this scoring system?

MR. GONZALEZ: Object to the form of the question.

A. Yes.

Q. Does the scoring system in the areas of respiration, circulation or consciousness, as you understand it, have you ever been trained that sometimes these things are reversed or altered as a function of time?

MR. GONZALEZ: I object.

MR. ALTMAN: Will you shut up for five seconds and let me finish my question? Just stay off my back, and when I am done you will object at the end of the God damned question. You are the biggest horse's ass.

James would just keep asking the question until he got the answer he wanted, but he had only so much patience.

We had wrung every possible drop of remotely relevant

information out of Nurse Roberts in just over an hour. Ten minutes after that, the curtain went up on Act Two, starring Sharon Todd. Benito Gonzalez was still smarting from James' outburst, and glared at him as James reviewed Sharon Todd's eleven-year career as a nurse, including operating room experience and her infrequent substitutions as a recovery room nurse. As soon as James asked a question to which Gonzalez started to object, James pounced on him.

MR. ALTMAN: In order for us to have a meaningful dialogue without any interruptions, Mr. Gonzalez, I am going to acknowledge that from here on out you have objected to the form of every single question. I am doing that now, so you need not make the objection. I am asking the court to note that you have objected to the questions.

MR. GONZALEZ: That is not necessary.

MR. ALTMAN: I would prefer it. Your record is protected. And that was, she and I—I can ask some questions, and you don't have to worry about it.

Q. (MR. ALTMAN:) Go ahead, if you would, and tell us when it was that you became familiar with this patient. Do you know who we are talking about, Louise Khavari?

Sharon, as it turned out, had assisted on Louise's first surgery, and had seen Narcan administered at the end of that surgery. She noted that Louise had spent some two hours in the recovery room at that time. Yes, she had assigned Nancy Roberts to relieve Gail Geraldo on the 15th. It was her job that day to decide who did what, and Nancy substituted in the recovery room all the time.

Quite a few minutes passed before Benito Gonzalez squeaked another "object to the form." James let it pass without acknowledgment. Then, this testimony followed:

Q. With respect to the duties of a recovery room nurse at this particular hospital, do you know whether or not the physician or the anesthesiologist is supposed to examine the patient prior to a patient's being discharged from the Post Anesthesia Recovery room to their floor?

MR. GONZALEZ: Object to the form.

MR. ALTMAN: Did you hear that your objections are on the record? Are you just troubled, nervous, upset, and inexperienced?

It was already past noon, and the Vultures found that they really had no further business with this witness. We were all out of there by 12:15. Score for the morning: ninety-five minutes total testimony, 96 pages.

One task I was especially grateful that James was handling was collecting on our insurance policies. I had been fortunate at the time I had hired Peter Fox's firm, in that I had insisted that the firm not charge their usual forty percent fee on proceeds from my own insurance policies, and that they had agreed to provide this service without charge.

I am sure that they knew that this was a much bigger favor than I had imagined. For example, the amount of paperwork required to collect the small death benefit included in our AAA membership would have cost far more than the $1,250 I finally received, if the office had charged by the hour for it. Upon notification by James that he was representing me and that we wanted to collect on the death benefit, the AAA Life Insurance Company wrote to James as follows:

"We regret to hear of this unfortunate loss; please convey our condolences to the family of the deceased. Please send us:

(a) Death certificate bearing raised seal.

(b) Obituary notice.

(c) Newspaper account of the accident.

(d) Police accident report.

(e) Copy of autopsy report.

(f) Claimant's signed statement. (Blank enclosed). It must be completed and signed by the surviving spouse.

(g) Doctor's signed statement.

We enclose our return envelope for your convenience."

Convenience. But this was only a foreshadowing of the machinations that would be involved in collecting on the Uninsured Motorist coverage on our Allstate policy.

The driver of the car that had caused the accident had not had insurance, or a driver's license for that matter. Our Allstate policy included "Excess Uninsured Motorist" benefits of $50,000 per person, $100,000 per accident. I had offered $50,000 of this to Ed Park's widow, Dorothy, and her attorney had notified us that she would accept this and sign a release stating that she would not seek further damages from me or my insurance company. The remaining $50,000 was to be apportioned between Louise and me for our injuries and her death, and of course, this was academic because the money would all come to me anyway.

After waiting for four months, I began to wonder just how good those hands I was supposedly in were. I complained to James about this delay, and asked him what the hell was the point of having insurance anyway. I mean, when AAA wanted all that paper to release a lousy $1,250, was it going to take some kind of lawsuit to get $100,000 in coverage I had paid for?

James took me out to lunch, and there I got an education on insurance companies and insurance coverage. And I gained a new appreciation of James' cleverness. There would have been no problem getting the money before this, James explained. In fact, even Howard Bellman could have collected it—and taken his forty percent—easily. There was one important thing to consider, however, and that was called "subrogation." In the context of this insurance coverage, this meant that by accepting payment of the Uninsured Motorist coverage I would subrogate any claims I had or would have against any other parties. This would mean that the insurance company could get their $100,000 back if I, or anyone acting on my behalf, were to win money from anyone else. In other words, if I took the $100,000 and then won $100,000 in my case, I would have to give it to Allstate.

I realized that most attorneys would have taken the easy way out, gotten the $100,000 and taken the quick $40,000, leaving me with $60,000. Then, if they had won in my suit, $100,000 of my share would have gone to the insurance company. That would have meant that the first $167,000 awarded to me would have gone to repay the $60,000 I would have gotten in the beginning.

This didn't seem right, but there it was. The solution to this predicament turned out to be relatively simple, but arriving at it was taking some time, and James had to retain another attorney to help him with it. Under the circumstances, I was pretty impressed that James had thought about the potential problem at all.

The other, potentially much greater, problem which had to be circumvented was that by taking the money from the car insurance, I might compromise the outcome of the lawsuit. If any action of mine could be interpreted as stating that Louise's death had occurred as a result of the car accident, this could ruin our claim that her wrongful death was a result of medical malpractice, which it plainly was. And we certainly didn't want to give the hospital or the doctors—or their insurance companies—any help.

The resolution of both problems was contained in a short agreement that James and his attorney cooked up. This agreement stated that $40,000 was accepted for Louise's bodily injury only, and specifically not for wrongful death, that $10,000 was for my injuries (concerning which there were no lawsuits anyway), and that Allstate had our permission and would have our complete cooperation to attempt to recover from the driver of the other car if they wished to do so. Ed Park's widow got her $50,000, or whatever was left after her lawyer got his check.

In all fairness, I must commend the Allstate "good hands" folks for their understanding and cooperation in accepting non-standard releases, and generally being very helpful. And I was truly sincere when I told James how much I appreciated his help. I signed some papers and received two checks totaling $50,000 on July 30, a mere seven months after Louise's death, and not even eight months after the accident.

6

Circling for the Kill

Summer is really the slow season in the justice business, especially if you have to coordinate the schedules of eight busy lawyers, and then cross them with those of two busy doctors. We were finally able to corral all parties on August 20 and 21, six weeks after our last deposition. These were our last two defendants, Drs. Walters and Martin.

I felt badly that we were suing Dr. Walters. This guy had done a fine job as my own anesthesiologist, had had nothing to do with Louise's second surgery, had just happened to come along and find her in the process of being dead, and had resuscitated her. I didn't feel quite as badly, though, after I heard his deposition.

Dr. Walters was accompanied by his (and Forstmann's) attorneys, Paul Sparks and Mr. "object to the form" himself, Benito Gonzalez. We got down to business at 9:45 a.m., with James running through the doctor's curriculum vitae, and determining that on December 15, 1978, he had been the Medical Director of the Anesthesia Department at Colonial Hospital. The job gave him the right to screen all candidates coming into the department, and he had overall supervision of the members of the department, who were Forstmann, Cooley, and himself.

James then called Dr. Walters' attention to the hospital's "Recovery Room Policy and Procedure" manual, from which James had the doctor read one statement, and then another which contradicted it.

Q. How about page 7, Roman numeral VII?

A. Discharge criteria? Well, there is a conflict. If you will read VI and if you go back to the "Anesthesia Policy" manual, page 9, number 6. Number 6 says that the patient may only be released from the recovery room by direct order from an anesthesiologist, and C says that a written discharge by the physician directly responsible for the patient while in the recovery room. So, I would say that the term written discharge by the physician means the written discharge after discharge by the physician; that the physician does not necessarily have to specifically handwrite the discharge order but he can direct somebody else to write that discharge order for him

This was a convenient interpretation, because Dr. Walters rarely saw his own patients at the time they were declared fit for discharge from the recovery room, either. He routinely relied upon the observations of Gail Geraldo or Nancy Roberts.

I could not believe how completely casual the doctors and nurses in that hospital were about Post Anesthesia Recovery. They feed you enough drugs to kill an elephant, keep you alive only by means of machines, and bring you to the point where you can open your eyes and mumble, and then they're done with you!

In the weeks since the last deposition, I had gradually become distanced from the lawsuit as I became more accustomed to living my life without Louise. She was gone, and that was that. I talked with James every day, but the case became more of a background event that we mentioned in passing.

Now the old frustration and anger were coming back. And then I was suddenly paralyzed, reliving that whole terrible afternoon. I sat helpless as my heart was ripped open.

Q. On December 15, 1978, how was it that you happened to come to her room?

A. I was going to the floor where she was situated either to see my patients for the next day or make post-operative visits—I don't recall—and as I came past the nurse's station I saw Mrs. MacMillan stooping to open the crash cart, the emergency resuscitation cart. I asked what was going on because it was general practice that you do not open the emergency cart unless there's an emergency, and she said that Dr. Forstmann's patient—she may have referred to Louise specifically—was having trouble breathing and that she was getting an airway for Dr. Forstmann, that she had just finished talking to him on the telephone and had walked over to the cart to get an airway because the last time that Dr. Forstmann had assisted her with a patient who was having trouble breathing he asked for an airway and she wanted to have everything ready for him.

Now, why James didn't leap on this blatant statement that Louise was not the first of Forstmann's patients to have difficulty breathing, I do not know. For all I know, a couple of more questions could have established that Forstmann was the angel of death. I was as stunned by James' ignoring it as I was by the offhand way that Walters talked about it.

Q. Had you heard a code called at that time?

A. No, I had not.

Q. Can you tell us that a code had not been called at that time?

A. I do not believe that a code had been called at that time.

Q. So we understand each other, your walking down that particular hall was something that you were doing in the ordinary course of the discharge of your duties and not in response to any emergency known to you?

A. That is correct.

Q. Did Barbara MacMillan tell you anything about the conversation that she had with Dr. Forstmann, other than what you have told us?

A. She told me that she had spoken to Dr. Forstmann and that he was going to be up shortly.

Q. Did Barbara seem anxious about the patient's condition?

A. She did not seem panicked. She seemed appropriately concerned.

Q. Appropriate for what? By that I am saying appropriate for—

A. Somebody who was sitting in front of an emergency cart opening it up. She had a look of concern in her face and a tone in her voice, I would say.

Q. There is no doubt at that moment on December 15, 1978—and you correct me if I am wrong—Louise was not your patient?

A. That is correct.

Q. Nevertheless, did you render some assistance to her?

A. I asked—

MR. SWIMMER (Wiesel and Ebner's attorney, sensing what was coming): I object to the form.

Q. Did you render some assistance to her?

A. I asked Mrs. MacMillan if I could be of some help until Dr. Forstmann could arrive and she said that she would appreciate my presence, or words to that effect.

Q. Why did you offer to help?

A. Again, she was opening an emergency cart and I felt that if she were opening an emergency cart there may be an emergency going on and that I do not like bad things to happen to any patients in the hospital whether they were mine or not.

Q. Was your reaction towards this situation—and, again, you correct me if I am wrong—but you did not know at that time that it was an emergency, one way or the other, correct?

MR. SWIMMER: Objection to the form.

A. I presumed it was an urgent situation.

Q. Was the taking care of a patient in this fashion—that is, becoming involved in someone who was not your patient previously, something that you consider to be expected of physicians in this community?

MR SWIMMER: Objection to form.

A. Since I was not asked specifically by anybody to see the patient, I would say I was under no obligation to do what I did.

Q. You could have just ignored the whole situation?

A. Exactly.

Q. That would be okay?

A. Yes.

Q. Do you have any recollection as to the time that this was?

A. I have seen various times printed in parts of the chart. I do not know exactly what time it was.

Q. What did you do about this situation?

A. I walked with Mrs. MacMillan into the room and I saw Louise in bed. Her husband and I believe it's her parents were standing by her bedside leaning forward and staring at her.

Q. What were they saying?

A. I do not remember them saying a thing.

Q. They were standing at her bedside staring at her?

A. Leaning. They were—as you approached the bed, you would approach her from her left. They were standing at her right and, as I approached, they stepped back to the foot of the bed.

Q. How did she appear to you? Tell us what you saw, Doctor.

A. When I walked into the room, she was in bed with the head of the bed elevated maybe twenty or thirty degrees. She was facing straight forward. Her arms were down by her side. I would say she looked pale. She did not look cyanotic. She had nasal packing in place. I put my hand over her mouth to see if I could feel her breathing. I did not see any movement. I did not feel any warmth come out of her mouth.

Q. You saw no chest movement?

A. I saw no movements of any kind. I saw no chest movements. I put my hand on her neck to feel for a carotid pulse and I did not feel one. I then turned to the family and asked them to please leave. I walked around the foot of the bed to get to her right side, put a stethoscope on her chest. I heard no heartbeat. I immediately started mouth to mouth resuscitation and asked the girl who was behind Mrs. MacMillan—I don't know who that was—to call the Code Blue while Mrs. MacMillan started CPR.

Q. She was unconscious then?

A. She was, I believe, in full cardiopulmonary arrest and you are unconscious within fifteen seconds after your heart stops beating, as a general rule.

Q. Yes, she was unconscious at the time, correct?

A. I believe she had a cardiac arrest. It is a term different that unconscious. She was not conscious.

Q. I appreciate your educating me on that matter. I can only speak in terms of what I know, and that is fine. What was your diagnosis of the patient at that time?

A. My diagnosis was cardiopulmonary arrest.

Q. You instituted CPR?

A. Yes.

Q. Did that cause her to breathe?

A. No.

Q. Did she ever regain normal breathing by virtue of CPR?

A. I believe that she started some respirations afterwards, but I will have to say that as I did the CPR, I had the smell and taste that I can only describe as sour milk and that is a descriptive term of the smell and not necessarily anything that was present.

Q. By the way, I am curious about the diet that Dr. Wiesel put her on involving dairy products.

A. I was not aware of that at the time. But, in any event, I became so nauseated after the chest massage was started that as soon as Dr. Forstmann arrived, who I believe was the first physician to arrive after the code was called, I immediately had him take over and I was turned to the side for fear of vomiting and it was a while before I could turn back to the patient from my own physical disabilities having started the CPR and so I cannot tell you all of the events because I did not witness some of the original events clearly.

Q. Did you have any conversation with Dr. Forstmann after he arrived?

A. Yes.

Q. What did you say to him?

A. I told him that I came upon her and that she had arrested. The conversation was made that at the time no drugs had been given.

Q. What was the cause of her condition, please?

A. I don't know the exact cause of it, of the cardiopulmonary arrest.

Q. Do you have a hypothesis?

A. I have no way of really putting all the events together to make perfect sense. The details just do not fit completely. There are too many things that do not fit.

Q. What are the things that do not fit that cause you not to be able to arrive at a cause of the cardiopulmonary arrest that you have diagnosed?

A. She was awake enough to—according to Dr. Forstmann's comments. I don't know if it is written in the chart or even in the deposition, but at one point he told me that she was awake enough to move herself from the operating table to the stretcher that takes her to the recovery room. She was awake on several occasions in the recovery room and she was also awake, by the nurses' reports from the depositions that I have looked through, on the floor after leaving the recovery room. Subsequent to that time she developed—

Q. Forgive me. Have you read anywhere where she was not awake or where she was sleeping soundly and breathing with difficulty?

A. Sleeping soundly is different than—one can be awake and fall asleep and sleep soundly and not be depressed (i.e. not have depressed respiration).

Q. Go ahead.

A. Subsequently there were reports that she became depressed as near as I can understand the way things were put, and was subsequently not arousable and then she suffered her cardiac arrest.

Q. What do you think caused her not to be arousable?

A. I don't know. I have seen the laboratory report where she had barbiturates on board, which were not administered by anybody who reported their administration in the record. And that brings to my mind as to when those drugs were administered and if, indeed, they were administered to her post-operative, that could explain exactly what happened. However, there is no documentation that they were ever administered to her in the hospital.

Q. If the drugs in fact were related back to the anesthetic drug that she was given, if that were true—

A. I was told by the hospital laboratory that they asked the Muller-Gross Laboratory if sodium pentothal could be confused with the Amobarbital and Secobarbital at all and they then subsequently asked the laboratory and it was reported back to me that sodium pentothal could not be mistaken in the laboratory test used.

Q. Let me ask you this: assume that the drugs that were found could be related back to the anesthetic agents that were used during the procedure. Would that be an acceptable explanation to you as to the cause of the condition that was diagnosed?

MR. SPARKS: I am going to object and instruct the witness not to answer since there is no predicate. I do not think he should be asked to make the assumption.

Q. Pharmacologically, do you think the drugs are related, that is the anesthetic agents, to those found at Muller-Gross Labs?

A. Pharmacologically there is a relationship between sodium pentothal and Amobarbital and Secobarbital and Pentobarbital and a number of others. They are pharmacologically related.

Q. The answer to the question is, yes, or it could be one or the other?

MR. SPARKS: What question?

Try as he might, James could not get Walters to say that the drugs found in Louise's blood and urine could have resulted from the anesthesia. So he took another tack.

Q. Fine. With respect to the cause of her condition, that is her lack of consciousness and the cardiopulmonary arrest, is it your belief within probability that it was probably caused by some form of drug as opposed to anything else?

A. That could be one explanation.

Q. Any other explanations?

A. Other explanations include possibility of pulmonary embolus, the possibility of aspiration, none of which have been confirmed by any of the tests that were done.

Well, further questioning ruled out aspiration; after all, the airway was "absolutely clear" when Walters performed the CPR. So it came down to Louise's cardiopulmonary arrest being caused by one of two things, in Walters' opinion: drugs, or pulmonary embolus. None of the tests performed on Louise could have detected a pulmonary embolus, if there had been such a thing.

Q. We come down to, and correct me if I am wrong, either drugs which may be related to the anesthetic drugs given, or, if you accept what Dr. Forstmann may have hypothesized, from some other source, be it nurses or husband or some other source. That is category one. Category two would be pulmonary embolus.

MR. SPARKS: You said drugs, and the only one that he has identified as being similar to the ones found at Muller-Gross was the sodium pentothal.

A. Or the possible administration by somebody of Amobarbital and Secobarbital. So there's three possible drugs.

Q. Now I have information to lay the predicate, and I want you to listen to a letter. I am going to read it to you and give you a copy of it.

"Dear Dr. Pollock: This is written conversation of our telephone conversation of July 18, 1979..."

By the way, I went to Muller-Gross Labs after Dr. Pollock's deposition was taken where I was not able to attend, and I went to ask some questions. I did a couple other things.

"...during which we explored the methodology employed in the toxicology screen on the blood and urine of the late Louise Khavari. We also discussed the report submitted following the analysis performed by Muller-Gross Laboratories.

"It is my understanding that neither the `Emit' system distributed by Silverman Laboratories nor the `Toxilab' system distributed by Analytical Systems can differentiate between small amounts of closely related barbiturates such as Pentobarbital, Secobarbital, and Amobarbital."

Do you understand this so far?

A. Yes.

Q. "These analytical techniques, in all probability, could detect small amounts of thio-derivatives resulting from the biotransformation of thiopental." Are you with me?

A. Yes.

Q. It is within the realm of medical probability that both the

Emit and Toxilab systems were detecting Pentobarbital, an end product of thiopental metabolism which is excreted in the urine." Do you follow so far?

A. Yes.

Q. "Since you had no clinical history and are most often called upon to perform such tests on the blood and urine of patients who ingested drugs and since Tuinal intoxication is common in your area, your report read, `positive barbiturates (possible Amo and Seco).' This statement was made on the basis of frequency of occurrence rather than upon positive analytical identification of a specific barbiturate. Had you been told that Louise was induced into anesthesia with a thiobarbiturate known to be metabolized to an oxybarbiturate your report would have been quite different.

"The report on the results of the GC analysis of the blood sample should have read `none detected.' Peaks identified on the basis of retention time, in reality were too small to allow for either qualitative or quantitative analysis.

"The report was once again based upon frequency of occurrence rather than upon definitive analytical data. A GC-Mass Spectrograph was not employed in these determinations.

"I believe this summarizes our conversation and I would be grateful if you would provide confirmation of the accuracy of my understanding of the results of your analysis by return mail, with a copy of your confirmation to James Altman. Many thanks for your cooperation." The letter is signed by Howard L. Powder, M.D., Ph.D. I have a confirming letter from Dr. Pollock, which is written to both Dr. Powder and myself, in which he confirms the accuracy of that conversation, which took place in my presence, Dr. Powder's presence, and his. To put to rest this drug business, if you assume that what is contained in this letter is true, and Dr. Pollock will so testify, and that is the predicate that Mr. Sparks was talking about, what then would you think was the cause of the cardiopulmonary arrest?

The other Vultures stopped the show to examine the letters, and they found another one, too. James had been doing his homework. The letter was from Silverman Laboratories in Palo Alto, California, the manufacturer of the urine test that Muller-Gross had used, stating that: "Using our Urine Barbiturate Assay it is not possible to differentiate between the various barbiturates. Our assay has been designed as a screen to detect the presence of any of the barbiturate compounds. Many of our customers who wish to differentiate use EMIT as a presumptive screen and further test positive samples with another methodology such as Gas Chromatography."

"As you know," James said, "That was not done in this case. Doctor, I want you to take into consideration this particular report of Dr. Pollock and Dr. Powder and would you tell me now, sir, based upon the information contained therein and assume that is what is going to be the testimony in this case, what then would you say about the cause of these drugs or the origin of these particular drugs?"

A. Well—

Q. If that is true.

A. Then I would have to say that pulmonary embolus is as good an explanation for her sudden arrest as any.

Q. What would you say about from where the drugs came?

A. I would say that the only drugs that we have identified were drugs that were administered either pre-operatively or post-operatively that we have a record of.

Q. At the conclusion of this lawsuit, the one we are involved in, we may want to know who it was or from whom you heard anything about the involvement of Farid insofar as either administering illicit drugs to his wife, if you have heard any conversation about that particular conclusion. So for now, did anyone ever tell you that they thought that Farid had administered drugs to his wife?

A. I never heard anybody say that they had any evidence that he had administered any drugs.

Q. Were you successful or unsuccessful at your attempt to revive Louise?

A. I was initially successful at ventilating her. The fact that she returned to heartbeat without the aid of electrical defibrillation and all, indicates that we were successful from a mechanical point of view in resuscitating.

Q. What about in terms of bringing her out of what you call her state of "was not consciousness"?

A. We, she, to my knowledge, she never awakened.

Q. Why? Why do you think she never awakened?

A. I presume she had brain death along the way. That is hard to say.

And indeed it was. Bit by bit James wound him through all of the factors that could lead to a logical conclusion. Finally Walters came up with, "I would say that she could not have been ventilating properly prior to my entering the room...it is possible that her ventilation was inadequate for a period of a half hour or more."

Then James went to town about Louise's anemia, low hemoglobin (red blood cells) level in the blood. And since red blood cells carry oxygen, the less red blood cells one has, the shorter the time one has to be breathing inadequately before the body would have insufficient oxygen.

Q. Who tells the people up on the floor the lady was anemic? Who tells them that?

A. Probably nobody.

Q. Nobody. I see.

After a few more minutes, it was Dan Weiss' turn to crossexamine the witness. Gradually he led the dialogue to:

Q. Have you subsequently had any conversations with any of the nursing personnel about this case?

A. No.

Q. By that, I mean talking about Nurse Geraldo, Nurse Roberts, Nurse MacMillan, Nurse Lang, Nurse Knopfloch, Nurse Masters?

A. Nurse Geraldo was in tears the next day in the hospital and I asked her why. She said because she felt very upset over Louise's death and I asked her why.

Q. The next day she was not dead.

A. Over her arrest. I asked her why. She said that she felt upset with the fact she had left the recovery room in what appeared to be a good condition, or at least she left the patient in what appeared to be a good condition. The patient left the recovery room shortly after she (Geraldo) left the hospital and the patient had a subsequent cardiac arrest and in her own mind she was trying to figure out if there was anything that she did or could have done differently that related to the situation and that she couldn't; that she was very concerned and that she had done all she could do and she was just extremely distraught over the whole situation. I asked her what happened. She said, "She was awake when she was here. I don't understand what happened," and she wanted to—she needed reassurance that there was nothing that she missed, that she should have done differently. I can't think of any other specific conversations with any of the nurse over this. One of the reasons that I did not—that we did not specifically go into this was that considering the situation, and retrospectively it was proven right, there was litigation involving the incident and I think although it is counterproductive because the longer you wait before you get all of the facts, the fuzzier the facts get. Everybody advised don't discuss anything with anybody because you never know what conversations you have is going to be brought up. What statements you may make and, therefore, the medical community suffers because we cannot discuss what happened and how to prevent it next time.

I guess that was not the first time that the legal system ever flew in the face of common sense, but Walters had an interesting point there.

James asked some more questions next, about whether the nurses should have reacted sooner, and Walters allowed that, well, in restrospect it is plain to see that they should have, but we shouldn't be too hasty here because they may not have had the necessary data at that point to make the right decision.

All told, we kept Dr. Walters for nearly three hours (108 pages) and finally quit when the Vultures got hungry. We broke at 12:30 p.m.

The next morning we got right to work with Dr. Michael Martin, the neurologist whom Koss had called into Louise's case at 7 p.m. the evening of December 15, some four hours after her cardiopulmonary arrest. Martin was under the wing of Francis Gautier, who James told me was the best defense attorney around for such matters.

After the formalities concerning Martin's education and career, Martin said that when he had examined Louise, he had found her to be in a coma, and that his examination had determined that there was damage to both sides of her brain, which ruled out a stroke as the cause of her condition at that time. It was apparent that the brain damage was brought on by the cardiopulmonary arrest. Then, James fished patiently for Martin's opinion as to the cause of Louise's arrest.

Gautier, the *eminence gris* took the opportunity to give James a lesson in the art of interrogation:

Q. How about reviewing the chart, Doctor?

MR. GAUTIER: He is not going to do it.

MR. ALTMAN: He will not?

MR. GAUTIER: He is not going to sit here and do it.

MR. ALTMAN: Is he going to testify at the time of the trial as to the cause of this lady's condition?

MR. GAUTIER: You can ask him if he has an opinion on what he has reviewed and so on.

MR. ALTMAN: I am more concerned not so much today as some date in November when he comes in and may at that time have an opinion, and I want to have your assurances as to what he is going to testify to or not testify to.

MR. GAUTIER: You can ask him today. He reviewed the chart prior to his consultation. He told you that already.

MR. ALTMAN: I am not talking about that. I am talking about him potentially as an expert witness or—

MR. GAUTIER: With that in mind, I think you can ask an appropriate question to get the answer you are proposing. That is all I am telling you.

Q. Suppose, Doctor, you take a moment and review the blood gases that really are only one or two for that particular day.

MR. GAUTIER: Let us not have him do that. (to the witness:) You reviewed this chart for your consultation, did you not?

THE WITNESS: Yes, sir.

MR. GAUTIER: After that review of the chart, and his exam, he must have formed some opinion, would you not think?

MR. ALTMAN: I asked him that.

MR. GAUTIER: No, you did not.

Q. (MR. ALTMAN:) What was your opinion, answering Mr. Gautier's question?

A. I do not know what caused the cardiopulmonary arrest.

Q. Why do you not know?

A. I beg your pardon?

Q. Why do you not know?

A. Because with the information available it is not possible for me to formulate a meaningful opinion.

James read Dr. Martin the entire chart all over again and asked:

Q. Taking that into consideration, and taking into consideration what you saw when you examined her on December 15, 1978, do you have an opinion then as to what caused her to sustain the brain damage that is described in your consultation?

A. Mr. Altman, let me see if I can answer your question with information that will clarify where I am in my thinking. I am sure it is of no interest for me to abstract back to another level of saying I don't know. Her damage was done by a combination of the consequences of cardiopulmonary arrest. The circumstances, to the best of my knowledge, to reconstruct from the nurses' notes, is that she had a period of hypoventilation prior to the arrest. The etiology (root cause) of the hypoventilation is unknown to me.

Q. You defined hypoventilation as what, Doctor?

A. Diminished respiratory function.

James and Dr. Martin reviewed each part of Martin's treatment of Louise, including what each of the several drugs he had given her was supposed to have done for her. At no time, Martin said, had he contemplated any surgery for her.

Q. Did you think, on the 16th, in terms of as to whether or not the patient was going to recover, or did you think at that point in time that her percentages of recovery either in terms of active brain usefulness or in terms of mortality, were going to—that she was going to make it on either score?

A. I do not understand the question.

Q. Did you think she was going to live on the 16th? Just plain flat survive?

A. I thought she might.

Q. What about in terms of having any useful brain function?

A. I thought she might.

Q. Your hope was based upon what?

A. I have seen patients, read of patient who have recovered from similar circumstances.

Q. Let me take this all the way to the end. She did not survive, correct?

A. Okay.

Q. Was her death based upon her brain injury?

A. Yes, it is my belief.

Q. What does that tell you about the severity of her brain injury?

A. In restrospect, from the time that the case was completed was that it was profound.

MR. ALTMAN: That is all I have.

The rest of the deposition was fairly uneventful. We heard one last refrain of "Wiesel and Ebner Had Nothing To Do With It" from Joel Swimmer, and then James picked up the ball for a little "re-direct." This time he wanted to talk about the potential harmful effects of saying pessimistic things at the bedside of a comatose patient.

Q. Is it something that Intensive Care nurses know to avoid unless it involves the patient care, obviously?

A. I would say by the frequency with which I make the comment that it is something that is not very well appreciated by hospital personnel, especially those working in critical areas where they are exercising special responsibilities and are preoccupied with those responsibilities, as well they should be.

Q. You make the comment, "Don't say that"?

A. To take care to avoid saying things in front of the patient. To treat the patient as though they may, in fact, be hearing what is said.

Q. Is that true of the care this lady should have received in December of 1978 from the nursing personnel in the ICU?

A. That is the care that any patient should receive in December of 1978, or otherwise.

MR. ALTMAN: Those are all the questions. Thank you.

But Dan Weiss wasn't going to let this slap at his nurses go unanswered.

Q. Doctor, you said the cause of death of this lady was likely a combination of the initial brain insult and the cerebral edema?

A. Yes.

Q. That is your opinion within reasonable medical probability?

A. Yes, that is right.

Q. Assuming that some comment was made to the husband in the form of a consolation remark concerning the patient that—let us assume it was in the context, as he said it, that perhaps you better brace yourself for the worst, or something of that nature.

MR. ALTMAN: That is not what he said.

Q. Let us assume that it was a pessimistic remark about the possibility of her recovery. Assume that is made by an ICU nurse. In this case, assume that it is made by Trudi Berns. Do you think that was a precipitating cause of her death, the comment made?

A. No.

MR. WEISS: That is all.

We finished deposing Dr. Martin, our last defendant, by 11:30 a.m., after less than two hours. The Vultures were all happy to be able to get to their favorite lunch spots ahead of the crowds. Dr. Martin had added 51 pages of testimony to our library.

There is an elite subspecies of Vultures known as Expert Witnesses. Like defense lawyers, they win whenever there is a case, regardless of the outcome. There are two kinds of expert witnesses: those on the plaintiff's side and those on the defendant's.

All that the ritual taking of depositions and the melee of paperwork that had gone on thus far had done was to gather the few facts and figures relevant to our specific case. In many respects, the only difference between this case and any other would be the names and dates, and literally a few words on a few thousand pieces of paper, most of which are copies. Now it was time to assemble the expert testimony which would really make the case.

Basically, in a medical malpractice suit, the victim (or the deceased victim's family) says that the doctor treated him improperly, or failed to treat him properly, causing irreparable and eternal harm, for which reason a tremendous amount of money is due to the victim or his family.

Depositions are taken, and the doctor says he didn't do it. And here is where the expert witnesses swoop down to feed.The plaintiff (victim) team hires the most qualified experts with the greatest credentials—and therefore the highest fees—that they can find, who will say that the victim is right.

Then the defense hires its own experts to say that everything the doctor did was within the bounds of what is normal practice. So somebody died? Oh, well.

Then, after everyone sees what the other side has mustered, the courtroom drama can begin.

Like every successful law firm, Peter Fox had a regular rogues' gallery of expert witness from which to choose. And here is a case where the most successful lawyers tend to attract the best expert witnesses. Everyone wants to be on the side of a winner in this arena. So I was very fortunate to have a collection of amazingly imminent doctors and surgeons on my side. When I found out how much money they got for a little bit of paperwork, I realized that the expert witnesses were not so sad that Louise had died.

Of course, the insurance companies have their stables of experts, many of whose ideas of acceptable medical practices seem to involve leeches, straight razors and bleeding basins.

In the context of the System, the existence of the expert witness phenomenon is as inevitable as the resulting testimony is predictable. And you can bet that no insurance company is going to settle without a fight, even if you have an X-ray that shows a scalpel with the doctor's name on it sewn up in your gut. You would have to pay a few experts to say that leaving a scalpel inside the patient is not good medical practice. The insurance company would find a few doctors who would say, "What do you expect? This isn't the Mayo Clinic."

In my case, Peter Fox had started contacting his array of experts in early April, furnishing them copies of my statement, the hospital records, the toxicology report, and a good idea of the testimony he wanted. As the depositions came in, copies of these were forwarded to the experts. Encouraging reports came back almost immediately, and these were forwarded to the other experts for guidance.

Now it is not always easy to find a doctor who will testify to the ineptitude of a colleague in the same community. And, of course, if you want your experts to have the best credentials in the world, you have to search the world over for them. Or, as in my case, your lawyer has to know where they are. Among our distinguished flock was an eminent surgeon who taught at Harvard Medical School and was also Chief of Hand Surgery at Massachusetts General Hospital, Dr. Jonas Fussel. Pretty credible, I had to admit.

Our most prolific expert in terms of reporting to us (and consequently our most expensive exit) was Dr. Harold Powder, Chairman of the Department of Anesthesiology at Upstate University of New York in Syracuse. In his first report, he reviewed the anesthesia given to Louise and stated: "...considering the muscle relaxant and 66% nitrous oxide, this is one hell of a large dose...Evidence has accumulated in recent years that Fentanyl is not a short-acting narcotic and in the doses employed here it can be quite long-acting." He summed up the situation this way: "Basically this was lousy anesthetic and postanesthetic care, compounded by poor nursing care."

7

Bone Picking

A couple of weeks later, after receiving the toxicology report, Dr. Powder wrote, "Why was a drug screen ordered? This is not common in a case of this type! Who suspected what? Why? How did the Secobarbital and Amobarbital get there? Unless we can answer the last question I fear there may be a big problem...It is important that you determine which of these drugs was in use at the time at Colonial General Hospital."

Powder asked some questions concerning the laboratory's methodologies in arriving at the statements in the toxicology report. These questions are what directed James to further question Muller-Gross Labs and ultimately determine that their "findings" were more guesswork than anything else, their methods were sloppy and that the report was meaningless.

Regarding where the supposed barbiturates had come from, Powder added, "James, when you see large doses of Fentanyl you wonder if the patient is getting it all or if there is some kind of drug abuse. Is this a case of barbiturates having been injected while the narcotic went elsewhere? Is this another Ann Arbor V.A. case where a kindly employee decided to take matters into their own hands? How sure are you of Mr. Khavari? Does he and did he protest too much? I realize that these are ugly questions, but someone suspected something when they sent blood off to Muller-Gross. What? Why?...I look forward to hearing from you as this saga unfolds."

By this time Powder was James' guiding light through the medical intricacies of the case. Less than two weeks later, Powder wrote with more hints for James to investigate, and a few observations.

"I have reviewed the deposition of Gail Geraldo. It adds little to what we know except to confirm that I would not want to be hospitalized in that puspocket." Regarding the casual release of Louise from the PAR, he said, "A phone order is a violation of the standard of practice in most respectable institutions. Most anesthesiologists insist upon seeing the patient prior to discharge."

Referring again to the hospital records, Powder pointed out that the clocks in the hospital must not have all told the same time as each other. Then he noted that Walters had administered Narcan during his attempt to revive Louise. "Apparently I am not the only one who thinks she got an overdose," Powder wrote. "But why the toxicology screen? It bugs the hell out of me...I look forward to the depositions of the anesthesiologist and the floor nurses. When this is over, we could write another Coma."

The very next day we received Powder's reaction to Valerie Masters's deposition, finding: "What I consider to be deviations from the standards of care." When she saw the patient was having trouble breathing, "she thought of calling an anesthesiologist but rather went through the `chain of command.' Why? She said, `It's like calling a code before a code.' Indeed that is the time to call a code. I have reviewed this with some of our nursing people, who cannot believe that a 'chain of command ' like this exists." He suggested that James review written nursing practice at the hospital. He summarized: "Briefly, Ms. Masters comes on duty, sees a patient in trouble, half-recognizes the problem, knows the patient needs to be watched, does nothing, does not stay with the patient and calls an inappropriate person for help so she doesn't get in trouble. All in all, not the level at which an R.N. with the experience she claims to have should function."

On June 29, Dr. Powder wrote James a lengthy, scathing review of Donna Lang's performance before the members of the deposition club. "It is evident that Mrs. Lang was not informed by the recovery room nurse that the patient was being returned to the floor, what the patient's status was at the time and what anesthetic was employed. This certainly is not consistent with any practice in any hospital I have knowledge of...Mrs. Lang again and again refers to the fact that the patient was not ventilating adequately and that she had to be reminded to take deep breaths. An experienced surgical nurse should have recognized that this was the lingering effects of a narcotic that could have been very easily reversed pharmacologically had she the presence of mind or the knowledge to call for appropriate help. In any event the patient should never have been left unattended...

"There are several statements in the deposition that refer to the nose packing. Mrs. Lang indicates that she believes that the patient's abnormal respiration could be accounted for on that basis. James, I would ask you to squeeze your nose and breathe through your mouth and listen very carefully. When I do this, even lying down, my respirations are still relatively quiet and do not change in character. The noise that was heard was related to upper-airway obstruction that is secondary to the depressed state induced by the lingering anesthetic and is completely and totally independent of the occlusions of the nasal passages. I would venture that the patient had been mouth breathing for the entire period of her hospitalization; the massive trauma she had suffered would have left her nose and face too swollen to do otherwise.

"This entire business of the Vaseline gauze is a snare and illusion designed to befuddle you. It is basically a lot of bullshit...

"It is not normal for a patient to be returned from the recovery room in this state and it is certainly not normal for the patient who has not been medicated on the floor to remain in this state for so many hours. It is not normal for the patient's ventilation to be obstructed and inadequate and it is certainly not normal for the patient to arrest some hours post-operatively. The question is, did Mrs. Lang's negligence contribute to the outcome? I fear that inevitably the answer must be `yes'...Though Donna Lang must share the responsibility, she is not alone. The entire operating procedure and nursing structure of the institution must share in the responsibility...

"In summary, we once again have one who purports to be an experienced surgical nurse who receives a patient from the recovery room, recognizes the patient as having a problem, does nothing about the problem, does not remain with the patient, fails to communicate that the patient has a problem and who must assume responsibility for the injudicious neglect that led to the ultimate outcome of this case. Not only did Mrs. Lang neglect to take adequate steps to prevent this outcome, but she demonstrates in response to direct questions an abysmal ignorance of the care of the surgical patient in the post-operative period."

In a postscript Dr. Powder added that he had located an ENT (ears, nose, throat) surgeon who would perform a tracheotomy on any patient who had had surgery similar to Louise's.

In a brief letter dated August 10, reviewing the report of another expert in our case, Powder agreed that "...the operating surgeons had the right to expect that the anesthesiologist would see to the maintenance of the airway. Unless you can say that the upper-airway obstruction was specifically due to operative trauma and edema secondary thereto, I fear these boys (Koss and Grossinger) are home free. The entire blame would rest with Dr. Forstmann and the nursing staff."

Dr. Powder wrapped up his work for us on August 16, with a five-page review of all of the other depositions and documents. He noted that according to the recovery room policy and procedures manual, an anesthesiologist was required to sign a patient out of the recovery room. He stated that Wiesel and Ebner were blameless.

He once again blamed Forstmann. "I am convinced that Louise was overdosed with narcotics, that she responded on the table and in the recovery room because of the pain of the surgical procedure and because someone was constantly stirring her up. When she was taken to the floor where the stir-up regime was not carried out, she acted like the typical overnarcotized patient who would breathe upon command but who would otherwise fall asleep, hypoventilate, become hypercarbic and hypoxic and suffer all of the sequela there of."

I was impressed by the fact that Dr. Powder had reviewed the records of fifty random patients in his hospital who had had the type of anesthesia used on Louise. None of the patients had received over 400 micrograms of Fentanyl, and most had gotten between 200 and 300 micrograms. Louise had been given 800. Of the fifty cases Powder had studied, only a few patients had required any Fentanyl after the second hour, and in the few cases where it had been readministered in the fourth hour of surgery, it had always been reversed by Narcan before the patient left the operating room. "I am convinced that this is the heart of the matter," Powder wrote, "and that Louise was grossly mismanaged from the point of view of anesthetic overdose...I cannot impress upon you strongly enough the magnitude of this overdose."

Forstmann had given Louise 200 micrograms in the last hour of her surgery, enough for the entire operation in the case of many other patients, and enough to require the patient to be mechanically ventilated in any event. Then they had shut off the machine, taken out her air tube, and Forstmann had gone to lunch.

"My opinion (that Fentanyl is a long-lasting drug) is based on personal observation, primarily. If Dr. Forstmann has the great experience he claims to have with balanced anesthetic, he should have made the same observation. He should have cut back his dose significantly. My opinion is secondarily based on a review of the literature. Admittedly, my review of the literature is more thorough than one might expect of a practicing anesthesiologist at Colonial General...(Forstmann) relies to a great extent upon what he is told by the detail men (from the drug companies) and the literature he receives from the pharmaceutical company. I am enclosing one of these pieces of trash and wonder if the Critikon Division of McNeil Laboratories is not partially responsible for what happened to Louise. The fact that Dr. Forstmann did not have these journals or knowledge (that I had) available to him, does not however excuse him from not being conversant with the article I sent you from Anesthesiology. He is listed in the directory of the American Society of Anesthesiologists as a member of that society, and as such receives Anesthesiology, the official organ of that society. This was not an esoteric article that dealt with unapplied dog physiology but was rather one of the few articles in that journal that directly related to the everyday care of patients. I would certainly hold him responsible for the contents of that article. It was published by reliable investigators at a reliable institution and is not to be ignored. Especially when it explains what happened to Louise and indeed what might be happening to a lot of other patients."

Another of our expert witnesses was an old favorite of James', Dr. Christian Jeffries, a Miami neurosurgeon. His report reviewed the hospital records and then said, "This was a seriously injured patient whose death was directly related to her operative treatment and subsequent care...After the second operation in which there was complete obstruction of the nose and partial obstruction of the oral cavity she was held in the recovery room only thirty minutes. This is too short a time for an operation of this duration under general anesthesia and particularly in one in which the normal airways have been partially obstructed and no alternative airway had been provided. This must be considered a grave error... The inadequacy of the post-operative orders in regard to vital signs and neurological checks in a patient with a compromised airway must be borne by Dr. Koss. It would have been prudent in this particular case to have ordered vital signs and neurological checks to be done at least every fifteen minutes. This would have prevented the one and a half hours of non-observation during which her condition became irreversible...

"In summary, this patient was operated upon and left with a significantly obstructed airway. She was not held in the post-anesthesia room an adequate period of time, she was sent to the floor with inadequate observation orders, she was observed inadequately on the floor and allowed to develop a degree of cerebral hypoxia that led to her death."

Another local neurosurgeon, Dr. Albert Deutsch was even more blunt. He wrote: "The errors made by the physicians were: 1) sending an individual without adequate airway back to floor care after a short period of time in the recovery room; 2) No orders were written to observe the airway or suction the patient; 3) not performing a tracheotomy. Nursing errors were not notifying a physician when the patient was complaining of difficulty in breathing, leaving the patient with a poor airway alone from 1:20 p.m. until almost 3 p.m. and a fifteen to twenty minute delay in calling a Code Blue. This lady should not have expired and would not have with proper medical and nursing care."

A month later, in a brief letter dated July 24, Deutsch wrote, "Mrs. Khavari probably could have been saved by a tracheotomy. Nowhere in any of the testimonies does the question ever arise why a patient with her nose packed and multiple procedures in her mouth was not sent to the Intensive Care Unit rather than to general floor care. Intensive Care Unit nurses are specialized nurses and would have recognized respiratory difficulty and unresponsiveness and it is hoped would have acted more rapidly. The undersigned continues to believe that this healthy young female of thirty-two years would not have died had she received adequate nursing care."

Janet A. Pinkley, Ph.D., the Dean of the School of Nursing of the University of Alabama, denounced every nurse individually, and then collectively. She wrote: "In summary, within all reasonable probability, the surgery of 15 December 1978 should not have led to the demise of Mrs. Khavari. This patient was a healthy thirty-two-year-old female prior to the accident and with adequate nursing care she probably would have survived."

Dr. John C. Klaus, an anesthesiologist from Jacksonville, Florida, had brickbats for Forstmann and the nurses. "I think that this case boils down to...that the problem Mrs. Khavari encountered was residual narcotic, which caused her to become depressed on the floor. This again is a problem of recovery and if this patient had been retained in the recovery room long enough, if this patient had been adequately monitored on the floor, if the nurses on the floor had been more aggressive in their treatment of her readily apparent problem, none of this might have happened...the violation of the standard of care involves her early discharge from the recovery room, inadequate monitoring on the floor and inadequate action taken too late to protect her from permanent injury and death." Klaus also noted that Dr. Forstmann had stated in his deposition that he had seen drug-induced respiratory depression in that hospital before.

To me the most impressive witness on our team of experts was Dr. Jorge Bernetti, Director of the School of Anesthesiology at the University of Colorado in Denver. Dr. Bernetti was the man who had invented the Bernetti Scoring System for determining when patients are ready for discharge from Post Anesthesia Recovery.

Bernetti wrote, "Although this is truly a tragedy of errors with a sad culmination, I will limit my comments only to the events of the day of the second surgical procedure, December 15, 1978, though I hope that eventually some of the other deficiencies of health care (by the hospital, doctors and nurses) provided to the above-named patient are addressed properly in this litigation...

"I myself have never given 800 micrograms of Fentanyl to a patient who I have not definitely planned to leave intubated and on the ventilator (heart surgery, liver transplants, etc.) after the operation. However, the fact is that many anesthesiologists do give large doses of narcotics and get away with it. My feeling is that they have been led astray by some people in the academic world who work under quite different circumstances—staffing recovery rooms with competent nursing personnel and even a full-time anesthesia resident. Reality in private practice is quite different, though in this particular case carelessness and neglect were carried to the extreme.

"At any rate, 800 micrograms of Fentanyl was too much for this patient...there is a paradoxical depression of respiration and central nervous system after the administration of this drug. This happens more often than everyone realizes. Two years ago there was such a case here in Colorado involving a patient that received 750 micrograms of Fentanyl for a two hour and forty-five minute operation. The patient entered the recovery room talking, only to have a cardiac arrest thirty minutes later, while the recovery room personnel were trying frantically to find the anesthesiologist. The defendant lost this case and the plaintiff was awarded a substantial sum...

"In our ten years experience with the PAR scores we have found that consciousness is a crucial factor that influences other signs such as respiration and activity. I find it hard to believe that this patient received scores of 2 in activity and respiration while she was given a 1 in respiration and a 0 in activity...It is clear to me that Mrs. Geraldo, the first nurse that received the patient in the recovery room, was in some kind of hurry to accelerate the passage of this patient through that facility. That attitude may have influenced the artificially high PAR score given to the patient initially...

"The replacing nurse, Mrs. Roberts...should have known better than to send a semi-conscious patient to the ward...

"The nurses can write anything they want on the chart, but what counts is the actual facts. The latter certainly contradict their written numbers. Moreover, the aggravating circumstances of one nurse wanting to leave and being replaced with another R.N., unfamiliar with recovery room procedures, speaks poorly of their pretensions on being professionals and the hospital's nursing practices and rules...

"Last, but not least, are the repeated negligent acts of the nurses in the ward..." which he then went on to list. He concluded his eloquent condemnation of all concerned by saying, "Sad indeed are the last events when she was again found unconscious and the nursing personnel were negligent to do something about it either by themselves or summon the attending physicians. They also were insensitive to the patient's husband's alarming requests to check her or seek medical assistance. I found this to be unacceptable in any J.C.A.H. approved hospital. The lack of professionalism and sensitivity for a patient in need shown by these nurses must be shared by the hospital, since as their institutional employer it must set the pace in organization and responsibility. The procedure manuals mean very little, if they are not followed and implemented. The physicians involved must share this responsibility since we all face problems of this nature and it is up to us to make sure that the hospitals where we work maintain proper standards of patient care to take the choice of dissociating from them."

Dr. Jonas Fussel, the plastic surgeon from Harvard Medical School and Massachusetts General Hospital, may have had the most impressive credentials of our gang of experts, but he turned in the briefest report of all. He said, "I believe many reconstructive surgeons would have opted for a tracheotomy in this patient's case, but if not certainly would have considered leaving an oral tube in until the patient was fully alert and awake. In some hospitals, it is not possible to send a patient with an endotracheal tube back to the floor, and because of the holiday season and because of limited personnel available in the recovery staff, this may have swayed the surgeon's judgment as to whether a tube should be left or not. The time interval over which the patient stayed in the recovery room was extremely short and I believe much of the patient's problems could have been avoided even with the absence of an endotracheal tube by a close observation in the recovery room setting...

"In reviewing this patient's case, I believe the most likely cause for her respiratory arrest and subsequent cardiac arrest was upper-airway obstruction. This obstruction no doubt occurred in the setting of heavy sedation. My reasons for expecting this are that the patient's husband recognized her struggle in breathing and a patient who is paralyzed usually does not struggle to ventilate."

It certainly could not have been his fiery rhetoric or anything exceptional about his views, so it must have been his credentials or the fact that Dr. Fussel was in Boston that made James decide that we needed a full-blown deposition from him. Of course, it would be too much to expect for Dr. Fussel to pop down to Miami for a few profitable hours of interrogation, so the whole damned flock of Vultures flew up to Boston for a day of profound billings to the insurance companies, and what turned out to be predictable and particularly inane testimony. I didn't go, but I was pretty incensed when I read the transcript, and outraged when I saw Fussel's bill and James's travel expenses, which were mine to pay.

In three hours (128 pages) of testimony, much of which was interrupted by squabbling Vultures pecking at each other, Dr. Fussel made the following statement into the record for our cause: "In my opinion, in a case such as Mrs. Khavari's situation, the managing surgeon or surgeons deviated from accepted standards of care in that they failed to elect any one of the three acceptable methods of maintaining this patient's airway in the post-operative period. Those three methods of airway maintenance would include a nasal-tracheal tube, that is to say and airway placed through the nose into the trachea;

an oral-tracheal tube, that is to say a tube placed through the mouth and into the trachea; or a percutaneous tracheotomy, that is to say a tube placed through the skin of the neck and into the trachea...I believe that the failure to exercise one of these three acceptable options contributed to Mrs. Khavari's death."

On the first of August, James went to see Dr. Gozar, the Iranian doctor with whom Louise and I had become friendly with at the hospital. Gozar had been furious when I had seen him outside the Intensive Care Unit on the evening following Louise's arrest, and had raged about inept nursing practices and stupidity and so on. James hoped that Gozar would testify on our behalf.

Gozar told James that on the evening of December 15, he had been approached by Drs. Forstmann and Koss, who had asked him to talk to me and tell me how sorry they were about what had happened up in Louise's room where she had not been breathing properly, there had been some confusion during shift change, and consequently she had not gotten the airway management that she had needed.

Gozar said that he did not want to get involved in this case, and had not gotten involved in it before, because he was concerned about his hospital privileges. "After all, I have to work here." He also mentioned that since he and I were both Iranian, he imagined that some people might see his participation in the case as a "Persian conspiracy."

Two days later, James received a bill from Gozar for $70.00, which was of course posted immediately to my account.

Part of the opening barrage of paperwork, way back in the beginning, required the defendants to tell us whom they would be calling as expert witnesses, and what these witnesses were expected to say. James looked over the list and decided to "depose" a few of them. This was the final move in the discovery phase of the lawsuit. I, for one, was very interested to see what could possibly be said in defense of the actions that our experts had identified and so thoroughly condemned.

We began at 11:30 a.m. on October 2, in a conference room at Jackson Memorial Hospital, with Anthony J. Hernandez, M.D., appearing to defend Koss' share of the debacle, accompanied by Charles Wilson, Koss' attorney. Hernandez was a professor of Otolaryngology (ears, nose and throat) at the University of Miami's prestigious School of Medicine, Chief of Otolaryngology at Miami

Veterans Medical Center, and also practiced at Jackson Memorial Hospital. He should have told us that he did all of that in his spare time, between appearing as an expert witness.

Under repeated questioning, he said, "I have so many malpractice suits I have testified in I could not number them to you because through the years I have been an expert in many, many cases... maybe twenty, thirty, or forty, something like that."

Hernandez was barely acquainted with Koss. He was familiar with the records of Louise's case, having reviewed excerpts of the depositions and read the hospital records. As far as he was concerned, everything about the surgery was just fine, absolutely within the standards of good practice.

Q. (MR. ALTMAN:) Do you have an opinion, within probability, reasonable medical probability in the standard we talk about, as to why the patient had a cardiopulmonary arrest?

A. I believe that this patient was asleep and she was not breathing well while she went to the ward, and the nurses who were watching this patient failed to call a physician when the patient complained to the nurse that she could not breathe. The nurse actually passed judgment interpreting that the patient said she could not breathe through her nose and told her to breathe through her mouth. At that point in time I feel that the nurse who is in charge of the patient in the ward or in a hospital room should have called a physician. The physician's—the first one should have been the anesthesiologist because the anesthesiologist is the one who follows the patient after the patient is completely recovered and, if necessary, calls the surgeon because sometimes the surgeon is needed, being the captain of the team. So, based on medical probability, I feel that the care, nursing care, should be the key factor in the complication that this patient had at that afternoon, which was around three o'clock or so.

James had him repeat each segment of the answer a few times to make sure everyone understood what Hernandez's opinion was. The deposition lasted an hour and a half, generated 81 more pages of testimony, and made it clear that this eminent physician blamed the whole mess on the nurses. This was, of course, why Koss' attorneys had hired him.

It made sense that Koss would point the finger at the nurses rather than at another doctor. For myself, I was especially curious to find out what anyone could say on Forstmann's behalf.

Less than two weeks later, on October 15, I found out. At 2:30 p.m. Paul Sparks, Forstmann's attorney, ushered Dr. M.N. Brian Cassius into the conference room at Peter Fox's office to meet the panel of Vultures. Dr. Cassius was professor and Chairman of the Department of Anesthesiology at the University of Miami, and Chief of Anesthesiology Service at Jackson Memorial, the V.A. Hospital, and at the Williams Player Eye Hospital. He had trained Forstmann.

James concentrated on the dosage of Fentanyl, which our experts considered excessive. Cassius said repeatedly that the correct dosage was however much it took to anesthetize the particular patient.

Q. Is there some relationship or supposed to be some relationship, Doctor, between Fentanyl and the body weight of the patient?

A. I do not think so.

Q. If the manufacturer thought so, you would disagree?

A. No. I think as a general statement there is a range within which you work which can be related to body weight, but if the patient starts to move and holler, you do not say, "You are only sixty pounds, you can't have any more."

Q. But that did not happen here, did it?

A. I presume not. It is not in the chart.

Q. Would you disagree that this is four times the amount of Fentanyl that should have been administered to this lady were one to follow the product information?

MR. SPARKS: I object. The product information sheet would be the best evidence.

MR. ALTMAN: I am asking if he knows.

MR. SPARKS: Quote chapter and verse. You have the thing.

Q. Here is the product information. I will have it marked as an exhibit. I will give it to you and I would like you to say that this lady's body weight—do you know what it is?

A. Refresh my memory.

Q. About 120 pounds. Assume she said 120 pounds. Take a look at this and you tell us for a woman who weighed that much, how much Fentanyl she should have according to the product information.

MR. SPARKS: For what period of time? For what period are we talking about, four hours?

MR. ALTMAN: Yes.

A. To put this into a medical context rather than a legal one—

Q. Look, I am putting this in medical. I have not asked you legal questions. I am not asking principles of law.

A. The point is, answering as a physician from the medical point of view, the patient requires the amount of Fentanyl she requires regardless of general guidelines. So that I do not want to mislead you with an answer that would relate to one thing but not to this patient.

Q. Before you read this product information, just imagine we have a lady that weighs 120 pounds, a young woman. Do you think 800 micrograms of Fentanyl is a normal dose for this patient?

MR. SPARKS: For what period of time?

Q. For the length of time of this surgery. Was that your opinion, Dr. Cassius?

A. That is a reasonable dose.

Q. That is a reasonable dose?

A. Yes.

Q. Not even high normal?

A. If the patient were moving, it would be low.

Q. Come on. Why do we have to come back to this mythical moving patient?

A. I am getting away from the mythical patient.

Q. I am asking you to talk about this lady. There is no movement here.

A. Presumably. Presumably the patient was anesthetized adequately. There is no evidence of it otherwise. Now if this is what it requires to anesthetize somebody adequately, that is the dose for that patient and I do not care what any product information sheet says.

Q. Then you do not care what it says?

A. I want to know in general. For this patient it does not matter, I would give her what she needs.

Q. Tell me, Dr. Cassius, is the way that anesthesiologists arrive at what is going to be the appropriate dosage of narcotic for a patient who is going to undergo general anesthesia something that you arrive at afterwards to see if the patient lived or is it something that you have a general idea before you get into the venture itself?

Dr. Cassius didn't have any problem with the anesthesiologist discharging a patient from the recovery room in thirty minutes or less, or doing so by telephone. Forstmann apparently epitomized modern medical ideals, in Cassius' estimation. So it was no surprise that he blamed everything on the nurses.

"I cannot speak of specific individuals. I do not know who they are, but it would seem it is obvious to me if a patient comes back to the floor in good condition and over the next two or three hours becomes either obstructed or comatose and where this is noted and discussed over a period of time, and nothing happens prior to the point where the patient is ready to arrest, there is something missing in the nursing care." That was what we got out of two hours and twenty minutes (112 pages) of the good Dr. Cassius.

A week later, James and the deposition club heard from two more defense experts, both registered nurses. They were Frances Powell, the Director of Nursing at the orthopedic-neuro division of Jackson Memorial Hospital, and Jane Reno, an assistant professor of nursing at Miami-Dade Community College. Other business prevented me from attending, but James gave me a brief report—interrupted by his choking on dry laughter—on the proceedings.

Apparently they had pointed to the indisputable fact that the doctor's had not given the nurses adequate orders, and that was all they had to say for themselves. The defense was sunk, and they knew it, James said.

8

The Carcass Rests

At the time of this case, Florida had a law requiring medical malpractice cases to be heard by a mediation panel consisting of a judge, a doctor, and a lawyer, before any jury trial could take place. Our mediation hearing began on October 26, 1979. James said that this case was zooming right along. Of course he meant as far as things go in the World of the Vultures.

The selection of the panelists other than the judge is something that the Vultures all have ample opportunity to squabble over, and they have the right to reject a certain number of candidates. So I never understood how Dr. Wharton became the physician panelist. Possibly James had used all of his challenges prior to the final selection on purpose, so that the mediation panel would turn out the way it did. Lawyers didn't care for the mediation requirements one bit, and for all I know they may have all conspired to get Wharton into position.

Almost immediately after the hearing commenced following a brief meeting in the judge's chambers with James and the other Vultures, Judge Francis X. Connors announced that Dr. Wharton was prejudiced, and disqualified him, thus ending the mediation. It seems that Peter Fox and James had sued him for malpractice a couple of years earlier, and had won. Wharton made remarks to Judge Connors that here was his opportunity to "get even."

Well, that was fine with all of the Vultures. For our part, James said that we would prefer a jury trial without having to introduce the findings of the mediation panel, preferring to trust the common sense of a jury to find that all of the defendants were guilty to some extent. The defense Vultures, and their clients, the insurance companies, were satisfied, because however grim things were looking for them, the wait of six months or more for the jury trial would allow them to hang onto their money collecting interest for that much longer.

There was nothing to do now but wait for the trial date, which Peter guessed would be sometime in April or May. He said we would hear from the court well in advance, and that I might as well just relax.

It was about time I paid a little attention to the business anyway. Somehow the export company that Louise and I had started had managed to grow and prosper, through no fault of mine. By this time, I had fairly well gotten over my desire to be dead, but that was still a long way from having any great will to live.

I was completely unmotivated, and the momentum of the business was winding down fast. The car insurance checks had come in time to prevent me from running out of money. Ironically though, this was a kind of negative motivation, isolating me from the need to get off my ass and do something.

My brother in Germany, sensing this and realizing that it might be months before anything happened in the case, insisted that I come to Germany and visit some of my customers there with him. I agreed to come in a few days.

James and I had dinner together three or four times a week, but I no longer frequented the office. In arranging my affairs so that I could take an extended trip to Germany, if I felt like staying there, I wrote a letter to Peter Fox and asked him to provide me with a total of the expenses on the case to date, and a reckoning of his firm's hours spent on the case. I added that I had some decisions to make about the future.

I am not really sure why I wrote that letter. Perhaps because I was frustrated that nothing was going forward; maybe I thought I might pay them off and get myself a new lawyer. Or maybe I was picking up on some Vulture tricks and just wanted to remind them who was boss.

I immediately got back a letter from Peter Fox that stated: "With respect to the costs, please be advised that thus far we have spent $41,288.00.

"I am unable to estimate the hours our office has put in. As you know, we have not kept hourly time sheets, and for me to attempt to reconstruct the amount of hours that James and I have spent on this case would be unwise at this time..."

$41,288. And counting.

I made an appointment and went down to Peter and James' office that same afternoon. The three of us met in James' office. After the usual pleasantries, I asked if I could see the expense records and pointed out that this was considerably more than the seven, eight, maybe ten thousand we had discussed in the beginning. Had they figured out their hours at all?

James was pretty nervous while we were waiting for Kathy to bring in what was, of course, an immense pile of bills and receipts. He fiddled with his gold Rolex watch while I sifted through the $7.60 postage receipts and found things like $584.00 dinners for him and Peter in Boston, not to mention several expert witness fees in the $3,000 and up range. I really didn't know what to say. As I opened my mouth, snap! James had wound his gold Rolex too much and the winder came off in his fingers. I had to laugh.

"James," I said, "have it fixed and I will pay for it."

"No, I did it myself. Shit." He shook his head sadly.

"How much more do you think it will be?" was all I could think to say.

"Not much, the worst is behind us, really, the trial will only be a few days, and they'll probably settle before that."

James became quite solicitous after that. When I left for Germany a few days later, he drove me to the airport and carried my very heavy suitcase all the way to the ticket counter. It is interesting to note that this same guy today has his own practice and spurns cases of less than a million dollars. The bigger they are, the higher they fly.

I stayed in Europe until after the first of the new year, of 1980. My brother and I toured Germany and visited the stores that sold our products. We went out a lot in the evenings. I liked the smoky, crowded night clubs where the incredible noise blanked out my memories for an hour or two. The cold in Hamburg was a shock after the tropical climate I was used to, but it cleared my mind. I saw old friends with whom I had gone through the university with, and each of them offered his condolences and unwittingly rubbed salt in the wound.

I went to Holland to visit Louise's parents at Christmastime. They did their best to be cheerful, but their eyes were hollow. Louise's mother would drift out of the conversation and sit looking sadly at something far away. Louise's sister Winnifred had chattered and laughed every waking moment for as long as I had known her. Now she was eerily quiet.

Although I had always felt completely at home with Louise's family, I was uncomfortable for the entire two days I was there. I relived my grief, as strongly as I had felt it a year before. And I wondered, even though I knew better, whether these people whom I had loved for ten years somehow blamed me.

On the first anniversary of Louise's death, I took the train back to Hamburg. My New Year's Eve was dismal.

Shortly after the first of the year, my brother and I flew to New York and on to Las Vegas for the International Consumer Electronics Show, where we met with our suppliers and entertained a couple of our German customers who turned up. After five days in that city, where the air was charged with enough electricity to both stimulate me and short-circuit my memory, we flew to Miami, where my brother stayed for a week of sunshine before he went back to the frozen gray of Hamburg.

The previous January, a month after Louise died, I had purchased a new four-bedroom house not far from my brother's home. I couldn't stand going home every night to the townhouse Louise and I had shared for our two months in Miami. I moved into the house even before the landscaping was finished.

It turned out that the builder, a large firm from Texas, was less than conscientious about finishing the yard, there were leaks in the roof, leaks in the air conditioning, problems with the bathroom cabinets and so on, and even a few pieces of the exterior wood had split. I contacted the builder repeatedly and got only empty promises.

Then, after a month had gone by, I got my bank statement and noticed that one of the checks I had written to the builder for $2,500 had not cleared the bank. Apparently it had gotten stuck in the builder's home office in Texas. I called the bank and stopped payment of the check.

It was probably April by the time the builder got around to contacting me, and they weren't very friendly about it. I told them that as soon as they repaired the house they would get their money. They said as soon as they got their money they would fix the house. I told them that I had had enough of their promises.

The stand-off continued until the following January when I came home from Europe. The builder hired a local attorney who filed suit in the County Court for the $2,500.

I told James about this, and he thought it was pretty funny. He said not to worry, he would take care of it, gratis. Now when a lawyer is working for nothing, it is amazing how quickly matters can get resolved. The next day James presented me with a copy of a little six-page lawsuit he had whipped up and served as a counterclaim against the builder. It ended, "Wherefore the Counterplaintiff/ Defendant, Farid Khavari, demands judgment against the Counterdefendant/ Plaintiff, CLIMAX HOMES, INC., in an amount in excess of $2,500 in compensatory damages, and in an amount in excess of $100,000 in punitive damages and further demands trial by jury of all issues triable as of right by jury."

Of course he didn't expect to win, or even to try the case. But it stopped the builder in his tracks. I kept the $2,500, and got the house fixed myself. I am certain that without James's nuclear counterattack I would have been better off just giving the bastards the money.

I was devoting a great deal of my time to the business, and the attention was paying off. I still had dinner with James a couple of nights a week but really did not concern myself with the case; I was too busy. One February morning, James called and wished me happy birthday, and told me he was taking me to a great place for lunch. I hadn't even thought about the date, but thanked him and agreed to meet him at the office around noon.

He drove us out to Coral Gables and pulled up in front of Christy's, one of Florida's most prestigious restaurants. We had a very fancy lunch, and James insisted that we must have champagne. We toasted the future, the trial, James's new BMW, and the hostess. James picked up the tab of $160.00 and wished me happy birthday.

I felt pretty good, and it wasn't just the champagne.

On March 19, we received notice that the trial was set as the first to be heard starting Monday, June 2. Peter told me to notify Louise's parents and a few of our friends from Europe who were planning to come and testify to Louise's qualities, that they should plan to be here for five days or so at that time. He would make certain that all of our experts were on hand.

Peter said that there was still a chance that there would be a settlement offer, and that we could avoid the trial. For the first time since I had met him, he seemed a little concerned. I realized that I was starting to seem like a risky investment; the Iranians were holding American hostages at the embassy in Tehran. Iran and Iranians were not very popular in America in those days. This could have affected the outcome of the case, or at least the amount of the verdict, when the case went to the jury.

Fortunately, we didn't have to find out. On April 24, Peter called with the good news: the case had been settled for $755,000, a record amount for an out-of-court settlement at that time. He congratulated me, and welcomed me to the ranks of the wealthy.

Of course, I was excited by the money. But the main thing I felt was relief that I wouldn't have to suffer through the trial, where I would relive the nightmare a hundred times a day. I was glad not to have to see any of the defendants ever again. And, more importantly, by settling the case before trial, especially for such a sum, the insurance companies admitting that their clients were responsible for Louise's death. That made me feel pretty good, too.

I wasn't the only one to learn the good news about our settlement. James immediately sent a letter to every one of our experts, as follows: "Please be advised that the above case has settled (with your help, I might add) and, hence, you need not settle your intended trip to Miami on this matter.

"Please forward any outstanding bill for your time and services to this firm immediately.

"On behalf of Mr. Khavari and this firm, our sincerest thanks.

"For your information, the case settled for $755,000.

"Best regards."

In other words, "Gentlemen, serve yourselves." (And in the future, remember how generous we are.) Of course, James could afford to be generous—it was my tab.

None of the experts had been the least bit shy about sending us bills for their services in the first place. But the day he received the letter, Dr. Bernetti, who had already to the tune of $3,000, suddenly remembered that there was another $2,000 due him. Dr. Fussel discovered that he had another $500 coming, and several of the other Vultures swooped down for one final bite. Once the new bills were all in, James and Peter could total the expenses and inform me as to the exact extent of my good fortune.

On May 16, I went to Peter and James' office to sign the papers. The settlement was actually four settlements. Three insurance companies covering the hospital and the nurses contributed $500,000. Forstmann's insurance company came up with $225,000, Koss' insurance company with $25,000, and Grossinger's chipped in $5,000. There was a separate document to sign for each of them, which released them from any further liability in the matter, in exchange for the money.

My favorite document was the hospital's and nurses'. "Know All Men By These Presents:" it began, that I, for the money paid, "Hereby remise, release, acquit, satisfy, and forever discharge the said second party (the hospital, the nurses and their insurers) of and from all, and all manner of, action and actions, cause and causes of action, suits, debts, dues, sums of money, accounts, reckonings, bonds, bills, specialties, covenants, contracts, controversies, agreements, promises, variances, trespasses, damages, judgments, executions, claims and demands whatsoever, in law or in equity, which said first party (I)ever had, now has, or which any personal representative, successor, heir or assign of said first party, hereafter can, shall, or may have against the second party, for, upon, or by reason of any matter, cause or thing whatsoever, from the beginning of the world to the day of these presents."

I promise you that I did not make that up.

"Who thinks these things up?" I asked James. I signed the papers, which were then witnessed and notarized. James could then exchange these releases for the checks, which he said would take a couple of days. Peter then presented me with a closing statement, as follows:

Total amount of settlement	$755,000.00
Less:	
Attorney's fee, 40%	$302,000.00
Costs incurred to date:	49,059.06
	-351,059.06
Approximate balance due at closing:	$403,940.94

"Forty-nine thousand in expenses!" I started. But Peter was ready for me. He handed me another paper that showed that if he had charged me his usual forty-five percent, his fee would have been $37,750 greater, so even if expenses had only been $10,000 I would have come out about the same.

"How in the hell could you have spent $49,000? I simply don't believe it!" They were ready for that, too, and gave me a large envelope full of photocopies (for which I had certainly been charged) of all the bills to take home, and told me that the checks would be at their office within a few days.

I went home fuming, and threw the pile of receipts on the kitchen counter, and went about my business. A couple of days later, James called to tell me that the checks had arrived. They were payable to the law firm and me, jointly. He asked when I could come down and endorse them. I didn't feel like dealing with it, so I made up an excuse about my car.

That afternoon, a courier arrived with a letter from James: "When you first came to this office as a client you were indeed a man in acute distress who did not know where his next dime was coming from. Since that time you have obviously done quite well in business and your lawyers have succeeded royally in the handling of your case. I find it hard to believe that you are unable to afford a car which operates properly.

"Therefore, by the time of your next visit to this office, be certain that you have purchased a new deluxe automobile if you wish for us to continue your representation." Very funny, I thought.

That evening I sat down at the table and looked through the bills in the case. First I read the statement:

Clerk's filing fees:	$ 85.50
Service of summonses	442.00
Circuit Court, Probate Division, opening estate and certified copies of letters	102.00
Miami Review: notice re: estate	47.60
Service of subpoenas	109.00
Witness fees	69.00
Investigation expenses	812.76
Photostatic copies	6,317.95
Telephone expense	403.79
Postage	129.96
T.E. Foley, Mediation Hearings	39.29
Fla. Society of Anesthesiologists, PAR manual	7.00
Deposition fee: A.J. Hernandez	300.00
Colonial Hospital, records	397.00
Univ. of Texas Health Care Ctr., review case1,	875.00
Professional Anesthesia, P.A., review materials, preparation of report1,	800.00
Basil M. Gates, M.D., consultation fee	200.00
Reza M. Gozar, M.D., conference fee	70.00

Jane Reno, R.N., M.S., depo. fee............................350.00
Roger F. Player, M.D., review of records,
depositions, and consulting fee1,.........................1,650.00
H.L. Powder, M.D., review depos, etc................1,875.00
H.L. Powder, M.D., review hospital
records, lit., opinions and report..........................3,625.00
H.L. Powder, M.D., travel expenses,
hotel, etc...927.39
(all together Powder got nearly $6,500!)
A.J. Deutsch, M.D. review records, depos,
lit., opinion and report..2,250.00
T.F. McDaniels, M.D., review , etc., etc..............1,375.00
C. Jeffries, M.D., review records and report........ 2,500.00
J.C. Klaus, M.D., review material and report..........800.00
J. Antonio Bernetti, M.D., M.S., expert
anesthesia evaluation..3,000.00
consultation, research, reprints, phoe..................2,000.00
Janet A. Pinkley, Ph.D., review records, etc.........2,825.00
professional svcs., travel time & exp...................1,869.84
Jonas Fussel, M.D., review records, etc................1,125.00
preparation of case 2,750.00
National Medical Advisory Service, review
records and report.. 600.00
Court Reporter fees, depo.'s & hearings..............4,876.27
Travel expenses, Altman & Fox,to
Boston, 9/11/79, airfare, hotel & exp...................1,366.37
Estimated bank charges for collection
of five insurance drafts.. 81.25

$49,059.06

Most of the experts' bills were pretty vague, saying, "...reviewing records, reading depositions, and consultation, ten (10) hours at $150..." or something like that. Of course, guys like Dr. Fussel got $250 an hour, and conscientiously spent several hours preparing for their depositions. Some experts didn't specify how they had spent their time on our behalf, but simply billed us for $600 or $1,000 or whatever. A couple of our experts, I suppose to show us how conscientious they were, actually detailed the time spent reading each deposition. Now, my English was not so good back then, but I could read a hundred-page, double-spaced deposition quite thoroughly in half an hour. Our experts took about two hours and a half, and their charges amounted to something like $6.00 a page.

All of this in front of me in black and white was astonishing enough. Then I started looking into the travel expenses. Dr. Powder had come to Miami for one day and one night, and his airfare had been only $210 of the $927.39 he had billed us for his expenses. Dinner had come to over $500. Vultures, I was finding, have insatiable appetites. James and Peter had run up a $584 dinner tab one evening in Boston. Dr. Fussel had billed us four hours at $250 per hour for having dinner with them.

And then, stuffed into the sheaf of "investigation expenses" I found a copy of a charge slip on James' American Express card for $160 from Christy's Restaurant. And the date? Happy Birthday to me!

James called the next day, and the next. I suddenly found myself far too busy to take an hour to drive across town and collect four-hundred-odd thousand dollars. James pointed out that, in those days of eighteen percent interest rates, I was losing over $200 a day. I said, "Who cares?"

I doubt whether any client before or since was ever so indifferent to collecting his jackpot. James and Peter were nonplused. They were losing a couple of hundred a day in interest, too, and to them that was like having to pay for their own lunch every day. But they couldn't cash the checks without my signature.

I avoided them for nearly a month. It was worth $200 a day to know how frustrated and helpless Peter and James were. I got a lot of value for my money. Finally, Peter himself got on the telephone, and asked me very respectfully if I might sit down with him and talk about whatever was bothering me. I told him that if he wanted a hint, he could look into the dinner tabs of doctors whose names began with 'P' and lawyers whose names began with 'F' and 'A.' He might also take note of certain charge slips from certain people's birthday lunches. If I were going to spend $160 on lunch, I told him, I could imagine more pleasant company than a lawyer.

I finally let them off the hook on June 10. Peter was obviously quite embarrassed, particularly by the birthday lunch, which he insisted was merely a mistake. The firm had intended to pay for that. As for the other things, well, if I didn't think they were absolutely fair, well, he wouldn't want me to get upset over such details. He magnanimously reduced the tab by a full thousand dollars. What the hell, he could afford to be generous.

I signed the checks, and what do you know? They told me the checks had to be deposited and cleared, and that I would receive my money in fourteen days. I smiled, and made them promise to give me my share of the interest they earned on the money during those two weeks. And I told them it might be a good investment to get a remedial reading course for their expert witnesses.

I got into my old friend, the BMW, and headed south from downtown, down U.S. 1, past the place where the accident had happened, and just kept on driving south.

It had taken nearly a year and a half, which was light-speed in the legal system, and I had "won." But how could anyone think in terms of winning, when I had lost the dearest person in the world?

As I drove, I asked myself for the thousandth time whether justice had been served. We had identified those responsible for Louise's death, and they were more or less everyone. Cooley had gassed Louise so heavily that when she came out of her first surgery she was convulsing and had to be tied down. Forstmann had so narcotized her that she couldn't wake up or even breathe properly. Koss, Grossinger and Forstmann had not placed a tube in her for breathing. The nurses had more important things to do than to keep Louise for even thirty minutes in the recovery room, such as getting their hair done and buying Christmas wrapping paper. Wiesel had turned his back on a woman in acute distress. The floor nurses had watched her slowly suffocate and had not called a doctor. And the hospital had contributed its lackadaisical indifference to blatant stupidity and professional neglect.

And as for them, those who had as much as murdered my Louise, and ruined years of my life as well, what was their punishment?

They had to take time out from their busy days to give a deposition. It would be idealistic to imagine that they would have suffered the least bit of embarrassment; hey, doctors get sued all the time. In the case of the hospital and the doctors, their insurance rates would probably go up a little. So it is the insurance companies, and ultimately really everyone, who pays.

And who really won? Not me, of course. How could $400,000 even pretend to compensate me for my loss. And who could possibly compensate Louise herself? James and Peter won, all right, over $300,000 for a few hundred hours of their time, if that. The expert witnesses on both sides hit the jackpot. And, of course, all of the lawyers and expert witnesses each had numerous cases going on simultaneously. These Vultures got the eyes, the brains, the heart and the liver.

The defense lawyers, who resented every minute of the time they spent in the presence of the plaintiff lawyers (who made so much more money than they did) bravely did all they could to stretch the case out. If you are an insurance company making a good return on your money, it makes sense to spend a couple of hundred thousand to avoid paying out a million for a couple of years. And, as an insurance company, you get to write off the million on your taxes when the case begins! The hatchling Vultures even got to the lower intestines of this corpse.

In the final analysis, insurance companies aren't going to lose money, so who pays? You guessed it—all of us. And what did we pay? The $755,000 award, plus at least $300,000 in defense lawyers and defense expert witnesses; all told over a million dollars so that I could get $400,000. And so a bunch of Vultures could get fat off it.

As I drove through Key Largo, it occurred to me that if someone would have simply come to me with a little sympathy when Louise died and said, "Sir, we represent all of the doctors and nurses and their insurance companies, and we are very sorry that something terrible happened. We do not know exactly what it was, but you shouldn't have to suffer through a big long process. Please accept this $300,000 (or whatever) as compensation, and we will conduct an inquiry because we don't want something like this to happen ever again. And you can believe that we will get to the bottom of this because we insurance companies don't want these bastards costing us money. We'll send you a copy of the report in six months if you wish," I would have been vastly better off financially, and over sixty percent of the expense—and the sheer waste of countless thousands of hours of people's lives that might otherwise have been spent meaningfully—would have been saved.

I didn't stop driving until I got to Key West.

My parents came to visit that summer, from Iran, where my father was a well-off businessman and a spiritual leader of great fame in the Baha'i Faith, a religion that is very peace-loving and promotes unification of mankind. The revolution had not been kind to anyone who was not a lower-class Muslim, and I was concerned for my parents' safety. We had a pleasant two weeks together, and I am glad my last memories of my father are good ones. I never saw him again.

Shortly after they returned to Iran, their house was fire-bombed by anti-Baha'i Muslim fanatics. A couple of weeks later my father was dragged out of bed at 3 a.m. by members of the Islamic Revolutionary Guard. Six weeks later, my mother learned that he had been executed, and all of their property was confiscated. My mother got out of the country with papers in her maiden name, and went to Germany.

I mention this, because shortly after that, in December of 1980, I was sued by Dr. Grossinger for his $6,000 fee from the surgery that had killed Louise. His insurance company had paid me, and now he wanted the money back! This was when I learned the extent to which my being Iranian could have affected the outcome of the trial in those days.

James went to court with me to defend me against the claim. Incredibly, the judge asked me disdainfully, "What would your Ayatollah Khomeini do with someone who wouldn't pay his bills?"

"Your Honor," James leapt up," "Khomeini would have killed his father and then charged him for the bullets, which is what did happen." (The Iranian Revolutionary Guard demanded payment from my mother for the bullets used to execute my father.)

The judge was pretty embarrassed. He looked at Dr. Grossinger and his lawyer and said, "Will you withdraw your suit voluntarily, or shall I dismiss it for you?"

And so, two years after Louise's death, the Vultures moved on. James, my great "friend" never called me again. I guess that should not have been surprising; when the Vultures clean the bones and there is nothing left to eat, they are done with you. I was left with a shattered life, an inconsequential sum of money, two years of pain behind me and who knew how many more to come. And the tattered memories of the dearest person I had ever known.

I placed a massive charcoal gray granite headstone on Louise's grave. It reads:

"Memories are all that remain.
Mine of her are my dearest treasure."

PART TWO

No End In Sight

9

Doctors: Greed and Incompetence

Under the Hammurabic Code of ancient Babylon, the penalty for medical malpractice was chopping off the doctor's hands!

One thing our nation is not short of is doctors. With some 550,000 of them to choose from—and nearly 17,000 new ones graduating every year—we have more than enough. The problem is, almost all of them are greedy, and a good number of them are incompetent, too.

Don't get me wrong. I have a great deal of respect for the miracles of modern medicine, and admiration for its hard-working and rigorously-trained practitioners. I certainly don't begrudge them the highest standard of living in the world. If I had a broken leg or acute appendicitis, I would certainly prefer the services of even a below-average doctor to those of the very best lawyer, no question about it.

In many fields, the costs of greed and incompetence are measured solely in dollars. In medicine, greed and incompetence translate into suffering and death as well.

Of the half-trillion dollars this country spends annually on health care, about twenty percent or $111 billion in 1988 goes for physicians' services. This works out to an average of $200,000 per physician, or $400 of the nearly $2,000 for every man, woman and child in the U .S. that is spent on medical care annually. (After paying such expen ses as office rent, nurses' salaries and malpractice insurance premiu ms, the average physician nets $110,000.) Physicians receive 2.2% of the Gross National Product of the U.S.; health care as a whole, 1

1%. Doctors, of course, prescribe how the other 8.8% is spent.

These numbers are not declining; they are escalating by the minute.

No one is certain how many of our doctors are incompetent. The Federation of State Medical Boards tells us ten percent. The American Medical Association questions such estimates, but other conservative medical authorities say the range is from five to fifteen percent, or some 27,500 to 82,500 doctors who should not be practicing, in the opinions of other doctors. Add to this the five percent or so, another 27,500, who are simply unlicensed! We are talking about 55,000 to 110,000 or more incompetent physicians, being paid some five to fifteen billion dollars a year, generating another twenty to sixty billion dollars a year in hospital and other medical costs. Incompetent doctors create twenty-five to seventy-five billion dollars in medical costs for our nation, which means up to $300 a year for every last American is wasted. But the real toll is in the suffering and needless death, and the ruined lives surrounding them.

Malpractice claims are filed against nearly twenty percent of doctors annually, and no one knows how many incompetent doctors avoid this honor. Of course, they can't all be guilty—can they? Yet, with only 400 doctors losing their licenses per year, it seems obvious that plenty of guilty ones are getting away with it.

Getting rid of all the incompetent doctors would not make malpractice disappear. Doctors are human, mistakes will be made, and that is just one of those things about life that is too bad. Still, it is a good bet that incompetent doctors kill or maim more than their share of victims, so eliminating them would be a good place to start. It is difficult to say with certainty how many lives would be saved, but I would suppose that to qualify as incompetent, especially in the opinions of other doctors, a doctor would have to be needlessly killing or maiming, oh, at least one of his fellow citizens per year. So now we are talking 55,000 to 110,000, or more, human lives per year, plus incalculable injuries and anguish.

I guess it would be too much to hope that we could send our incompetent doctors as goodwill ambassadors to North Vietnam.

Or we could sell them to the Pentagon, and they could add to their arsenal of M-16's, M-1's, M-60's and MX's a new deadly weapon: M.D.s.

We may need to export a few of our competent doctors, too. The American College of Surgeons has said that we need as many as sixty thousand board-certified surgeons, and another ten thousand interns and residents, to cover us for the next forty years. We have a good sixty thousand more than that right now. Fish gotta swim, vultures gotta fly, and surgeons will perform surgery. Sometime whether we need it or not.

Estimates from such conservative sources as a congressional subcommittee say that 2.4 to 3 million unnecessary operations are performed each year. Other recent estimates range as high as 4 million. Various studies put the number of useless operations at eleven to thirty percent. Extreme estimates range from half to even ninety percent. If indeed we are blessed with a surfeit of surgeons, 3,000,000 operations a year is only one per week for each of 60,000 surgeons. The real number of needless surgical procedures performed is almost certainly much higher, but two or three million is plenty anyway.

Each year, up to half of the 200,000 lower back disc operations performed, seventy percent of the nearly 800,000 hysterectomies, tweny percent of the 1,300,000 cataract operations, and fourteen of the 250,000 coronary bypass operations are not needed, for example. The death toll from these and other unnecessary surgeries is estimated at 40,000 to 80,000 every year. Similar excesses are found in ordering tests; fifteen to twenty percent of the 1,500,000 angiographies performed annually are inappropriate, for example.

Recent reports have exposed hospitals where in over fifty percent of births occur by Caesarian section, as compared with the average of "only" twenty percent. Certainly even this figure is far too high; but the doctor and the hospital can charge a lot more for a C-section delivery than for natural childbirth, and what woman is going to question her doctor's recommendation at a time like that?

It would be easy to suppose that all of these unnecessary surgeries and tests are simply the result of greed on the part of the doctors.

What is even worse is that a great deal of them are ordered out of plain ignorance, incompetence and just plain stupidity. (In this regard, lawyers are more honorable; at least a lawyer will tell you he doesn't know the answer to your question—no matter how trivial or common it may be—and that he will research it for you before taking any action. A doctor will prescribe medication or surgery or treatment or tests or something any time, rather than do nothing.) Some tests are dangerous; X-rays are known to cause cancer, but of course this will not show up for a long time. X-rays are not always informative, but they are always profitable, so doctors order X-rays, and plenty of them. Is this out of greed, or ignorance? What's the difference?

Medications can be dangerous, too. Reactions to medications prescribed by doctors kill another 100,000 people per year, and cause over 1,500,000 hospitalizations annually. Apparently the cure is more dangerous than the disease in many cases. Add to that the unknown number whose actual cause of death is not the ailment shown on the death certificate, but rather the treatment of that ailment. It gets kind of scary, doesn't it?

Now we raise holy hell when medical science practices on beagles and monkeys and bunny rabbits, but where is the outcry about the millions of senseless tonsillectomies that have been performed? Even victims of malpractice only file claims in ten percent of cases! That is, malpractice as we now know it. But doesn't needless surgery constitute malpractice as well? Black's Law Dictionary defines malpractice as: "...bad, wrong, or injudicious treatment...resulting in injury, unnecessary suffering, or death...and proceeding from ignorance, carelessness, want of professional skill, disregard of established rules or principles, neglect or a malicious criminal intent." Any time a surgeon cuts you, your life is at risk; there is no such thing as perfectly safe surgery, no matter how competent the surgeon. I call needless surgery blatant malpractice. And I call deaths from needless surgery murder.

Well, sick people go to doctors, and some sick people die. Doctors tell us who is sick, and doctors sign death certificates. They are in control from the moment we are born until we die, of natural causes or otherwise. But what would we do without them?

Recent history provides a few interesting examples of what happens when you remove a lot of doctors from the equation. In 1976, doctors went on strike in Los Angeles to protest malpractice insurance rates. A survey of seventeen major hospitals found that sixty percent fewer operations were being performed. The death rate in L.A. County during the strike fell eighteen percent, only to rise back to normal when the doctors went back to work.

In 1973, doctors in Israel went on strike for a month. Patient contacts were reduced from 65,000 to 7,000 per day. The death rate dropped by half for that month, the only time that had happened since the doctors' strike of twenty years before. In Bogota, Colombia, striking doctors withheld all but emergency care for fifty-two days; the death rate fell thirty-five percent.

For better or worse, we are at their mercy. So we must never forget where their self-interest lies. Doctors get recognition and reward for doing something rather than nothing. The doctor is a hero when he intervenes. If he saves the patient (or if the patient happens to survive his unnecessary treatment), so much the better. If the patient dies, oh, well. He was too far gone when he finally sought treatment. Who could blame the doctor who tried to save him? The doctor gets paid either way.

And, of course, the more services the doctor provides, the more he gets paid. Clearly, one reason for the high incidence of costly medical procedures is that doctors get paid more for expensive surgery than for less costly courses of treatment. Conversely, it is interesting to note that in prepaid group plans where surgeons are paid steady salaries not tied to how many operations they perform, hysterectomies and tonsillectomies occur only about a third as often as in the normal fee-for-service system. Given the fee-for-service system, it is not surprising that preventive medicine is a low priority for most doctors. It is well-known that proper nutrition can prevent many health problems, yet most doctors are less informed on the subject of nutrition than many lay people. Nutrition is rarely even taught in medical schools.

I don't know whether people become doctors because they are greedy, or people become greedy because they are doctors. Anyway, it is safe to say that doctors become greedy because they are people. It would be completely amazing if they did not succumb to greed. In the fee-for-service system why should we imagine that a doctor would be less likely to prescribe unnecessary operations than, say, a transmission repairman?

There are a number of factors that conspire to guarantee that a doctor will order every test, treatment and surgery that the patient will sit still for.

First there is the perceived notion that the doctor has power over life and death. We may have confidence in a mechanic, but we have faith in a doctor. And we know a lot more about our cars (and take better care of them) than we do our bodies. If power corrupts, then the absolute power of life and death the doctor holds over the faithful must comprise both the most sublime of temptations and boundless opportunities. When the doctor tells us to do something, we do it. When we have a problem, we expect the doctor to do something.

Second is the fee-for-service system itself, which provides the enterprising physician with plenty of incentive to stay busy, coupled with the fact that most consumers of his services are relatively insulated from fee-shock by insurance or government programs. Only twenty-five percent of the money spent on health care in America comes from direct patient payments, with thirty-four percent from health insurance and other private sources, and forty-one percent from Medicare, Medicaid and other government programs. The direct effect of open-heart surgery on the average patient's wallet is no greater than that of a haircut.

The threat of litigation itself has a perverse effect on the amount of needless medical tests, treatments and surgery performed. As malpractice insurance rates rise, doctors are forced to increase their incomes to pay their bills. This means that they have to charge more and sell more services just to stay even. (Naturally some of those extra procedures will generate a little more litigation.)

Even more ironic is that the best way for doctors to protect themselves against litigation is to do things the same way other doctors do. By making the same mistakes and practicing to the same level of excess as all the others do, a doctor both maximizes his income and minimizes his chances of being accused of practicing outside of accepted standards. Being too different can bring on liability problems.

Compounding these problems is the ever-expanding universe of diagnostic and procedural possibilities provided by technology. Each new discovery enhances the credibility of the profession and creates new wealth for it simultaneously.

From the standpoint of simple economics, you would expect that a surplus of surgeons and constantly improving technology would bring about better health care at a lower cost. But technology accounts for one quarter to half of the rise in medical prices and overall health costs, for several reasons. It is a fact that technology saves people who live to incur more medical costs than they would if they had simply died, but who could complain about that? After all, saving lives is the goal of the technology, and it is hard to quibble about money when we are saving lives.

But it is also a fact that even if a new technology cuts per-patient costs as compared with the old one, it can be relied upon to raise the total jackpot by expanding the total number of treatable patients. Coronary angioplasty is one recent example. This technology treats blocked arteries by insertion of a balloon catheter that widens them "non-surgically." Many patients who are too sick for traditional coronary bypass surgery (i.e. those who even the doctors feel would be too endangered by the surgery) can receive angioplasty. Doctors predict that the new lithotriptor machine, which pulverizes kidney stones with ultra-sound instead of surgical removal will end up treating asymptomatic (harmless) kidney stones that no one would ever consider operating on. As for now, the machines are not widely distributed yet, and treatment costs are much higher than conventional surgery, although risks seem to be far less.

The cost of keeping up with new technologies includes the latest equipment that a doctor has to buy to have an up-to-date practice. Once new equipment is on the payroll, you can bet that it will be used on every patient who provides the least excuse for its use.

Technology unquestionably adds to the number of expensive and unnecessary operations performed for the benefit of the doctor, who wants to use technology, rather than for the benefit of the patient. In a recent study of two million Medicare beneficiaries, the Rand Corporation investigated a procedure called carotid endarterectomy, which removes obstructions from an artery supplying the majority of blood to the brain. The study concluded that the operation had been inappropriate in one out of every three cases in which it was performed. In addition, 3.4% of the patients died within thirty days of the operation, and another 6.4% suffered non-fatal strokes during or immediately following surgery. Although the additional medical care required due to these mishaps is undoubtedly profitable for the doctors, many experts feel that a complication rate of almost ten percent suggests that the procedure is of questionable value in the first place.

But then, the decision regarding what is appropriate is made by the doctor. The judgment will not necessarily reflect the consensus of the medical community as a whole, because there may be no consensus on a particular operation. This leaves the field open for aggressive practitioners. If you live in Boston, for example, you are twice as likely to enjoy a carotid endarterectomy as if you live in New Haven, according to a recent issue of the New England Journal of Medicine.

Medical tests offer tremendous opportunities for income enhancement, especially if the doctor owns a piece of the laboratory, rather than just receiving a kick-back or a retail mark-up on the procedures he performs. Oh, they may not pay as well as surgery, but they make up for it in volume and relatively minimal risk. And who's ever going to get mad at you if you order a test for them and the results are negative? Testimony before the House Energy and Commerce Subcommittee on Health and the Environment in September, 1988, pointed to studies indicating that between twenty and sixty percent of the 30 billion dollars spent annually for routine lab testing is unnecessary (or $24 to $72 for every American wasted).

In other fields of endeavor, supply and demand tend to balance out, and tend to be reflected in prices. The physician is in the enviable, and almost unique, position of controlling all three.

When greed results in the performance of unnecessary tests or surgery, that is reprehensible but at least sadly understandable. But when petty greed results in emergency services being with-held, that is contemptible.

Six months after our wedding my lovely wife Janilla had an ectopic pregnancy, and the fetus died. One day she experienced terrific pain and cramps. Her gynecologist was out of town, and our call was referred to one of his associates. This doctor told us that we should come in at 5 p.m. the next day so that he could perform what is called a D & C abortion. His fee was $500, and he would expect payment in advance, since our health insurance did not cover pregnancy-related matters.

When we arrived at the office the next day and were greeted by the good doctor shortly after five o'clock, I presented my check already filled out for $500. "It has to be cash," he said. I assured him that the check was good, and told him I had less than a hundred dollars in cash and nowhere to get cash after five. My wife was in agony and had begun to bleed. He repeated that he required cash. I noticed an American Express sticker on the receptionist's window, and offered my platinum card. He shook his head, "Cash." I was never so angry in my life. "Then take the check," I shouted. "If I jam it down your throat you will shit cash, and then you will see that the check is good." He turned pale and started to shake. "Okay, okay," he said. But he was shaking too hard to be trusted with a knife.

We went home, and while we tried to find another doctor, the pregnancy was spontaneously aborted. Now I can only think of a few reasons why any professional would demand cash, in lieu of a check or at least an acceptable credit card, and none of them are good ones, especially when someone is in pain that could be indicating a life-threatening condition. My best guess is that his concern for saving a few bucks on his taxes outweighed his concern for the health and welfare of his patient.

Soon after that, we got new health insurance and a new doctor, too. My wife got pregnant again, and carried to term without complications. We had a son, and our health insurance covered eighty percent of the doctor's $2850 fee.

When we shopped for health insurance to include our new addition, we declined maternity benefits; we weren't planning to need them again for a while. We should have known that this would guarantee that my wife would become pregnant again, which is what happened four months later.

The state of Florida requires doctors to have liability insurance, or to have demonstrated financial responsibility of $100,000. When we went back to the same doctor, there was a sign in the waiting room informing us that the doctor was not carrying insurance. I also noticed, when I paid in advance, that his $2850 fee had not gone down. Once again, everything went smoothly and we were blessed with a baby girl. A week later I received a bill for $200. When I called the doctor's office to protest that we had been told that the flat fee covered everything, they said, "You have insurance. Why should you care?" I told them that I did not have insurance, that I had paid the fee myself, and that I cared very much. "Oh," they said, "if you don't have insurance, don't worry about it." The next day I received a letter from my health insurance company. Not only had the doctor not been satisfied by full payment in advance, he had tried to collect $3050 from my insurance too!

I will have to admit that not every doctor is completely consumed by greed. I recently went to an opthamologist who had been treating a minor eye condition for me, and at the end of the office visit he said, "No charge." I was so shocked I could have had a heart attack. Then, his having acted so far outside standards of practice—by not charging me—I could have sued him for malpractice!

Doctors get Special Recognition because their greed and incompetence provide the victims, bringing prosperity to all in the World of the Vultures. But the highest honor, the Order of the Golden Beak, is reserved for those doctors whose credentials qualify them to be Expert Witnesses. Since the issue in any malpractice case is whether the treatment (or abuse) the patient received was within the realm of normal standards of medical practice, both sides in the case must employ experts. The plaintiff's (victim) team hires a bunch of doctors who say that what has happened to the victim is a shocking and unconscionable departure from accepted standards of treatment. The defendant's (doctors and their insurance companies) team hires another batch of experts who will say that the victim got the best care available in the known universe. It is not surprising that a fee of several thousand dollars can make an expert extremely sympathetic to the cause of whoever is paying.

The victim has to pay his own experts whether he wins or loses the case. If you can't afford to pay, then you had no business letting the doctor commit malpractice on you in the first place, because there is a good chance that you will lose your case. You can bet that the doctor and his insurance company will have an army of experts on tap to testify that you have no complaint. How many people don't pursue malpractice cases for this reason? Who knows?

In 1987 medical care costs in the U.S. rose 6.6 %, nearly double the general inflation rate of 3.6%. The share of the nation's total income claimed by health care has almost doubled in the last twenty years, and already accounts for over eleven percent of the Gross National Product, considerably more than in any other industrialized country, and continues to grow unchecked. If we don't do something about it, our entire economy, and way of life, are at risk. Major industrial employers will face bankruptcy trying to sustain the rising costs of health insurance. Already health care costs add over $600 to the cost of every Chrysler automobile. How much more will it take to make American manufacturers completely unable to compete in world markets? Rising unemployment could bring the economy to its knees, while rising taxes to cover skyrocketing Medicare costs will deliver the coup de grace. The shifting of an ever-greater portion of personal income to medical costs can only have a depressing effect on other sectors of the economy, modern medicine will ultimately destroy the economy if it doesn't kill us first.

Ironically, as much as fifty percent of the annual increase in health care costs is due to improvements in medical technology. Every day new treatments are discovered that allow more patients to live longer, but at a price. True, many medical breakthroughs have contributed to improved health care at much lower costs. Antibiotics exemplify this; a few dollars worth of antibiotics can save a person's life and prevent a costly hospital stay.

On the other hand, more spectacular developments such as organ transplants may save lives, but cost hundreds of thousands of dollars per case, let alone development costs of hundreds of millions. I have always wondered how it is possible that a transplant operation, which takes only a few hours and involves a finite number of people, can cost $300-400,000. The transplanted organ is donated to begin with, and the operating room has space for only a few doctors. Each new procedure that becomes available adds immensely to our overall health bill when it is put into practice in addition to the traditional treatments.

Certainly no one wants to deny life-saving treatment to anyone. Indeed, ninety percent of Americans believe that each of us is entitled to health care "as good as a millionaire would receive." Yet increasing costs, which led to health insurance premium increases of twenty to forty percent in 1988 alone, actually make quality health care unattainable for a growing number of people. At this time, 37 million Americans are not covered by any form of health insurance at all, and rising costs will cause more employers to curtail or eliminate insurance coverage for employees and their families—or go out of business entirely.

As eager as the doctors are to embrace new technology that will line their pockets and boost their egos, they have shown a tremendous amount of antipathy toward any developments that would reduce the cost of health care or improve the quality of care for the patient. As far back as 1943, the American Medical Association (AMA) was found guilty in a federal court of a criminal violation of the antitrust laws because of its efforts to destroy the nation's first Health Maintenance Organization (HMO). In 1982 the Federal Trade Commission (FTC) found the AMA guilty of civil violations of the antitrust laws for trying to suppress new methods of health care delivery (including HMOs) and for its ban on medical advertising. In 1987 the AMA was found guilty in a federal court of violations of the Sherman Antitrust Act in its avowed attempts to destroy the chiropractic profession through boycotts and dissemination of misleading information. The American College of Radiology and the American

College of Surgeons, additional defendants in the case, were also found guilty. They settled financially and agreed to cease their illegal activities and begin professional cooperation with the chiropractors; the AMA did not settle and was ordered by the court to publish the court's nine-page injunction order against the AMA in its journal, which it did in December, 1987.

Why would the AMA perceive the 30,000 or so chiropractors such a threat to its hundreds of thousands of members? Probably because in selected medical areas chiropractic treatment has been proved more effective than "modern" medicine, at far less cost to the patient and insurance companies. While I don't wish to imply that chiropractic is a panacea, study after study shows that chiropractic is a most valuable weapon in our health care arsenal, and one whose benefits far outweigh its costs. (Interestingly, some of the studies cited here are from the files of the AMA as subpoenaed for evidence by lawyers representing the chiropractors in the trial.)

The California Workers Compensation Study comparing chiropractic to medical care for back ailments on 1,000 patients showed that chiropractic care was twice as effective. The Oregon Workers Compensation showed that people under chiropractic care for back injuries were able to return to work in half the time of those receiving conventional medical care.

In the trial, a noted orthopedic surgeon from Chicago testified that in orthopedic wards using chiropractic care, the average hospitalization time of patients was cut in half. Patient stays averaged five to seven days at JFK Hospital, incorporating chiropractic care, and fourteen days at its competitor, Lutheran General Hospital, not offering chiropractic care.

A two-year study conducted in Italy of twenty-two medical static backache clinics using chiropractors concluded that people under regular chiropractic care had their hospitalizations for orthopedic conditions reduced by 87.6% and work-time losses by 75.6%. The survey studied 17,142 chiropractic patients, and the research was one completely by medical doctors and university professors.

AV MED, the largest HMO in the southeastern U.S., located in Miami, sent 100 patients to a local chiropractor and recorded the results. Eighty of the one-hundred had previously seen an average of 1.6 physicians for their ailments and had been non-responsive to medical care. Seventeen had been medically diagnosed as having disc problems and twelve as needing surgery. After chiropractic treatment, eighty-six percent had their ailments corrected, none of the disc patients needed surgery, and none of the patients was made any worse. The HMO saved $250,000 on surgical and hospital bills, and the M.D. conducting the study gave full credit to the chiropractor.

A study conducted during World War II by a former AMA trustee reported to the AMA the impressive results a chiropractor had in an Army orthopedic ward and that the overall results compared with the best that the medical department had to offer. The study reported that chiropractic treatment had impressive results even with some cases where medical treatment failed, and that chiropractic treatment should be an integral part of all medical orthopedic wards. This study was suppressed for over forty years until it was subpoenaed from AMA files.

The AMA's contention that it has always acted in the interests of the public welfare wears thin in light of its demonstrated actions, which indicated plainly a higher interest in protecting the incomes of its members.

Despite the AMA's condemnation of chiropractors as quacks, the potential for harm to the patient from chiropractic treatment is reflected in chiropractors' malpractice insurance premiums of only $3 to 4,000 annually, compared with those of medical doctors which can run over $100,000 per year for doctors in fields where chiropractors compete. Yet, thanks to the diligence of the AMA, chiropractors are treated like the orphans of the health-care system.

What can be done about the doctors? We will look at that later. Reforming the World of the Vultures won't happen overnight. Meanwhile you must learn to protect yourself and your family from the Vultures.

I hope that I have made it clear that the only way to really win in a malpractice situation is not to be involved in one in the first place. If you think there is something wrong with you that your doctor isn't taking seriously, go to another doctor. If your doctor says that you need surgery, go get another opinion. And another. And another. From doctors that are not associated with each other. If you don't know where to get a second opinion on surgery, call the U.S. Government's Health Care Financing Administration hotline, 800-638-6833 (in Maryland 800-492-6603). Somebody is getting all of that unnecessary surgery; make sure that it isn't you. During hearings before the Senate Health Subcommittee, Senator Edward Kennedy recalled a skiing injury to his shoulder he had suffered as a young man. Four specialists were called in to recommend treatment; three of them recommended surgery. He followed the advice of the fourth, who had just as many degrees as the others and did not recommend surgery. The injury healed. A witness at the hearings, a Professor of Medicine at the University of Vermont, replied: "The senator's shoulder probably would have healed as satisfactorily if the operation had been performed." Probably.

If this tirade on the health-care industry has angered you and scared you, or shattered your image of doctors, good. I hope that you will never again look upon any doctor with blind faith.

10

Hospitals—Disaster Factories

Whenever the curtain goes up on a medical tragedy in the World of the Vultures, chances are that the stage is set in a hospital. This is not just because doctors practice the most dangerous aspects of their craft in hospitals, it is because the hospitals themselves often play an active role in transforming patients into victims.

Six percent of hospital patients get hospital-induced infections, which are often drug-resistant, and 20,000 to 80,000 people die from these infections each year in the United States. Hospital-induced infections are among the top ten killers in America!

Hospitals have no shortage of motives which run counter to the interests of the patient, and no end of opportunities to turn even a routine stay into a one-way trip to the morgue.

There are approximately 6,800 hospitals in the United States, with beds totalling over 1.3 million. Although it is probably no consolation for those who live in smaller cities and towns where the hospital has perhaps closed, America is faced with a dangerous oversupply of hospital beds. If you wonder why I say dangerous, consider that even with all of the unnecessary surgery and treatment that takes place, the hospitals are still operating at sixty-five percent of capacity.

Every empty hospital bed is a potential disaster just looking for someone to happen to.

Thirty-nine percent of our half-trillion dollar health care budget (about $200 billion) goes for hospital services. This is about 4.5% of the Gross National Product, and represents $800 per year for every last American. Still, with all that extra capacity, the not-for-profit hospitals are having a hard time breaking even, and the for-profits—well, there's no such thing as enough profit for those Vultures. Both types of institutions are motivated to cut costs and increase revenues.

A hospital is no better than the people who run and staff it. Very few hospitals can complain of being critically underequipped, or of inadequate facilities; it is people who make the difference.

Competent and conscientious personnel can, and do no doubt often do, save lives in spite of blunders on the part of doctors. All too often, though, as in Louise's case, incompetent personnel compound the doctors' errors.

Unfortunately, lighter patient loads do not reduce costs to the extent that they reduce revenues, and thus tend to cause reduced staffing, which lowers the quality of care while per-patient costs rise.

In other businesses, undertrained, tired or overworked personnel affect productivity and quality. In a hospital, inadequate training can, and does, kill the customer. In Louise's case, there were numerous opportunities for her to have been saved if the nurses had been competently trained. If a hospital is understaffed, even competent nurses' performance will suffer through overwork. And a hospital is one place where even the slightest mistake could cost a life.The wrong medication, the wrong dose, the wrong time, the wrong food, the wrong patient...even the linens on your bed could kill you if they aren't disinfected properly.

The ultimate responsibility for an institution that must be as shipshape as a nuclear powerplant rests with the administration, which determines staff requirements, sets its standards, and hires the staff. The administration is insulated from the consequences of its errors by its insurers. And if the price of liability insurance goes up, well, that's the way it goes, raise the rates, what can one do?

Ironically, the threats of litigation and increased liability insurance costs tend to make hospitals very defensive concerning their personnel. To dismiss a nurse or staff doctor, or to lift a doctor's hospital privileges after an incident of malpractice would be an admission, if not of total guilt, at least of partial responsibility on the hospital's part. On the other hand, if a hospital dismisses a doctor or nurse for incompetence, it risks getting sued by them.

And if a hospital's death rate gets out of hand and liability insurance premiums skyrocket, no problem. It gets passed along to the health insurance companies, who pass it right back to all of us.

Fortunately for the hospitals, most patients have insurance or government programs to insulate them from their hospital bills, so there is little pressure to reduce prices, and little resistance to increasing them. Unlike in other businesses, an abundance of supply in the face of weak demand does not bring prices down. Competition for the best doctors and the most patients causes hospitals to escalate expenditures on the latest expensive equipment, and on advertising. This does nothing to bring down the price of a five dollar aspirin.

As an economist, I have always found it curious that the price of a hospital room would cover round-the-clock nursing care in a luxury suite in a world-class resort hotel, where certainly the atmosphere would be more conducive to recovery, and the food would be a lot better. I doubt if the insurance companies would see things that way, but it would save them a lot of money. Meanwhile, hospitals charge whatever the traffic will bear.

I had one eye-opening experience that showed me just how arbitrary hospital pricing policies can be. A couple of years ago, my mother developed a cataract on her left eye. Although the surgery was a simple outpatient procedure not involving a hospital stay, we were advised that the hospital charges would be over $4,000. Since my mother did not have insurance, I asked the opthamologist whether he could get the hospital to give me a break. I had no problem with his fee of $1800, which is pretty standard in Miami. He said he would see what he could do.

The next day his nurse called us with the date for the surgery and the good news that the hospital would accept $1000, and that we would also have to pay the anesthesiologist $300. When we arrived for the surgery, I paid in advance, as arranged, and we went to the surgical wing. Six other patients were getting cataract surgery that day. At four grand a pop, plus doctor's fees, the hospital was taking in more money than a casino.

The operation was a total success, and we were very grateful to the opthamologist.

About a week later, we received a computerized bill from the hospital. Had I not settled in advance for $1,000, or if my mother had had insurance to take care of it, the hospital would have collected $4,735!

I cannot imagine the doctor having had enough influence to persuade the hospital to provide its services and facilities for a price below actual costs. And since this happened to be a private hospital, I would assume that the hospital made some money on the deal. After all, how much can an hour of operating room time, two hours in the recovery ward, and five minutes' attention from a nurse cost?

If it cost $1,000, then at normal prices the profit would have been nearly four-hundred percent.

Many hospitals employ some sort of risk management program to reduce the problems that lead to malpractice suits. These programs involve training of nurses and staff in the use of new equipment, new discoveries, treatment methods, etc., and alerting them to potential problems with various procedures. These programs undoubtedly help to reduce sloppy practices, and save lives and money. Still, most malpractice incidents involve doctors, and hospitals have little control over doctors.

Hospitals are faced with a dilemma: doctors who perform unnecessary surgery and commit malpractice cause problems for the hospitals, yet these same doctors generate revenues for the hospitals. Efforts to clean up shoddy practices and reduce costs are also certain to reduce the hospitals' income.

Operating a hospital below capacity (the average hospital is only sixty-five percent full) is as great a challenge to the administration as running one that is overcrowded. With so many empty beds, it would seem that the quality of care would improve, yet the sad fact is that empty hospital beds do not generate revenue, and therefore hospitals operating below capacity also tend to be understaffed. In either case, any additional patients will further overburden the staff and exacerbate conditions, which further contribute to negligence and malpractice.

However outrageous hospital bills may be, hospitals cannot be accused of overpaying their most important employees. Nurses are not only overworked, but certainly underpaid. In spite of the tremendous responsibilities inherent in the profession, starting pay for nurses averages less than $21,000 per year. What is worse, nurses are confronted with a compressed pay scale; that is, after twenty years on the job, a nurse cannot expect to earn even $30,000. As nurses become more and more overworked, the profession becomes less and less attractive. Currently, there is a shortage of nurses—about 200,000 more are needed to fill vacancies. Three quarters of the nation's hospitals do not have enough nurses, and nineteen percent report severe shortages. At the end of 1987, the job vacancy rate was 11.3%, up from 4.4% in 1983. This situation will continue to worsen as nursing school enrollments dropped by nineteen percent and admissions to undergraduate nursing programs declined by thirty in the same period.

Nurses have never received the recognition that they deserve. A nurse can spend hours per day intensively caring for a patient, yet the doctor, who may only see the patient for a few minutes per day, gets the credit when the patient improves. Now, as hospitals cut staffs of nursing assistants, orderlies, secretaries and aides, nurses are further overburdened. This not only compromises the quality of patient care, but degrades the profession and makes nursing even less attractive as a career. The shortage of nurses has become a matter of grave concern to doctors; it makes it tougher to get patients into hospitals, and threatens the doctors' income. In its great wisdom, the AMA has come up with a solution for this alarming situation. The AMA proposes the creation of a new job category: registered care technologist (RCT). RCT's would be trained on the job and would handle routine bedside care. The American Nurses Association has predictably, and properly, denounced this plan.

There is no question that this plan would do nothing to enhance the attractiveness of nursing as a career. Worse, it would downgrade patient care, while doing little, if anything, to reduce the overall cost of health care.

As the nursing profession becomes less attractive, nurses like Nancy Roberts, Donna Lang and Valerie Masters will become more the rule than the exception. For this, we can only thank the shortsightedness of hospital administrators.

11

Lawyers—E Miseria Res Secundae

E miseria res secundae, out of misery, prosperity. Lawyers are the Vultures who most purely epitomize the species.They thrive on conflict, suffering and misery, of which there is plenty enough without the conflict, suffering and misery created by the lawyers themselves.

This is nothing new. 350 years ago, Shakespeare said, "The first thing we do, let's kill all the lawyers." Obviously, they didn't.

Today we have a plague of lawyers, about 800,000 of them (one for every 312 of us) taking in over $75 billion dollars a year, about 1.5% of the Gross National Product. This amounts to $300 for every man, woman and child in America.

The Japanese may be creaming us in electronics and cars, but they will never catch up to us in lawyers per capita: we have them beaten fifteen to one!

And the law schools are hatching more of these Vultures every year.

By the turn of the century we will be blessed with over a million of them!

One thing is certain: they will find something to do, and they will charge like hell for it.

The more I think about the lawyers I have seen in action, and the legal profession in general, the more I am convinced that these Vultures circling and swooping are a more imminent threat to our nation than ICBMs from half a world away.

There are about 12,000,000 lawsuits filed each year. When you consider that there must be at least two parties in each suit, this means there is about one suit filed for every twenty people in the country each year. If that's not scary enough, consider this: while a lawsuit can drag on for years, it actually only consumes a few hours of a lawyer's time; one lawyer could handle a hundred or more lawsuits every year. Just the number of lawyers we have today could gobble up the resources of the entire population with a wave of their word-processors, any time.

According to a study by the Rand Corporation's Institute for Civil Justice, presented to the Joint Economic Committee of the U.S. Congress in 1986, nearly one million tort cases per year (half of them auto accident cases) make it through a state or federal court, accounting for total expenditures of between $27 and $34 billion. Of this, $14 to $19 billion is spent for costs of the litigation, not including the compensation paid to the plaintiffs. Defendants (mostly insurance companies) pay $7 to $10 billion, including $4.2 to $5.7 billion for lawyers' fees alone. Plaintiffs pay $6 to $7 billion in legal fees, and the government spends at least half a billion on court processing costs. Of the $27 to $34 billion in annual tort litigation costs, only $12.6 to $15.3 billion gets to the plaintiffs in net compensation.

High-stakes malpractice litigation exemplifies the best and the worst of the legal profession. If there is a hero in the World of the Vultures, it is the malpractice attorney, who stands up to the big insurance companies for the victim. Without these brave champions, the victim wouldn't have a prayer.

I was extremely fortunate, and grateful, to have one of the most successful malpractice firms in America on my side after Louise's senseless death. We are all fortunate that these lawyers work on a contingency fee basis, meaning that they get paid a percentage of the amount awarded to their client, usually one third to forty percent. Otherwise, there would be very little malpractice or personal injury litigation at all. Who could afford tens, or even hundreds, of thousands of dollars in legal expenses to bring the culprits to account?

But do not be mistaken: it is not warm concern for the rights of the victim that motivates these lawyers, it is cold cash. They make a lot more on contingency fees than they could get by the hour, and they get a lot more business that way.

The defense lawyers hired by the insurance companies, on the other hand, do their best to see that the victim doesn't have a prayer anyway. A malpractice case affords them the opportunity to push "due process" to the limits of legality. And push their billings to the sky.

The defense lawyers win as soon as there is a case; defense lawyers charge by the hour. It doesn't matter to them if their clients are guilty or wrong; either way, it is to the advantage of the lawyer and the client to drag the case out for as long as possible. Our legal system gives the lawyers the role of determining the pace and complexity of the proceedings, and therefore how much they will cost.

The contingency fee lawyers make a lot of money, but only if they win (which, in the case of personal injury and malpractice cases is about forty percent of the time). This encourages them to be diligent, resourceful, and as efficient as possible, but as thorough as the opposition dictates. On the other hand, it also encourages frivolous lawsuits, hysterically large demands, and rampant greed.

Defense lawyers can only charge as much as the client is able to pay. In the case of an insurance company, it can add up. The System provides virtually unlimited potential for a skillful lawyer to keep a case from being resolved for years, and sometimes decades. The repertoire of stalling tactics is inexhaustible as long as the money well doesn't run dry. This encourages them to be meticulous, painstaking, redundant, obfuscatory and to act with the relentlessness—and at the speed of a glacier.

Ironically, what makes a lawyer a skilled lawyer is his ability to use the law to defeat the law, to use the letter of the law to subvert its spirit and intent. The System serves the lawyers a hell of a lot better than it serves us.

This should surprise no one, since it was lawyers who created the very system whereby they earn their living. They built a system full of protections that are known as "due process," which allow both sides fair access to information and witnesses, including an elaborate discovery process. This itself can consume months or years of high-priced hours. Naturally, they don't protect anything but the lawyers' incomes, least of all the people they are supposed to protect.

For some reason, American lawyers get away with outrageous behavior in the courtroom, such as would not be tolerated for a second in any other country. Shouting, screaming, making belittling and sarcastic remarks, insulting the opposition, intimidating witnesses, and various other grandstand tactics are routine. European lawyers find their American colleagues incredibly uncivilized. Seeing a couple of legal titans doing battle might lead one to think that these guys hate each other, but that would be a mistake. This is all a smokescreen; of course, the two sides need each other. The sound and fury is as sincere as that of two professional wrestlers in the ring; they may put on a great show, but they will be careful that no one really gets hurt because they have to go on again tomorrow.

The System is structured to protect the income of lawyers from outside influences. Although lawyers are allowed to advertise heavily to generate business for themselves, and to pay referral fees and other "sales commissions" to other lawyers for bringing them business, lawyers,- as part of their "code of ethics," are not allowed to share their fees with non-lawyers or to have non-lawyer partners. This would prevent, for example, any participation in a law firm by an entrepreneur who might want to provide legal services to the public at reduced rates.

In a malpractice suit, it is the victim against the doctor and/or hospital and one or more insurance companies. The advantage always belongs to the bad guys. The worst thing that can happen to them is that they can lose. Meanwhile, the longer they can avoid paying out money, the more money they make. The fact that this simply compounds the injury to the victim is not just, but it is legal. And if, after dragging things out as long as possible, they can settle the case for less than they should, they win.

Litigation is a drain on the wealth of not only the opposing parties, but of the nation as well. In terms of the economy, the costs of litigation are far greater than the amounts paid out by the participants.

When malpractice premiums rise to recoup payouts, the price of health care goes up, and therefore the cost of health insurance rises. This forces companies who pay for health insurance to raise the prices of their products and services to an extent that covers their increased costs, and more to protect their profit margins. These costs compound at each step in the chain of distribution. So everybody loses. That is, except for the doctor (he raises his fees), the hospitals (they raise their prices), lawyers (they get their fees; this is how they make their money), and the insurance companies (they raise their rates). All of us pay, in the form of higher prices for everything we buy, and in the form of diminished purchasing power and a decline in the general standard of living. The impact on the economy is far greater than the paltry few billion that changes hands directly in these matters.

We have to thank the lawyers for a great deal of this. In fact, what is wrong here is epitomized by my case. I got $400,000, paid $50,000 in expenses, and my lawyers got $300,000. You can bet that the insurance companies paid the opposing eight law firms no less than $300,000 all together, and probably another $50,000 for their expert witnesses and so forth. Easily more than a million was spent to pay me $400,000. And I was lucky; many settlements are eaten up entirely by the victim's lawyers and expenses. Meanwhile, someone had to pay that million so that I could get $400,000. And they got it from someone else.

Lawsuits do not create new wealth, they transfer wealth. If it were just a simple hand-off, that would be one thing; the net wealth remaining in the system would be the same. But when the majority of the money is lost in the transfer, this takes wealth out of the system, and the net result is a loss. You don't have to be an economist to see that if you keep taking wealth out of the system, whether it is your own checkbook or the U.S. economy, the System goes broke.

When the lawyers prosper on the misery of others, it is not just that of the victim. Remember Vultures will feed on all of us.

INSURANCE COMPANY COSTS OF MEDICAL LIABILITY INCURRED IN 1985

* Insurance Company Expenses	17.02%
* Legal Defense Costs	18.36%
* Claimants' Legal Costs	21.54%
*Compensation for Claimants	43.08%
	100.00%

Source: Academic Task Force for Review of the Insurance and Tort Systems, Preliminary Fact-Finding Report on Medical Malpractice; Gainesville, Florida; August 14, 1987; p. 198.

While contingency fee arrangements offer the victim access to the legal system he could not otherwise afford, and the lawyer a bigger piece of the pie than he would otherwise get, not to mention a lot more cases to choose from, a victim of malpractice or injury is still not assured of representation, fair or otherwise. The costs of dancing to every little tune the defense will call, in terms of time and cash outlays, often outweigh the potential benefit to the lawyer.

This means that a person whose injury isn't "worth" $100, 200, or say 500,000 simply cannot attract the attention of a proven trial lawyer. If you haven't had the wrong leg amputated, or been paralyzed or better yet senselessly killed, a heavyweight plaintiff lawyer won't even return your call. If you are lucky his office might assign an investigator to examine your potential case and report the facts for possible consideration by the boss. Even if a lawyer decides to take your case, it's "Don't call us, we'll call you" from that point on. You will, however, get a card each Christmas while you are a client, and, if you bring in some big money for the firm, for the next three years as well. You can only expect this royal treatment from law firms with exceptional class.

Nowadays James Altman will not even consider a case involving less than a million dollars. Recently, he was nearly defeated and was forced to accept only $700,000 for a young woman who twisted her ankle in a discotheque. (Well, more precisely, he got $280,000 for James, probably $50,000 for expert witnesses, and maybe $370,000 for the woman. As well as a few-hundred grand for the defense lawyers.)

You don't find guys like James Altman advertising on television. They may get their names in the paper from time to time, but guys like James generally keep a low profile. Many of their cases are referred by other lawyers, who get the customary one-third of the lawyer's forty percent share of the jackpot.

Now it may seem absurd for some lawyer to pick up a hundred

grand or more just for picking up the phone, but consider the Federal Trade Commission's position that this benefits clients by providing an incentive for lawyers to refer them to more competent specialists. However lamentable that reality is, it is also reality to be considered.

Consider the case of the daughter of one of my friends. She drove a BMW 320i, a model that was known at that time for its tendency to throw itself into a spin under routine conditions. I had one that did it a few times. Hers, unfortunately, spun off the road and dumped her in a canal. She suffered brain damage and now does little but sit around taking up space, and will require care for the rest of her life.

My friend called in his business lawyer who was a competent enough business lawyer. This lawyer was doing all right for himself billing by the hour. Here was a classic goldmine case, the kind that can make a lawyer rich. He didn't see how he could lose, and he decided to handle the case himself.

He had all the elements necessary to propel him into membership in the Order of the Golden Beak: a young girl, tragic brain damage, and an easily provable economic loss, due to a known product defect. (All this in a legal environment where a woman who, driving her husband's Porsche when drunk, had an accident which killed her passenger, sued Porsche for making a car too fast for an average driver to handle, and won $2.5 million.)

This poor hatchling fought a brave, at least expensive, battle, and ended up "winning" $100,000, obviously not even a meaningful fraction of what it would take to care for this girl. The lawyer presented the expense accounting to the family in the amount of $60,000, but gallantly refused to take his rightful forty percent fee. So the victim got $40,000 (instead of nothing) out of the kindness of the Vulture's heart. How gracious.

The real fact is, this Vulture's greed probably cost her in excess of a million dollars because he failed to act in the interest of his client—and ultimately himself—by referring her to a competent specialist.

Many aspire, but few achieve, membership in the coveted Order of the Golden Beak.

Such a case as this one might be comparable to a proctologist performing brain surgery. Although the proctologist has a medical license, performing surgery outside his realm of competence and achieving disastrous results would plainly be malpractice. Although lawyers are always ready to sue doctors, it is not so easy to get a lawyer to sue another lawyer for you. While lawyers will stand in line with contingency fee agreements in their hands when you want to sue a doctor, you had better bring cash in advance, and lots of it ($10,000 to $50,000 just as a retainer), if you want to sue a lawyer. However ineffective government regulators may be in controlling shenanigans in the medical and other professions, the lawyers answer to no one but themselves. The only place you can turn to complain about a lawyer is to a grievance committee (e.g. part of a state or local Bar Association) made up of yes, you guessed it, lawyers. This process of self-policing the legal profession has, predictably, worked out very well for the lawyers. Of course, a few lawyers do get disbarred from time to time, if they should become too much of a black eye on the face of the profession.

But don't expect too much satisfaction from the Bar Association grievance procedure. The Florida Bar, for example, has a convenient "gag" rule to protect lawyers from embarassment due to their wrongdoing. Even if the disciplinary board agrees that a complaint against a lawyer is valid, and reprimands that lawyer, anyone who discloses that he has filed a complaint against the lawyer can be held in contempt of court! That is, unless the Bar itself reveals that the lawyer has been disciplined. In ninety-seven percent the few cases where the board reprimands a lawyer, the reprimand is a "private" one which cannot be disclosed. This measure only protects the unethical lawyers and the legal profession, at the expense of the general public.

It is lucky for lawyers that they only have to answer to themselves, because if they had to do business like the rest of us they would be sorry indeed. There are not too many professions I can think of where you have to pay up front for a certain estimated amount of proposed services (the retainer), and then pay by the hour for however much time the professional decides to spend on your problem. What is especially curious is that, often as not, if you take a problem to a lawyer, he will tell you that he does not know the answer to your problem, but he will research the issue at your expense, of course. Talk about earning while you learn! These guys charge you for the time it takes to make a note to charge you for something, and you will find that lawyers generally bill in quarter or half-hour increments. And for the time they spend talking to another lawyer who has referred you to them. And so on.

Heaven help you if you have to hire a lawyer to deal with a matter in another state or country. Not only will you have the pleasure of paying two law firms (your local Vultures and their out-of-state cohorts) but you will be blessed with the hourly charges and telephone bills as these two champions of your cause jabber by the hour like long-lost friends.

Once you have paid a retainer, you can kiss that money good-bye. If there is one single person out there who ever had a lawyer finish a matter for him for less than the amount of the retainer, and who actually got part of his retainer refunded, I have yet to meet him. Once the retainer is exhausted, you can either continue to feed the Vultures at whatever rate they decide to charge you, or you can start over with another Vulture. No matter what, you are screwed.

Curiously, since you are privileged to pay for all of these services before any results can be known, it may be wisest to pay the highest rates possible, because the best lawyers are the ones who charge the most. Although, as any lawyer will be quick to remind you, there are no guarantees of success in any legal undertaking. Circling at heights less lofty than those reserved for the Order of the Golden Beak is another echelon of contingency-fee lawyers. Open the yellow pages and look at the full-page ads, or turn on the television during the day or late at night. If the offending party had sufficient liability insurance at the time of your injury, you will find a sympathetic ear even if your surgeon did not cut off the wrong leg, or remove the wrong kidney, or even if you are not a pretty girl with a twisted ankle. In fact, you can often get plenty of sympathy and guidance even if you were not hurt at all.

These more democratic Vultures employ flocks of hatchling lawyers, with legions of secretaries and powerful word processors. They may not rack up the spectacular verdicts of Golden Beak class, but they more than make up for it in volume. The majority of their cases are settled without even leaving the office, which keeps the expert witness and other trial expenses down. Any lawsuit, however flimsy or small-time, can still cost an insurance company tens of thousands to defend against it.

A few telephone calls, letters, a suit filed here and there—these things don't take much time or cost a lot of money. They know that the insurance companies know that even a flimsy or small-time lawsuit can cost tens of thousands to defend. So, a settlement offer that covers the lawyer's fees and expenses, and maybe a few thousand for the victim is a cheap way out for the insurance company. Of course, the insurance company's lawyers won't recommend this course of action—at least not until they've bled the case for all it's worth.

Small-time deals with insurance companies can be so easy that even a bungling boob of an independent practitioner (maybe a hatchling that no firm wanted) can make a living out of them. A lovely young woman, Janilla, whom I was later to marry, fell into the clutches of a quintessential jerk whose sole purpose on the planet, so far as I see it, is to provide a bit of comic relief here.

Janilla operated a successful cosmetics business in Akron, Ohio. On April 5, 1984, a year before I met her, her car was hit by a car driven by another nice young woman. While she was in the hospital, a girlfriend came to visit her, and told her that this calamity could be worth $100-150,000, according to her husband, who just happened to be a personal injury lawyer.

Janilla consulted with the husband, Ed Schwein, who contacted the other driver's insurance company. The insurance company immediately offered Janilla $15,000, and when this offer was not accepted, they raised their offer to $25,000.

Ed Schwein, Esquire, assured her that this offer was an insult, the product of scheming insurance claims adjusters to screw the defenseless victim, etc., etc., etc. Nevermind the insurance company's willingness to hand over the money today; that was no demonstration of their good faith and intentions, but clear proof of their undeniable responsibility! After all, they were offering to pay money; normally they would have denied liability altogether. So said Mr. Schwein, who convinced her to sign his standard contingency fee agreement.

Schwein on Janilla's side turned out to be a great boon for the insurance company, and a surprise bonus for the insurance company's lawyer. A month went by, three months, six, a year. "Nothing yet, these things take time." Soon Janilla met a handsome guy from Miami at a conference (me), got married, and moved to Miami. Two more years passed, and finally in late September, 1987, when our son was over a year old, she received a letter from the insurance company.

The letter was from the auditing department, which had noticed that we had not cashed their check for $35,000 which had been issued the third of June and mailed to her lawyer.

If you ever want your credulity strained, ask a guy why he held a check of yours without telling you for over three months. This check had to be signed by my wife and the lawyer, so he hadn't exactly stolen the money. He said that he didn't trust the mails, and didn't want the check to get lost. How about if Janilla came up to Ohio? And so on. I was flabbergasted by the very idea that such a thing could happen, and to top it off I had to end up arguing with this turkey. Then I realized that he was no Vulture; I could have respected him more if he had stolen the money instead of wondering why he wouldn't send the damned thing by Federal Express.

After a week of getting nowhere, I called the head of the claims department of the insurance company. Thus began a most remarkable correspondence. The insurance company sympathized with our position, but stuck up for the lawyer. They couldn't pay the money directly to my wife, out of fear that the lawyer would sue them, and he almost certainly would win.

As the correspondence stacked up, one day I ran across Janilla's copy of the lawyer's contract. Neatly typed into the blanks detailing his share of the booty was "one third percent. Normally, the lawyer gets one third of the jackpot if he doesn't have to file suit to get it. That is, thirty-three and one-thirds. This illiterate legal genius had written a contract entitling himself to one-third percent, or 0.0033-1/3 of the settlement. We decided to take him up on it, and authorized the insurance company to pay the lawyer his contractual fee, which came to $117.00, and give my wife the rest, for which she would sign a release holding the insurance company harmless from a lawsuit by Ed Schwein, Esquire.

No dice. Okay, we said, put Mr. Schwein's alleged money in escrow while we settle this between him and us, and give my wife two-thirds of this money to settle a four and a half year old claim. Sounds good to me, said the insurance company's lawyer. Sounds good to me, said the insurance claims manager. That was in October, 1988.

Through December, 1988, the insurance company managed to avoid paying one cent to anyone but their lawyers. Finally, on January 16, 1989, we received two-thirds of the settlement directly from the insurance company, and a check for the other one-third was made payable to my wife and Ed Schwein and forwarded to the insurance company's lawyer, pending a resolution of the matter between Mr. Schwein and us.

The resolution was not long in coming. A month later, the insurance company resolved the situation by cancelling that check and making another payable directly to Ed Schwein. Once again the nobility of the species shines through: Vultures may eat up everyone else, but they look out for each other.

In the meantime, we wrote a letter and presented copies of all documents to the Disciplinary Council of the Supreme Court of the State of Ohio, the folks who oversee the behavior of lawyers in those parts. We received a prompt reply. It read: "We have reviewed and investigated your complaint against the captioned attorney and find that he has not violated any of the Disciplinary Rules as set forth in the Code of Professional Responsibilities. Therefore we are closing our file on this matter." It was signed by, you guessed it, a lawyer.

While Ed Schwein is a mere turkey who can scarcely aspire to be a Vulture at all, the more creative and productive hatchling Vultures strive to enter the Order of the Brass Beak, achieving income, if not professional status, comparable to that of the Golden Beak gang.

Should you think that the case of Ed Schwein and the results of our complaint to the Disciplinary Council of the Supreme Court of Ohio is an isolated case, then you had better think again. Less than a year later, I found myself filing a complaint against two more lawyers, this time with the Florida Bar.

You know, some people seem to attract mosquitoes. I seem to attract Vultures. The "case" I'm referring to arose out of an old business deal involving a group of people in Germany, two guys in California, and myself. Someone in Germany wanted $40,000 from one of the Germans, who didn't have it, so they got the bright idea of coming after me for it. Fortunately, the deal was very well documented and I had absolute proof that I was not the guy responsible.

But that wasn't good enough for two Miami attorneys, Mel Lummel and Ted Unerfahren. These guys were hatchlings working on contingency, and if they had to let go of me they wouldn't get a red cent. They didn't anyway, but they sure tried their best. For over a year they took depositions, flooded my desk with senseless paperwork and endless interrogatories.

Finally, they gave up, but not before I had spent $6,136.57 in attorney's fees to defend me. This was unavoidable because as long as they were pressing the case, and had I not responded properly to the suit, I could have had a $40,000 judgement made against me. When Lummel and Unerfahren finally faced the facts and voluntarily dismissed the case, I was relieved. I was also furious.

So I filed a complaint with the Florida Bar Association, seeking reimbursement of my legal expenses and reprimand for Lummel and Unerfahren. You can guess the outcome; so could I. Several attorney friends told me that I was wasting my time; that the Bar wouldn't do anything at all unless it was completely outrageous.

What was really outrageous was how the thing proceeded. The Florida Bar wrote a letter to Lummel and Unerfahren asking them for their response to my complaint, reassuring them that "A reply from you will assist this office in determining whether this is a matter which must be referred to a grievance committee." In other words, tell us whether you are the bad guys.

Not surprisingly, Lummel and Unerfahren did not admit to being "bad guys." On the contrary, the first two pages of their response concerned their educational background, the fact that one of their bosses was a former branch staff counsel with the Florida Bar, highlights of their illustrious careers to date, and even the fact that one of their mothers was a judge. They then spent a page or so recapping the history of the case, carefully avoiding the facts that led them to its withdrawl.

I knew then that the game was over, but I wrote a letter to the Bar pointing out that "the only shortcoming in Lummel and Unerfahren's otherwise eloquent diatribe is that it ignores the facts which would weaken their otherwise logical case." I reminded the Bar that "the pedigrees and past glories of Messrs. Lummel and Unerfahren and other members of their esteemed firm are not the issue here," and I went on to list the facts and to respond to the obfuscatory points in Lummel and Unerfahren's letter.

Ten days later, I received a letter from the Florida Bar advising me that: "The matters you raise are civil in nature and are not within the proper scope of the Florida Bar's investigatory authority. If you have any questions concerning your rights and responsibilities in this matter you may wish to secure the services of an attorney. Accordingly, our file in this matter is now closed."

What the Vulture who wrote that letter was telling me was to go feed another of its kin if I wanted to pursue the matter further. So if incidents like these with Schwein and Lummel and Unerfahren aren't within the investigatory scope of bodies that the lawyers set up to police themselves, then what is?

If a lawyer makes a bad decision in accepting a worthless case on contingency, why should everyone else suffer for his error in judgement? If a lawyer knew that filing a groundless case against someone who he would have to pay for the defense, then there wouldn't be so many specious cases filed.

It seems that the only way a lawyer can get a reprimand from the Florida Bar is by starring on the front page of the Miami Herald for a few months in a row. Then the lawyer gets a reprimand for doing something that you or I would hang for! Florida isn't unique in this respect, but what can we expect as long as the people who pass judgement on the lawyers are lawyers?

The Bar Associations don't get too concerned if it's only us getting ripped up. But they do get really pissed off when a few lawyers try to get more than their share of the pie. So instead of reprimanding lawyers who screw the public, they spend a lot of time trying to curtail the rights of lawyers who screw each other.

What gets them hot under their button-down collars is advertising. When, say, a personal injury lawyer bombards the airwaves with his "unethical" advertising, he gets his claws on countless clients before any other Vulture gets a chance. Then, at his leisure, he can sort through the potential cases, put his staff of hatchlings to work grinding out paper and settling by phone, making a third of the action in the process. The big money comes from selecting the few big cases, farming them out to the heavy hitters in town, and getting a third of the other lawyers' fees without doing anything. Ethics is not the real issue here, money and simple jealousy is.

Advertising is expensive, so not very many Vultures can afford to take to the airwaves. Thank God! If one percent of them did, there wouldn't be time for I Love Lucy.

Other complex Vulture rituals, completely adaptable to production line methods, include personal injury and malpractice suits. Whether the issue is medical malpractice or personal injury of a more mundane nature, the lawyer's trump cards are his expert witness doctors, who will testify to the extent of the indignities and damage inflicted upon the victim by the "tortfeasor(s)" (legal term for "bad guys"). Sometimes after working as a team, the relationship between the lawyers and the expert doctors becomes especially cozy, creative, and profitable.

The Miami Herald, one of the world's great newspapers, recently uncovered a spectacularly successful cooperative enterprise that has been quietly prospering in South Florida. The Sunshine State is a haven for Vultures, but these guys take the cake for chutzpah.

First the lawyer's staff would discover whether the proposed defendant had sufficient insurance to qualify to get sued. Then, reasoning that high medical bills are the best evidence that an injury occurred, the lawyer sent his clients, who were virtually all poor blacks, to a certain orthopedic surgeon and a certain neurosurgeon.

There the victim would be treated to a costly battery of medical tests, including one for syphilis, and often Nuclear Magnetic Resonance and other esoteric augurs to show that the victim had suffered lower back injury. This is a favorite malady in that it generates a lot of sympathy, represents a serious disability, and is pretty difficult for the defense to disprove.

In an overwhelming display of concern for the victim, the doctors would then proceed to remove a disk from the "injured" back, thus running up the medical bills to help the client demonstrate the extent of his injury. Medical bills as high as $37,000 became the obligation of the client, of course.

Memos from the lawyer's office bear witness to the lawyer's proficiency in the field of medicine, as he prescribed treatment that would best help orchestrate his case.

Now that these creative practices have come to light, I am sure that more Vultures are already swooping down to sue these doctors for malpractice.

But the doctors needn't worry. Their insurance companies will go straight to the membership of the Order of the Silver Beak for the best defense lawyers money can buy. The Silver Beak is an honor that a Vulture earns by saving big insurance companies lots of money for a long time, generally in combat with the champions of the Golden Beak class. Achieving this status qualifies the Silver Beakers to enjoy earnings which can approach those of the elite Brass Beak.

Hatchling defense lawyers, the kind who defend insurance companies in the great majority of cases, are aspiring Silver Beak candidates, working their way up from the common ranks of the Tin Beak class.

Hatchling defense lawyers resent the fact that the contingency fee lawyers make so much more money than they do, and envy them for it. They may also resent the fact that they owe their livelihoods to the contingency fee lawyers. If victims had to pay their lawyers by the hour, there wouldn't be much need for defense lawyers.

On the other hand, if defense lawyers didn't make things so damned difficult, the contingency fee lawyers' services wouldn't be worth so much, either.

Whether this symbiotic synthesis is serendipitous, or a simple conspiracy, is moot.

Sometimes the hatchlings are amazingly resourceful in creating money for themselves out of next to nothing. My brother was involved in a fairly minor car accident a couple of years ago; his Mercedes was hit by a drunk driver who turned out to be his next door neighbor. My brother's knee was banged up pretty badly, and there was about $2000 damage to his car.

My brother had had his share of distasteful experiences with lawyers, and when his neighbor's wife came over to settle the matter directly with him, he was cordial. She said that if their insurance company found out about the accident, they would be canceled and have to pay a fortune in insurance. Would my brother accept $2500 and her paying the bill to repair the car as compensation?

My brother signed an agreement, and put his car in the shop. When it came time to pay the repair bill, the woman was $250 short. When she refused to pay, my brother turned to her insurance company, which, on the advice of their attorneys who certainly cost more than $250 to begin with, declined to pay.

My brother's good faith had been abused, his knee was hurt and he was walking around with a cane. So he went to see a Golden Beak lawyer of our acquaintance, who as a favor decided to sue the insurance company for only $100,000 in damages.

Of course, it was nearly two years, and lots of lawyer hours, before the trial date, which is usually about the time cases get settled. The insurance company lawyers decided that they might as well make another few grand and take the case to trial.

Unfortunately, my brother lost, on the strength of the agreement he had entered into in good faith with the neighbor. But the final triumph for the insurance company's lawyers is that the case, having gone this far, is now being appealed, and the defense lawyers will have another feast out of what began as a moldy little scrap. The whole thing could have been settled amicably by a claims adjuster for less than the price of an hour of the Vulture's time.

So the insurance company lost some money, but why should they care? You and I will more than make it up to them, that's for sure.

Does any doubt remain in your mind that we have Government Of The People, By The Lawyers, and For The Lawyers? One person of every twenty-two in Washington, D.C. is a lawyer.

Does anyone out there doubt that lawyers can continue to expand their piece of our action to whatever extent they choose? The lawyers created the System. Certainly they have no incentive to create a system that serves us better when they already have one that serves themselves so well.

Any complaints? You could write your Congressman. But he's probably a lawyer. A Vulture too.

12

Insurance Companies— The All-Time Bloodsuckers

Now we come to the vehicles that transfer wealth to the doctors, lawyers and hospitals: the insurance companies. Insurance companies are an essential part of the Vulture Crisis, because they are the reservoirs of money which are tapped by the process.

Liability insurance, and especially medical malpractice liability innsurance, exemplify the best and worst of the insurance business. We will concentrate on these forms of insurance here.

Insurance is a means of spreading risk around so that an individual is not wiped out by an unforeseen catastrophe. Everyone pays a small share of the potential loss into the insurance company, and if disaster strikes, the insurance company pays for the loss. That is the theory.

Insurance companies enjoy an enviable and unique position in the world of business. Everyone needs their product, and its consumers are often required by law to purchase it. The insurance company can deliver its product as fast as a computer can type it, and doesn't need an inventory, because the product is only a promise. There aren't any year-end clearance sales on last year's policies, because the product is made to order every time someone buys some.

It has always amazed me to hear the insurance business referred to as an "industry" as one would talk about the steel industry or the automobile industry.

In recent years we have heard woeful cries from the insurance industry about how much money it is losing, and why it must raise premiums to cover losses. Between 1984 and 1987, insurance companies nearly quadrupled the amount of money they took in from general liability premiums to over $20 billion in 1987. At the same time, income from medical malpractice premiums nearly tripled, to almost $4 billion.

All together that $24 billion amounts to just about $100 per year for every citizen in our great land. In 1987, our nation's 3,555 property-casualty insurance companies, the ones who sell liability insurance, reported after-tax operating profits amounting to $13.7 billion, or nearly $55 for each U.S. citizen.

If they were "losing" money before that, they have certainly made up for it in the meantime. A look at the 1986 figures for twenty top casualty companies, which follows gives no indication that insurance companies were candidates for federal bailouts then, either. They certainly weren't wasting any of their money paying taxes. In fact, property/casualty insurance companies had net income of $5.7 billion for just the first half of 1986.

PROPERTY AND CASUALTY INSURANCE COMPANIES' PROFITS FOR 1986

Insurance Company	Net Income	Federal Taxes Incurred	Surplus as of 12-31-86
State Farm Mutual	$1,615,655,255	$ -0-	$12.1 Billion
Aetna Life & Casualty	1,013,771,074	-0-	3.5 Billion
Allstate Ins. Co.	656,541,268	-0-	4.1 Billion
Hartford Fire Ins. Co.	542,851,117	-0-	2.3 Billion
Amer. Int'l. Group, Inc.	525,719,783	-0-	2.9 Billion
Liberty Mutual Ins. Co.	454,899,721	-0-	1.8 Billion
Ins. Co. of No. Amer.	454,103,785	-0-	1.4 Billion
United States Auto Assn.	369,640,282	-0-	1.7 Billion
Travelers Indemnity Co.	306,749,373	-0-	2.9 Billion
Crum & Forster Ins. Cos.	241,979,607	-0-	1.1 Billion
U.S. Fidel. & Guar. Co.	218,009,304	-0-	1.2 Billion
Lumbermens Mut. Cas. Co.	201,449,619	-0-	1.1 Billion
Safeco Ins. Co. of Amer.	159,342,578	-0-	622 Million

Ohio Casualty Ins. Co.	139,781,320	-0-	452Million
Continental Casualty Co.	359,141,107	1,019,038	1.8 Billion
St. Paul Fire & Marine	230,150,437	2,039,850	942 Million
Home Insurance Co.	199,158,152	5,331,045	770 Million
Continental Ins. Co.	272,778,921	13,778,687	1.3 Billion
Chubb Group	244,281,988	14,220,334	983 Million
Firemans Fund Ins. Co.	351,306,397	44,125,402	1.3 Billion

Source: California Trial Lawyers Association Forum, Sept. 1987.

I guess what really got the property/casualty companies upset was that in 1985 they only made $5 billion (twenty dollars a head for all of us). And this in a year when their surplus cash on hand was barely $77 billion, a scant 385% of what it was in 1974. Clearly, 1985 was a year of crisis for the insurance companies. Or at least they told us it was.

But then, they can manufacture a crisis any time they want to, even more easily than they manufacture their "product." All they have to do is decline to offer any particular coverage they may choose, and poof! A crisis!

What is really going on is that the insurance companies are telling us all the Big Lie. This becomes obvious when you recognize that insurance companies are out to make money, and when you consider how they make money.

Insurance companies make money two ways: through underwriting, and investments. Underwriting is assessing potential risks, and collecting premiums that, in theory, will cover the payouts that are required and leave a profit. Investments are assets that theoretically produce gain. In theory, income from investments is hedge against potential underwriting losses, and will help keep premiums down.

Since insurance company assets are between three and four times greater than the amount of premiums they take in each year, income from investments represents a significant part of the over-all income of an insurance company.

The amount of money that insurance companies make from underwriting will depend on how accurately the premiums they charge reflect the payouts they will have to make under the policies. How much they will make from their investments will be determined by the growth in value of their assets, plus the actual income they generate.

How much money the insurance companies make all together, then, is the sum of their income from premiums and investments, less all of their costs, from payroll and commissions to claims paid or payable, costs of defending against those claims, advertising and all other regular business expenses.

How much that really is, we will never know for certain, because the insurance companies cook the books. And who can blame them? It's legal.

One thing you can know for certain is that if the insurance companies admit that they are making any money at all, they are really making a hell of a lot more. Because insurance companies are bigger and more powerful than everyone else, they have some very advantageous laws working for them. They get to "lose" money on paper, while they make tens of billions in reality.

How do they do this? The secret lies in the rules involving their reserves. If you file a claim against the insurance company today, the insurance company estimates how much it is going to have to lay out to defend itself and how much it will ultimately pay you. Then it deducts this amount from its income this year, for tax purposes, and meanwhile it invests this money for a year or two while it feeds a few Vultures to hold you off, and someday it may pay this money to you, or it may not. Meanwhile, they have the money, but it's not, well, taxable income. A pretty neat trick.

Who determines how much these reserves should be? The insurance companies, of course. Who wins if they overestimate them? The insurance companies.

The real value of these rules to the insurance companies will never be known, any more than that of exemption from anti-trust law, another little benefit of being an insurance company.

Since the insurance companies get to deduct reserves for anticipated payouts every year, yet won't know the full extent of the payouts against this year's claims for years to come, it cannot be valid to judge the fiscal health of the insurance industry by looking at the figures for only a year or two at a time. You can only begin to get the picture when you look at what happens over a period of a decade or more.

Insurance is a cyclical business. When interest rates are high, insurance companies want to generate a lot of cash quickly so that they can invest it at the high rates. Insurance premiums plummet as the insurance companies scramble all over each other to get the cash. The insurance companies sacrifice profits from underwriting in favor of investment gains. In the ten-year period of 1976 through 1985, the property/casualty insurance companies reported terrific underwriting losses totaling $64.771 billion.

Lucky for them, the investment department was doing a little better than that. According to the United States Government Accounting Office (GAO), the property casualty companies had investment gains totaling $144.254 billion in that same ten-year period. The insurance companies say $27 billion less, because they paid out $15 billion in dividends and $12 billion was "unrealized" capital gains, assets which increased in value but did not produce cash income. So the GAO estimates they made $81 billion, and the insurance companies say $54 billion. What's the difference? (Other than the fact that $27 billion is about $108 out of every American's pocket, that is.)

Either way, that is after-tax income, because these wily guys actually had a negative Federal Income Tax bill of $1.6 billion for the period! Pretty slick, I'd say.

The next part of the cycle is what happens when interest rates and investment returns slacken and the insurance companies have to start paying attention to the insurance business again. Not content with their investment gains, the insurance companies now attempt to recoup their underwriting losses. Premiums skyrocket. Certain risks become uninsurable at any price. Availability dries up. Uh-oh, a crisis!

Much of the underwriting losses stated consist of reserve increases, which the GAO believes are overestimated. The GAO reasons that since the insurance companies will be earning interest on their money, the insurance companies should discount the amount of reserves they write off by the amount of interest they will earn before they pay the money out. If they pay it out at all anyway. Congress agreed, and discounting reserves became a part of the Tax Reform of 1986. Get ready for another round of lachrymonious squawking and even higher premiums from the insurance companies when they have to pay taxes.

Most of the underwriting losses are directly attributable to bad management and sloppy underwriting practices that took place in the years when the insurance companies were undercharging for their product to grab quick cash.

And then there are the claims which finally get paid. And the bills from the lawyers they pay to prevent having to pay the claims, and to stall as long as possible while the interest piles up on what money they ultimately do pay out.

When the insurance companies raise their rates and limit coverage to make up for underwriting losses, they blame society, lawyers, the jury system, the law, doctors, and anyone else they can think of. Then they spend tens of millions of dollars lobbying for "tort reform" to limit the number and size of potential liability claims. These investments in changing the system to further favor the insurance industry have paid off handsomely in forty-one states, which have taken action to protect the welfare of the poor insurance companies.

And is there anyone out there whose insurance bills have gone down?

The insurance companies cry that they are in terrible, terrible financial trouble. Even allowing for their inflated reserves, the figures in the chart show that property/casualty insurers gained at least $54 billion in net profits over the ten-year period.

The insurance companies cry that plaintiffs and lawyers have brought drastically increased numbers of suits, and that juries have played along with the lawyers to bring about a massive increase in the size of claims as well.

There is no doubt that lawyers cost insurance companies plenty of money, and not just by suing them. The insurance companies' own lawyers account for almost as much in the fees they collect for helping the insurance companies try to avoid paying on claims. Spending thousands on legal bills to avoid paying my brother $250 is a case in point.

But who could blame the lawyers? If insurance companies' management plays right into their beaks, the lawyers would be fools to deprive them of the pleasure of their services. A classic example of an insurance company bungling to the benefit of lawyers occurred recently in Miami. In the heat of a domestic argument, a husband shot his wife in the arm. She arranged a quiet settlement with the homeowner's insurance company's claims adjuster for the liability limit of $25,000 (the husband, who was insured, was liable for the injury). Wait! said the claims adjuster's boss. Maybe we won't pay that claim at all. Yes, wait! squawked the lawyers. We didn't get our piece of flesh yet!

The woman sought the counsel of a Golden Beak plaintiff lawyer. The case came to trial, and the jury awarded her $12 million, to punish the insurance company for acting in bad faith. Are the defense lawyers unhappy? Not on your life! Now they get to appeal and really run up some bills. After all, if the insurance company will let lawyers charge them five grand to avoid paying a $250 claim, what will they pay to avoid having to make good on a $12 million claim? When the insurance company finally pays four or five million, the lawyers will look like heroes.

To be fair, juries do sometimes pass out insurance companies' money capriciously, as in this case. However, as the chart shows, the so-called litigation "explosion" hardly qualifies as much more than a loud fart. True, the amount of tort lawsuits has increased, but when adjusted for population growth, that increase is only two or three percent. True, the average verdict has increased significantly, but that statistic is skewed by a few spectacular awards (e.g. $127 million against Ford for one claim), but the median verdict has increased only slightly.

And then, you have to blame the insurance companies themselves for simply insuring some of the wrong people. The majority of malpractice awards, for instance, are paid to victims of a very small minority of doctors. In Florida, for instance, nearly half of the money paid out in malpractice claims in the last ten years resulted from the actions of four percent of the doctors.

Now, if you have ever bought life insurance or car insurance, which are a hell of a lot cheaper than medical malpractice insurance, you know that your insurance company can find out anything it wants to about your health and your driving record. Is it credible that they do not know to whom they are selling malpractice insurance? If you had a habit of driving drunk and killing people, do you think the insurance "industry" would be beating a path to your door?

Insuring bad doctors is effective advertising for the insurance companies; as long as stories of big verdicts abound, the good doctors (who are the vast majority) will gladly pay whatever premiums the insurance companies demand.

So, in the end, why should the insurance companies care? They supposedly insure us against catastrophic loss, yet in the final analysis, we—society, you and I, all of us—insure them. If they start to lose money, we make it up to them by paying whatever level of premiums they demand.

The insurance companies tell us that this terrific amount of claims and massive verdicts are the cause of unavailability and unaffordability of certain types of insurance. Yet the simple fact is that the tremendous underwriting losses are not due to the civil justice system, but to mismanagement in slashing prices and irresponsibly grabbing for cash to invest when interest rates were high.

In the late 1970s and the early 1980s the U.S. enjoyed a period of high interest rates worthy of a banana republic. Of course, the insurance companies took advantage of the opportunity to open their doors to anyone who would feed them cash to invest. Insurance costs came down, easing the "insurance crisis" of the early 1970s, when insurance companies parlayed their trump hands into all manner of tort reforms throughout much of the country. Among other things, "no fault" insurance laws were enacted in many states. Well, folks, ten years is a long time to you and me, but it is nothing to a timeless institution like an insurance company or a bank. Most of us don't remember the great insurance crisis of the 70s; we were too busy worrying about gasoline prices.

And what about interest rates? Being cash rich by nature, and controlling hundreds of billions in financial instruments, which earn interest, insurance companies are a major force in the capital markets. Is it possible that the insurance companies, as such huge lenders, actually have a direct effect on interest rates?

When there is a lot of money available to borrow, interest rates tend to go down. When interest rates go up, who is in a better position to take advantage of the opportunity to grab a bigger piece of the pie than insurance companies, whose stock in trade is cash flow? And, as the flow of capital into the markets increases (as insurance companies cut rates and broaden coverage to raise cash, which is, by definition, very difficult to do otherwise in times of high interest rates), interest rates begin to drop, but only after the big investors have locked in the high rates for themselves.

This is not to say that there is anything wrong with insurance companies making money. On the contrary, it is essential that insurance companies not lose money if their products (promises) are to be worth anything.

But, when it comes to lending money, the highest rate of interest comes from the shakiest borrowers, and rampant greed coupled with an unlimited pool of cash to invest has inevitably led the insurance companies into the junk bond market. As an economist, and as a citizen of our nation, as well as an ordinary human being, I find that to be fundamentally wrong.

From less than $1 billion in 1981, the volume of junk bonds has rocketed to over $175 billion today, or about $700 of junk bonds in circulation for every U.S. citizen. What's wrong with junk bonds? If a corporation is willing to pay high interest rates to raise money and investors are willing to buy its bonds, what's the matter with that?

I have no quarrel with people investing their money any way they want to, but insurance companies? That's different, because society as a whole will pay if the insurance companies make risky investments and lose.

But that is not the only reason I object to insurance companies buying junk bonds; the main reason is that junk bonds are used to facilitate leveraged buyouts of companies, which can make piles of money in the short term for investors and key players, at the expense of the employees, the stockholders, and society as a whole.

A leveraged buyout is essentially a scheme whereby the purchaser uses the target company's own resources to acquire it. If you wonder who thought this up, simply look at who is making money at it. It is also interesting to note that the legal fees in a single leveraged buyout deal can be $100 million or more.

A leveraged buyout begins with an investor group, usually involving a company's top management and/or an array of buyout specialists, lawyers and so on, coming up with about ten percent of the purchase price in cash, then securing bank loans with corporate assets for another fifty to seventy percent, and raising twenty to forty percent by selling junk bonds to insurance companies and pension funds, among others.

The buyers simply bid high enough for all outstanding shares for the company that they acquire all of the outstanding stock and take the company from public to private. Once in possession, they immediately begin selling off parts of the company to reduce the debt.

Under a staggering debt burden, the company must race to cut costs to create the short-term profits needed to service the debt. These cuts can disrupt tens of thousands of jobs in the short term, and destroy the company in the long run by reducing research and development and capital equipment improvements required to keep the company competitive. In the meantime, the clever owners can take their amazingly profitable "new improved" company public again and really cash in.

With so much of its resources dedicated to paying the interest on its debt, the company could be bankrupted by even a slight recession.

If the $175 billion in junk bonds represents thirty percent of the total value of leveraged buyouts going on, then leveraged buyout action passed the half-trillion dollar point some time back ($2,000 per capita).

In all of that, there is no doubt that much good has been done for the economy, and that there are many companies who could not have survived and prospered and contributed significantly to the greater good. But at what cost? Consider that by plunging these companies in debt at interest rates as high as the market chooses to demand, and exhausting three to four percent of the money raised in sales commissions on the junk bonds (vs. one percent or less for regular bonds), the buyers are selling out the future of the company—and the employees—in return for instant gratification. This harms the economy by disruption and unemployment (one percent of unemployment adds over $30 billion to the budget deficit), and even moreso by pushing up interest rates as the high-paying junk bonds suck up a growing proportion of available capital.

Higher interest costs mean higher prices, while at the same time high interest rates drive up the value of the dollar and thus make U.S. products less competitive in the world market. So we enjoy not only higher prices at home, but growing unemployment as American products are priced out of the market and imports get cheaper.

Are insurance companies hurting? Hell, no. Are they hurting us? You bet.

13

How Fair Is The Judicial System?

I have a great deal of respect and appreciation for the American system of justice. Let me make that clear. But admirable though its spirit and intent may be, it is no secret that the American judicial system remains less than perfect, in practice.

We all know that things work out differently for the rich than they do for the poor, and generally better for whites than for blacks or other minority citizens. In similar cases, higher sums will be awarded in certain areas of the country, while certain cases would not even be pursued in other areas.

We all know that situations exist where prejudice on ethnic grounds has weighed on the scales of justice. My own case when Dr. Grossinger was suing me and the judge himself inquired what Ayatollah Khomeini would have done about my not paying a medical bill, and indeed the reversal of his hostilities when told about my father's fate, were blatant examples of such irrelevant influences.

These things will change as society's values change, and I think America has made phenomenal strides toward eliminating the scourge of prejudice from our land. I know of no fairer system of justice on earth.

But there are more insidious and dangerous things going on in the World of the Vultures that directly affect the quality of justice in our land. Take, for instance, the chummy relationships between some lawyers and judges.To begin with, lawyers generally have about as much hostility toward each other as professional wrestlers. They act fierce and crazy, but of course they are cool and respectful; otherwise someone might get hurt! This way, all the Vultures win.

Who are the judges anyway, but lawyers from the community who are elected or appointed to steady jobs? Given the fact that even a Supreme Court justice makes less money than a mediocre young lawyer, it is all the more a miracle that we have somehow found the number of great jurists that we have who are also noble enough to sacrifice personal gain for the public good.

I got a firsthand look at friendly relations between a lawyer and a judge a few years ago. At a trade show in Las Vegas, I had purchased a pair of very expensive audio amplifiers that were made in Great Britain. I shipped them from Las Vegas to Miami via a well-known trucking line, but they were damaged in transit. When I filed a claim with the trucking company, instead of paying for the damaged goods, they gave me a partial settlement and left me the damaged amplifiers and the prospect of shipping them roundtrip to England for repair. I was not satisfied with the settlement, and to top it off the trucking company sued me for $840 in freight charges for the ill-fated journey from Las Vegas!

I asked James Altman to help me out with this, and off we went to County Court. After the judge heard both sides, he gave James a meaningful glance and ruled in my favor. After we left the courtroom, I asked James whether he knew the judge. "Oh, yes," James replied. "He is a friend of mine, and our firm contributed substantially to his campaign."

I was glad that the judge was James' friend. In retrospect, I can see that the trucking company had a point, too. (Although if they had told me they would expect me to pay the freight bill after ruining my goods, I would have demanded a larger settlement to begin with.) Still, a chill ran through me when James spoke, when I realized that the trucking company's lawyer might have been the judge's friend instead.

When you consider that law firms are heavy contributors to judges' election campaign coffers, and that judges just might be in the market for cushy jobs when their tenure is over, it is not too surprising that such things can and do happen.

Occasionally relationships between judges and lawyers become more than courteous, that is, outright corrupt. For example, the F.B.I.'s recent Operation Graylord uncovered massive corruption in Cook County, Illinois, courts, with outright cash payoffs from certain lawyers to certain judges proving to outweigh other considerations (such as the evidence) in some cases.

The jury system theoretically places the responsibility for determining the outcome of many cases in the hands of six or twelve citizens. The attitudes and values of the jurors will be reflected in the verdict, and sometimes the jurors will sympathize with a plaintiff to a very great extent. Then along comes the judge, who can arbitrarily reduce the award mandated by the jury. It is asking a lot of a judge to uphold an award that will make the plaintiff's attorney more money for a few hours work than the judge may earn in two decades.

Similar situations often arise in arbitration proceedings, except the judge's role is filled by a "neutral" attorney who is acceptable to both parties. Arbitration is often used to settle auto accident cases, particularly when the victim is trying to collect on his own uninsured motorist coverage from his own insurance company.

Preparation for arbitration requires exactly the same efforts as for a court trial, including depositions, interrogatories, expert witnesses and all.

Then the plaintiff's lawyer and the defendant's (insurance company's) lawyer each select another lawyer to represent their points of view on the arbitration panel (if two lawyers are good, then four must be better). The third member of the arbitration panel is a "neutral" lawyer, who both sides agree is unbiased. Then, when the calendars of all concerned can be coordinated, the fun begins.

The plaintiff and defendant each present their case and parade their experts, summarize their arguments and so on, and then the three arbitration panelists decide what the verdict shall be. Of course the whole outcome turns on the whim of the "neutral" lawyer, who has the last word. The defense lawyer's appointed panelist will argue for no award, or a minimal award; the plaintiff's appointee will demand the moon. That is their job and they get paid well for it. The "neutral" lawyer is the tie breaker.

Many plaintiff lawyers prefer arbitration, with its flexible scheduling, less formal setting and relative efficiency, to the jury process. But often a victory can be hollowed by a small-time lawyer who earns a few hours pay serving as a "neutral" panelist. Here again it must be pretty hard for these panelists to watch their more successful colleagues, the insurance company's lawyers getting big bucks by the countless hour, and the plaintiff's lawyer in a position to earn more for one case than the small-timer might make in ten years.

I was a witness in one case where the victim was supposed to receive $325,000, but the award was reduced to $16,000. The reason for this outcome was that the plaintiff's lawyer had agreed to accept a "neutral" lawyer suggested by the insurance company. The guy was a neighbor of the plaintiff's lawyer, who wanted to see his acquaintance pick up a few bucks by getting the spot on the arbitration panel.

Unfortunately, this "neutral" party made about $40,000 a year working for a local law firm, and didn't have the money to buy the things for his family that the plaintiff's lawyer had. The neutral lawyer's son would always borrow the toys of the plaintiff's lawyer's son, and so on; the "neutral" lawyer had developed quite a complex about it. So, when this guy had his big day, he clipped the plaintiff's lawyer's wings (and clipped his pay by over $100,000, too).

At the same time, he was doing the insurance company a favor, which would certainly be repaid in future business from them. Insurance companies have a much more frequent need for a "neutral" lawyer's services than do individual plaintiff's lawyers.

The dilemma facing the plaintiff's lawyer in selecting a "neutral" panelist is that since the defense will not accept another plaintiff lawyer for the slot, the "neutral" lawyer has to be a lawyer from some other area of legal practice, who will take on the relatively paltry job, yet who is also comfortable with vast sums of money.

It is ironic that the American justice system's obsession with fairness to all is itself a part of the problem. The lamentable coddling of criminals (or alleged criminals) is one thing. Certainly the police agencies are only human and unquestionably a sizable number of people accused of crimes are innocent. I would rather have a system that is frustratingly cautious in judging people guilty and carrying out its sentences than a system that could allow innocent people to be unnecessarily penalized.

Still, the lawyers have found ways not only to protect the guilty, but to do so at the expense of the innocent. I am not just referring to the way lawyers cost us millions in their attempts to spare the lives of self-confessed mass murderers by means of endless technicalities. The same thing happens every day in just the sort of case that any one of us might find ourselves in at any time, like a minor traffic accident.

You may have the misfortune to be driving along minding your own business, stopping at an intersection, and having the fellow behind you fail to stop until his motor is in your back seat. A few minutes later the police come along and determine that the other driver is at fault, and issue him a citation. Assuming that he is insured, you may have the good fortune to find that not only is his insurance company not interested in paying you for your loss, but if you should sue them to collect, you will soon learn that not only is the other driver (who rear-ended you and got the ticket) not at fault, but that you yourself are the "bad" guy.

Now you have to prove that the other guy is in the wrong. It seems obvious to any reasonable person, you say? Don't worry, lawyers don't have to be reasonable. You will find that since the policeman didn't witness the accident, his assessment of what happened is irrelevant in the eyes of the law. If you are lucky, you may avoid paying the guy who hit you! God forbid that the guy hurt himself.

This is as preposterous as the burglar who breaks into your house and hurts himself suing you and winning, which has been known to happen. Hundreds of similar examples abound. A good friend of mine recently learned about the absurdity of the tort system in a case involving an automobile accident:

My friend Bob's car was hit by a teenaged driver who ran a red light. Bob's car was totalled, and he was lucky to escape death or severe injury (he was wearing a seatbelt). The kid, accompanied by his mother, also miraculously escaped with a minor cut, but was not wearing a seatbelt as required by Florida law. Although the mother presented an insurance card as the officer wrote the kid a ticket for running the light and causing an accident, as it turned out the insurance company had never been informed of the teenage driver and thus declined to pay. Bob sued the mother, who owned the car. Under Florida law, she and the kid would lose their licenses until they had paid for Bob's car.

Now, enter the Vultures. After over a year, the kid's lawyer responded by countersuing Bob, blaming him for the accident, and demanding damages for his "permanent disfigurement" (small scar).

Bob's insurance company's lawyer predicatably ran up thousands in billings over what should have been a simple matter, and then advised Bob to let the insurance company settle with the kid for the limits of his policy. Otherwise, if the kid prevailed in court, Bob would have to pay the difference out of his own pocket. The reason for this absurdity is that the facts that the kid was operating the vehicle illegally (uninsured and with no seatbelt on) and that the kid had been ticketed for running the light are not admissable in court. Therefore, who wins? The lawyers for both sides and the person who broke the law and caused the accident. Bob might have lost a valuable car, but learned a valuable lesson about the World of the Vultures.

By using the letter of the law to subvert its spirit and intent, lawyers have enriched themselves and impoverished us all. Our system of justice was founded upon reason and common sense. These have been replaced by legal manipulation and absurdity. Let's bring back some common sense.

14

What To Do About The Vultures

So that is our Vulture Crisis, in a nutshell (or a vulture's egg-shell). Now, what can be done about it?

The problems are not just those associated with each subspecies of Vulture, but the fact that these problems interact to produce a vicious synergy, a crisis that is greater than the sum of its parts.

It is clear that none of the players in this black comedy of terrors has the least motivation to change his own situation in any manner that would be beneficial to the rest of us. Each of the Vultures is quick to lay blame upon the others, however, and to propose reforms for them.

Doctors and insurance companies whipped up a solution to the "Malpractice Insurance Crisis" in Florida in 1988 and spent millions to sell it to the voters. Amendment 10, as this proposal was known, sought to limit non-economic damages in tort cases (i.e., damages for such nebulous things as pain and suffering) to $100,000. This probably would have reduced insurance premiums for the doctors, and certainly would have made a lot of money for the insurance companies. It didn't offer anything good to the victims, and it is unlikely that any benefit would have accrued to you or me. The proposition was defeated, thanks to a multimillion dollar counter-advertising campaign by the lawyers (of course).

Amendment 10 was doomed to failure not because it limited potential awards to potential victims, but because it would have severely limited the potential income of lawyers derived from these cases. On the other hand, if the amendment had proposed to limit lawyers' fees to $100,000 regardless of the size of the award, it almost certainly would have passed in spite of opposition by the lawyers.

The doctors and insurance companies had little to lose in any event. With the rejection of Amendment 10, no one can complain about high malpractice insurance premiums and high doctors' fees.

Voters in California, meanwhile, overwhelmingly approved Proposition 103, a short-sighted "solution" to the runaway auto insurance rates in that state, which requires insurance companies to roll back auto rates by twenty percent, and by an additional twenty percent for drivers with good driving records. While it is reassuring to see democracy in action stomping on the toes of Big Business, there is no way that California can force insurance companies to do business in California if they don't want to.

Now the insurance crisis in California will transform from one of high rates to one of unavailability, and then the cycle will begin anew. You certainly don't have to feel sorry for the poor insurance companies.

California's high insurance rates still do not approach those in South Florida, where estimates of uninsured drivers run from sixty to eight-five percent, due to the high rates as well as idiotically lax insurance laws.)

Our Vulture Crisis is multifaceted. Many plans have been propounded to relieve us, but each plan addresses only one facet of the crisis. Since what makes this a crisis in the first place is the fact that the Vultures are enriching themselves at our expense, it is not enough to limit legal fees, or reduce potential damages awarded to victims. Ultimately, the solution must involve clipping the wings of all of the Vultures. No one has yet proposed a comprehensive solution. Still, each aspect of the problem has been seriously studied, and some aspects of the resulting limited plans have merit and could be components of a comprehensive remedy.

Doctors

Let us begin with a clarification of the duties and responsibilities of doctors to their patients. Doctors are supposed to take care of sick and injured people and heal them to the best of their ability. What doctors are not supposed to do is perform unnecessary surgery, prescribe unnecessary drug or treatments, or kill people.

Certainly, with these responsibilities, no one can object to doctors making a lot of money. Still, the practice of medicine should not be just another business whose primary goal is to make money.

Ideally, we would have competent and safe medical care available to everyone at affordable cost. What we have today is moving ever faster, ever farther from that ideal.

Doctors contribute to our crisis in many ways, not the least of which is negligence or malpractice. The doctors create a lot of problems for us, and, to be fair, a lot of other influences cause problems for the doctors, which in turn become problems for all of us.

Where there is medical malpractice, you will usually find a doctor at the bottom of it. In a survey of 272 cases of proven medical malpractice, doctors were responsible in 49.4% of cases, while hospitals were at fault in 22.4% and a combination of doctors and hospitals were to blame in 28% of cases. The lawyers are right when they say that there is too much malpractice going on—too many doctors and hospitals failing to properly care for their patients, or performing unnecessary procedures on them.

Simple greed on the part of doctors, whether manifested as unnecessary treatment or in their astronomical fees, is cause enough for concern. Either way, the emphasis is financial rather than medical. Yet, a doctor would have to be superhuman to turn his back on the boundless opportunity for enrichment that exists under the present system. Although no studies have correlated rising income of doctors and incidence of malpractice, I do not think it unreasonable to suppose that some relationship is inherent there.

American doctors enjoy the highest median income of any professional group in the world, and the margin between the median income of doctors and those of other professions in the U.S. has continually widened over the past several decades. Of course the source of all these riches is all of us, either in the form of direct payments from patients, or from insurance companies or the government.

Insurance companies make it easy for greedy doctors to cash in. Health insurance covers a wide range of expensive services, and because the patient with insurance coverage, or Medicare, is insulated from the direct costs of his care, he is likely to sit still for any old operation his doctor demands, as long as it doesn't cost him too much. This is not much of a problem for the insurance companies. After all, the high cost of medical care is a good reason for people to buy insurance, and however high the most of health care, the insurance companies will find a way to make a profit. This is a great problem for the rest of us, however, as it runs up the nation's health care bill—yours and mine—and actually encourages excess and creates opportunity for malpractice.

Physician ownership of hospitals and medical laboratories, cannot possibly serve to reduce excess costs either. Kickbacks from testing laboratories would seem likely to encourage doctors to order as many tests as patients will abide.

And when doctors make money from selling drugs that only they have the right to order, is it any wonder that over $30 billion in prescription medications is part of our annual health-care bill, and millions of people are prescription junkies? Referral fees from other doctors encourage passing a patient around as far as his insurance will carry him.

A total of 71,930 physicians were involved in 73,472 medical malpractice cases in 1984. Of these physicians, forty-two percent had previous claims filed against them. Based on the forty percent success rate of plaintiff lawyers in such cases, this means nearly 30,000 cases of proven malpractice. Out of this a scant 400 doctors' licenses were lifted. Even this might have improved the situation, but as things stand, a doctor who loses his license in one state can simply go get a license in another.

This is not the way to control malpractice.

The involvement of doctors as expert witnesses in malpractice or personal injury cases does nothing to hold down the costs of such litigation, nor the cost of health care or insurance in general. Of course only a doctor can assess the extent of a person's injury, or whether the injury may be permanent, but as long as the expert witness business is lucrative, there will always be an opposing medical view for hire. What is the sense of running up all of the expense when we already know that in any given case the defense's expert witnesses will testify that nothing that the defendant did was wrong, and the plaintiff's expert witnesses are going to say that the defendant did nothing right?

It is only fair to note that doctors have problems of their own. One major concern is the escalation of malpractice insurance premiums, which have run parallel to those for all other forms of liability insurance. Although malpractice premiums have increased for all doctors, certain specialists have been hit with exponential increases, which have actually forced some of them out of practice in such critical areas as emergency rooms. Obstetricians have seen their rates go as high as $200,000 per year. Overall, neurosurgeons pay the highest premiums.

It is one thing for doctors to have to work under the constant threat of being sued for the slightest mistake, real or imaginary, of their own. But any doctor on the periphery of any other doctor's unfortunate mistake, real or imaginary, can find himself embroiled in a lawsuit involving another doctor's mistake, real or imaginary. As in our case, the doctor might just happen to come along and revive a patient despite everyone else's negligence, and then find himself a defendant in that patient's lawsuit.

By 1986, 37% of physicians had had at least one claim filed against them in their careers. Of the specialists, 64% of obstetricians and gynecologists, 50% of surgeons, 39% of radiologists, and 36% of anesthesiologists had had claims against them.

More and more, this leads to the practice of defensive medicine—the practice of medicine with an eye for a course of treatment, which would be maximally defensible should litigation ever arise. This could be somewhat beneficial, by encouraging conscientiousness, but it also encourages excessive tests, treatments and surgery.

Hospitals

The great majority of medical malpractice claims (80% in 1984) involved misdeeds alleged to have occurred in hospitals. Hospitals themselves account for 22% of malpractice cases, and share the blame with doctors in another 28% of cases.

Not every hospital can be the best-equipped, but with relatively few exceptions, American hospitals are among the best-equipped in the world. For the most part, the problems with hospitals are people problems. As hospital staffs are reduced due to lower occupancy rates and unavailability of qualified personnel, often nurses and doctors are overworked. This creates conditions conducive to negligence and malpractice by mere accident.

Hospitals are faced with a dilemma when they find staff members negligent or dangerous: if they fire the miscreant they in effect admit that misdeeds have been done for which the hospital itself is responsible under the legal concept known as respondeat superior or "let the master answer." Further, they risk being sued by the former employee. It is little wonder that hospitals tend to be very defensive of their employees, and to be slow to dismiss anyone. Under the present circumstances, who can blame them?

And, morally, as well as legally (respondeat superior again), the responsibility for the activities of a hospital rests with its administration, its management. Maintaining standards of competence must begin at the top.

Lawyers

In considering the role of the lawyers in our Vulture Crisis, it is necessary to distinguish between plaintiffs' (victims') lawyers, and defense (insurance companies') lawyers. Beyond the obvious potential for plain old malpractice on the part of lawyers themselves, different lawyers contribute to the situation in different ways.

Plaintiff lawyers have been known to file lawsuits whose foundations were less than substantial, and bogus lawsuits cost as much as any other kind to defend oneself against. How many billion a year does this add up to? Who knows how much it really is? By far the main contribution to our crisis by the plaintiff lawyers, however, is their high contingency fees.

Defense lawyers are a far greater problem. Defense lawyers win whenever there is a case, and the longer the case drags on, the more they win, regardless of the outcome; they get paid by the hour. They have the motivation—and the methods—to milk a case for all it's worth, and then some. This runs up the victim's costs (e.g. expert witness fees) as well.

If the case involves a potentially large award, the defense lawyers have a bonanza: the insurance companies will gladly pay whatever it takes to forestall having to pay the victim, for as long as possible. And in the legal system, that is a long, long time. If the case involves a trifling sum, not to worry; a good lawyer can still make a buck. If he just keeps churning out paper, he can earn himself many times what the insurance company could have settled for. Although this may deter plaintiff lawyers from filing so many suits, it can also backfire and cost the insurance company even more in punitive damages.

There is no limit on defense fees, unless it is set by the defendant. And, once he's in up to his limit, odds are he'll go as deep as the lawyer has time to take him. Although plaintiff lawyers, with their huge fees and flamboyant styles, get the worse press, defense lawyers contribute far more to the costs of litigation, and thus to rising insurance costs.

Insurance Companies

Insurance companies' contributions to our Vulture Crisis involve three general areas.

First, there is the instability created by their speculations in the stock and bond markets, particularly the junk bond market, which provides financing for leveraged buyouts. Selling policies below cost to grab cash when interest rates are high, and then ratcheting rates higher creates a recurring crisis situation, particularly when interest rates fall and insurance companies have to look to underwriting to solve their appetites for short-term cash.

Secondly, the insurance companies cost themselves, and therefore all of us, a tremendous amount of money and grief by not keeping their lawyers under control. Insurance company lawyers are a classic example of the tail wagging the dog.

Thirdly, insurance companies make it unnecessarily difficult, and expensive, for claimants to collect, even on their own policies. Apparently they would rather pay a lot, often in the form of punitive damages, tomorrow, than a fair amount today. This is certainly due, in part, to the influence of the lawyers.

Other than the jeopardy created for themselves by their marketing and investment practices, insurance companies are really vulnerable in only one area. Most policies cover incidents that occurred during the period of coverage, whenever claims may arise, up to the statute of limitations for a particular type of claim. Most tort laws allow a period of years after the incident for a claim to be made, and thus an insurance company can find itself defending a doctor that they insured three years ago for an incident alleged to have taken place three years ago, and forced to pay a claim out of current cash flow. Since all of us, in fact, insure the insurance companies, I guess we don't need to feel sorry for them. Don't worry, they'll squawk plenty loud before they lose a cent, so we can all have time to pay higher premiums to make it up to them.

The Judicial System

Another part of this Vulture Crisis is the American judicial system. The processing of tort claims in the judicial system is slow and extremely costly. No doubt this is thanks to lawyers, who, over time, have turned the legal system to their benefit.

In the case where the fate of a defendant is decided by a jury, the outcome can be skewed by subjective factors. Juries by their nature are not specialists, and are thus ill-qualified to objectively evaluate the appropriate award in many cases. A jury may arbitrarily award $700,000 to a pretty girl who twisted her ankle, $100,000 to a brain-damaged child, or $127 million to the family of a victim who died in the crash of an allegedly faulty car. (This judgment was handed down against Ford in a case where the gas tank of a Pinto exploded when the car was rear-ended.)

Arbitration, on the other hand, puts the fate of the victim in the hands of a panel of lawyers. The lawyers may have knowledge of the process, but most are not particularly qualified to assess what is truly fair financial compensation for a victim.

Further, by relying on the testimony of paid, and therefore guaranteed biased - experts, the judicial system prolongs the process of straightening out the victim's life. This creates needless suffering for the victim, and serious expense, too, while doing little to deter abuse of the System.

Victims

Our Vulture Crisis requires two groups of victims to sustain it: those people who are hurt in an accident or injured through malpractice or a bad product, and those who are injured financially by paying the tab for the whole Vulture feast, the general insurance-premium-paying public.

The tragedy of the victim's suffering is that without it, none of the Vultures would benefit. The Vultures should roll out the red carpet for the victim, for all he does for them.

The only active contribution to our Vulture Crisis on the part of the victims is in the small proportion of cases when the victim is actually over compensated. This, of course is as wrong as inadequate, or nonexistent compensation.

The general public pays for the Vulture Crisis not only in the form of higher health and auto insurance, and general health care costs reflecting higher insurance costs, but in higher prices for everything as the effects of higher health care costs ripple through the entire economy. Health care adds as much as $600 or more to the cost of a new car, for example.

It is conservative to estimate that the Vulture Crisis costs each of us $1,000 or more per year, and that number is growing at a greater rate every year.

The real victims of the Vulture Crisis outnumber the Vultures by better than a hundred to one, and if you are not a Vulture, you are a victim. It is time for the victims to demand a solution to the crisis, including a reform of the entire health care delivery system, to provide adequate safe and affordable medical care to everyone.

Partial solutions, as proposed by various interested groups and institutions, can provide some improvements, but unless comprehensive reforms targeting all of the Vultures are enacted, the Vulture Crisis will only loom larger in the future. It won't go away.

The American Medical Association (AMA) has proposed a system whereby malpractice complaints would be reviewed by a government-appointed board of doctors and representatives of other professions. The board would investigate malpractice complaints to determine whether they were merited, and suggest appropriate settlements. Any plaintiff or defendant dissatisfied with the outcome could have the case further reviewed by a hearing examiner, whose determinations would be further subject to review by the entire board.

If the party were still dissatisfied, he could appeal through the tort system, but only on matters relating to how the case was adjudicated. There would be no limit on damages for lost wages, medical costs and the like, but awards for pain and suffering would be limited to a maximum of $200,000.

The AMA says that this proposal would have several advantages over the present tort system. First, it would eliminate the need for plaintiff lawyers to collect the money. Secondly, successful claimants would receive their settlements within one year rather than wade through the tort system quagmire that can take years. In addition, the proposed system would police doctors' competence, and possibly find a way to keep an eye on bad doctors, or even take some sort of disciplinary action.

Although the AMA's proposal could be said to have merit, if for no other reason than that the lawyers don't like it, it does little to reduce the contributions of the doctors to our Vulture Crisis. The AMA proposal would clearly make things a lot easier on the doctors and insurance companies, at the expense of the victims and the lawyers. What the AMA is saying is, "Let's have a board of doctors decide whether malpractice has occurred. If so, pay for it according to what we doctors think is fair. Get rid of those pesky plaintiff lawyers."

What the AMA is not saying is, "Here is a proposal that will reduce malpractice and unnecessary surgery, and make medical care safe and affordable for everyone." That might cost them some money. Greed is a greater problem than incompetence.

The lawyers, predictably, think the present system is just fine. According to them, there is no insurance crisis, or lawsuit crisis, but too much malpractice; too many doctors and hospitals failing to attend properly to the safety of their patients. When people fail to receive health care meeting minimum standards, it is not the fault of lawyers, after all. The lawyers say, "Just get rid of the bad doctors and everything will be all better."

No one can argue against getting rid of bad doctors, and the lawyers know that. However, how unhappy can the lawyers be? If every doctor was a bad doctor, so much the better for the lawyers, both plaintiff and defense.

From the insurance companies' standpoint, the ideal situation would be to collect the highest premiums the market would bear, and to pay out nothing. Since this is not possible, the insurance industry supports such developments as measures to reduce the number of incidents which give rise to claims, "cost-spreading" measures, changes in tort law, and changes in traditional insurance and reserve systems to make them more favorable to the insurance companies' interests.

Certainly any of these developments would be of benefit to the insurance industry. In theory, they would also benefit the doctors in terms of reduced insurance costs, although there is scant evidence that when insurance companies get their way premiums are reduced. Predictably, the insurance industry is looking out for itself, but its proposals do not address improving health care or reducing health insurance costs.

Individual states have come up with some creative legislation to address various aspects of the Vulture Crisis. Virginia enacted the Birth-Related Neurological Injury Compensation Act. Lawsuits involving brain-damaged newborns contribute significantly to the prohibitive malpractice insurance premiums levied upon obstetricians, and in fact a great deal of brain damage suffered by newborns is not the fault of the doctor. (It is ironic that now, thanks to modern medicine, many brain-damaged infants live who would otherwise have died.)

The Virginia law takes all cases involving birth-related neurological injuries, some of which would garner awards of up to $10 million in the tort system, and provides medical and other expenses from a pay-as-you-go fund. At age 18, the victim also receives living expenses based on the state's average weekly non-farm wages. The plan is funded by voluntary payments of $5,000 per obstetrician or hospital with obstetric services, and $250 assessment from every other doctor in the state. Obstetricians who do not contribute are not protected.

California responded to the malpractice insurance crisis of the mid-1970s with the Medical Injury Compensation Reform Act, which caps compensation for non-economic damages (pain and suffering) at $250,000.

By the way, as much as this must have pleased the doctors and insurance companies, California doctors still pay some of the the highest malpractice insurance premiums in the nation. In addition, the law caps the share of an award that can go to a lawyer on a sliding contingency fee schedule. Lawyers can receive no more than forty percent of the first $50,000, one-third of the next $50,000, twenty-five percent of the second $100,000, and ten percent of any amount over $200,000. (In my case my lawyers' fees would have been $117,000 instead of $300,000.)

Florida's Tort and Insurance Reform Act of 1986 mandated the creation of an Academic Task Force to study problems involving affordability and availability of liability insurance, to review the impact of reforms included in the 1986 Act, and to report its findings and recommendations. The Academic Task Force consisted of members who were not associated with any of the interested groups, such as doctors, lawyers and insurance companies.

The Task Force recommended adoption of a Prompt Resolution of Meritorious Medical Negligence Claims Plan, including the following provisions:

(a) Claims against doctors, and denials of such claims, must be preceded by a reasonable investigation and accompanied by an expert's written opinion;

(b) Incentives should be provided for claimants and health care providers to submit claims to a binding arbitration to determine the amounts of economic damages, with non-economic benefit, not to exceed $250,000 and reasonable attorney's fees;

(c) If the defendant refuses to submit to arbitration, the plaintiff should retain all existing rights to a jury trial.

(d) If the plaintiff refuses to submit a claim to arbitration, plaintiff's non-economic damages at trial should be limited to $350,000.

The Task Force also recommended that physicians and hospitals be allowed to participate in a no-fault plan limited to birth-related neurological injuries. It recommended rejection of a plan to limit non-economic damages in tort cases, including medical malpractice, up to $100,000.

At the same time, the Task Force offered several proposals involving substantially strengthening the role of the state in the regulation of health care providers, calling for legislature to provide more resources and an improved administrative structure to enable the state agency to discipline physicians whose incompetence results in medical malpractice. It proposed that a separate division, the Division of Medical Quality, be created within the Department of Professional Regulation to discipline and license health care providers, and that this division should be funded by increases in licensing fees for health care providers.

The Task Force further proposed that legislation be enacted requiring the Division of Medical Quality to establish and supervise quality assurance boards on the local level, to identify health-care provider incompetence and disciplinary problems at their source.

The Task Force recommended a Premium Impact Equity Plan to provide equity payments to physicians who can demonstrate that high malpractice insurance premimums are causing genuine financial difficulties. This plan would be financed by a tax on medical malpractice insurance premiums. The Task Force recommended rejection of any plan calling for use of existing revenues to subsidize malpractice insurance premiums, or any plan requiring a state-operated insurance pool.

Other thoughtful proposals to cope with the Vulture Crisis were put forth by the United States General Accounting Office (GAO) in a report titled "Medical Malpractice: A Framework for Action." The GAO recommended the following measures:

(a) Shortening the statute of limitations for filing

claims, which would tend to reduce the number of claims filed;

(b) Revising joint and several liability rules, to require a defendant to pay damages commensurate with his share of fault in the case. This would be more fair to the defendants than the present system, which can make all defendants jointly and severally liable for the entire amount of damages, and encourages involving peripherally-involved people as defendants simply because they have "deep pockets;"

(c) Reducing malpractice awards by the amount of payments received from collateral sources (such as health insurance), which would prevent plaintiffs from collecting twice for the same injury;

(d) Limiting lawyers' contingency fees, to provide a greater portion of awards to the injured parties. This would encourage lawyers to settle larger cases sooner;

(e) Requiring periodic payments over the life of the injured party or over the period of disability, rather than lump-sum payments. This would better assure that funds are available when wages are lost or medical expenses incurred (and it would dramatically reduce costs for the poor insurance companies);

(f) Placing reasonable caps on awards for non-economic damages such as pain and suffering, which would bring more predictability to these damages, which currently are highly subjective, controversial, and not easy to quantify.

The recommendations of the Task Force and the GAO are certainly more broad in scope than those put forth by the interested parties. For the most part, they would be welcome improvements in the status quo. Even so, they are far from complete. In some cases they don't make a lot of sense. For example, the Academic Task Force recommended a ceiling on non-economic damages of $250,000 if a case is settled by arbitration, and of $350,000 if the case goes to a jury trial. Where is the incentive to submit claims to arbitration?

In any event, neither set of proposals attacks the real problems by getting to the roots of the Vulture Crisis, nor creates any incentive to improve the situation or to prevent all the misery from occurring in the first place. Neither provides for the establishment of a system to provide safe, preventive and affordable health care for everyone.

So far, this book has been about the problems. Is there any doubt of the magnitude of our problem? The latest "in" crisis is the great bail-out for the Savings and Loans. And it will cost the American public over $200 billion. The budget deficit alone runs over $100 billion so it's easy to see the magnitude of this cost. Well, folks, the tab for the Vulture Crisis may not be so easy to add up, but it certainly is costing us well over $250 billion per year, and climbing. That means just about a grand for every one of us. Every year. And counting.

My intention is to offer a sound, practical and comprehensive solution to the Vulture Crisis, looking out for the victims those who are physically injured, and the general public whose injuries are fiscal. This solution includes simultaneous changes for all of the Vultures.

15

Further Advice

The best way to deal with medical malpractice is to begin by doing as much as possible to prevent its occurrence in the first place. Efforts to accomplish this must include the following:

1. Elimination of financial incentives. This means prohibiting doctors from practicing in hospitals in which they have a financial interest, or from using any laboratory in which they own any share at all. I would prohibit doctors from deriving any financial benefit whatsoever from any laboratory, or from any enterprise involving the sale of medications. Unless doctors are salaried, the incentives for needless surgery exist. However, in the few situations where tissue review boards have begun to examine pieces removed from patients' bodies, the number of operations in those hospitals has declined dramatically. I am not saying that sometimes it is not better to be safe than sorry, but if a surgeon continued to turn in healthy appendixes day after day, the tissue review board would be in a position to document the extent of his excess. Establishment and enforcement of simple guidelines in this regard would quickly reduce the amount of unnecessary surgery.

2. Regulation of medical fees. As much as I believe in a free market, when we are confronted with a monopoly, we must regulate it. Modern medicine is nothing less than a monopoly, with a far more

significant impact on our lives, and economy, than the telephone or cablevision company. A tariff schedule of maximum charges for services rendered would make health care costs more predictable, and it would immediately reduce the cost (if not the price) of health insurance.

3. Weeding out the bad doctors. When a doctor is found guilty of malpractice once, he should be reprimanded and put on notice. The second proven incident should result in the doctor's license being restricted for one year to practice under the supervision of a doctor whose record is clean. Strike three—you're out. Revoke the licenses of three-time losers. And don't let the doctor get another license in another state. While we're at it, we should examine the credentials of every person who is practicing medicine today with at least as much scrutiny as the law requires a restauranteur to examine those of his dishwashers. It has been estimated that over 25,000 unlicensed doctors are practicing in the U.S. Many of these doctors are from other countries, and have not qualified for licensing in the U.S. Often licensed doctors hire these unlicensed physicians to work in their clinics for low wages, and cover for them by signing prescriptions and insurance forms. These practices are prevalent in urban areas with large immigrant populations. This measure would allow for human error, and would permit good doctors to improve their performance. It would also get the bad and unlicensed doctors out of the system abruptly.

4. Requiring a second medical opinion. To protect the patient from unnecessary surgery, at least one opinion should be from a non-surgeon in the appropriate field of medicine who is unrelated to the surgeon in the case. In the case of a head injury where a neurosurgeon recommends surgery, a disinterested practicing neurologist should review the case prior to the proposed surgery. In cases involving proposed back injury, the opinion of a chiropractor should be required. In many cases the chiropractor would not only recommend against the surgery, but would also solve the problem without the need for surgery. The benefits of requiring a second opinion will be determined by the extent to which the reviewing doctor is financially disinterested in the case. In no event should a reviewing doctor receive any form

of financial benefit from the case other than his fee for examining the patient; certainly the reviewing doctor cannot be allowed to receive referral fees from surgeons at all.

5. Integrating chiropractic into the health care system. Chiropractors should be included on the staffs of hospitals and general clinics, and more practitioners of this healing art should be trained. A portion of government medical reasearch funds should be devoted to evaluation of the potential benefits and savings that would result from widespread applications of this health-care discipline.

6. Protecting doctors from arbitrary lawsuits. When a malpractice case occurs, often every doctor who has even looked at the patient ends up as a defendant in the resulting lawsuit. This strategy may be useful for placing blame on the guilty doctor, but mostly it makes a lot of money for defense lawyers and expert witnesses at the expense of the innocent doctors, in lost income and wasted time. Doctors who are inappropriately sued should be entitled to legal fees, lost income and some form of punitive damages from the plaintiff's attorneys. At the same time, guilty doctors or their lawyers who try to blame innocent doctors for the malpractice should be required to compensate them for time and lost income. In this case, the plaintiff and the plaintiff's lawyer deserve extra compensation for their trouble. These remedies would protect good doctors, and would reduce the time and expense involved in litigation.

7. Preventing abuses of expert testimony. First, any doctor who is selected as an expert witness must have a record unblemished by malpractice. Second, fees for expert witnesses should be standardized according to a fee schedule. Third, doctors should only be allowed to act as expert witnesses in no more than six cases per year, and for the same lawyers (either plaintiff or defense) twice a year. This would help prevent cozy relationships between doctors and lawyers from developing at the expense of justice for all of us. Ideally, the testimony of an expert doctor should be credible at face value. Obviously, however, the plaintiff and the defense will each have doctors who will support their opposing positions, so neither side is particularly credible. What is required is a panel of neutral physicians who have no financial interest in the specific case; their compensation must

come from a neutral source. This could be funded by court fees paid by the losing party. This would reduce the prostitution of the medical profession by greedy expert doctors and reduce the costs of litigation and therefore reduce health and malpractice insurance significantly.

Implementation of these changes would help to defuse the Vulture Crisis and improve the quality of health care while reducing costs. However, even if an organized grass-roots popular movement demanded them, the appropriate regulations would have to withstand the lobbying of the American Medical Association and other organizations in the health care establishment, and somehow make it through Congress without being diluted to satisfy the interested parties. That is hard to imagine.

I propose a reform of the health-care delivery system in the United States, from the inside out. I propose the establishment of an alternate health care delivery system, an efficient system where people get quality health care, conveniently, at cost levels, which would allow health care to continue to be provided in the future. When the alternative exists, the free market will take care of the reform. The present medical establishment would have to fall in line or be left out in the cold.

I would like to clarify something. I do not favor socialized medicine; that is, I do not favor government as the health care provider. Still, health care is a basic raison d'etre of society, and whether it is paid for directly by the consumer, or whether the wealth is extracted from the economy in some other fashion, the health care delivery system affects every one of us on a very basic level. If I could believe it possible for such an alternative health-care delivery system to be instituted and operated efficiently by the government, I would favor that form of socialized medicine. I do not believe the government could do it well, if at all. The system I propose is different from the nationalized health-care systems of Eastern and Western Europe and Canada, in that it is based on principles of the free-market economy.

I believe that quality health care is within our grasp. Certainly the technology exists and improves daily, and its attainment is too essential to us all to trust to altruists or bureaucrats. I favor a profit-motivated system, whose profits depend on doing what is right for every single patient. After all, that is the same thing as doing what is right for society as a whole.

The system I propose differs from Health Maintenance Organizations (HMO's) in significant ways. HMO's have two major shortcomings: lack of control over medical costs, and lack of control over the uniformity of quality of treatment. HMO's are set up so that patients pay a flat monthly amount for most health care services, and they arrange with designated doctors and hospitals to treat their patients. However, the doctors and hospitals are paid on a fee-for-services basis, and this does little to discourage them from ordering excessive tests and procedures, especially since they generally charge the HMO's below-market rates. By contracting with doctors and hospitals, the HMO's relinquish control over the quality and nature of health care services delivered to their members. Still, HMO's represent a step in the right direction, and often make better health care more affordable.

Health care is as basic and essential as food, shelter and clothing to the maintenance of life, and I believe it should be as available and affordable as any other basic necessity. With a market consisting of the entire population, the potential for tremendous economies of scale exists, and must be exploited for the benefit of all of us today, and for the future.

In other areas technology and the free market improve our standard of living by making more and better goods available and more affordable. For example, the cost of a television set today represents a much smaller portion of a family's purchasing power than it ever has, and the television set is better than ever. While we complain about food costs, we pay a smaller percentage of our income for food than any nation on earth, and the quality and selection available to us is unrivaled anywhere. Yet improved technology and growth in the number of health care professionals and facilities has only caused health care costs to skyrocket. Health care delivery has escaped the influence of the free market long enough.

My proposed system of health-care delivery borrows liberally from organizational and management concepts that have been proven time and again to maintain quality control and hold down costs. One corporate paradigm of efficiency in these regards is the McDonald's fast-food empire.

It is inconceivable that anyone has not heard of McDonald's, and apparently a whole lot of us patronize them regularly. Wherever a given demographic situation exists, a McDonald's restaurant will spring up and become a fixture in the community. It will not be owned by the government, and economically it will be a positive contributor to the community, and represent a healthy return on investment for its owners. Standards of freshness and sanitation far exceed any that might be laid down by a government edict. All of this has come about by free-market forces.

In the context of this discussion, whether or not one likes McDonald's food is irrelevant. What is indisputable is that the product is consistent, the procedures structured and efficient, the facilities hospital-clean, and the individual outlet profitable. Whether you get your french fries in New York City or Grand Island, Nebraska, you can bet that they will taste the same, and be delivered to you at the same temperature. Standards of performance and quality are mandated by headquarters,.and strictly maintained by individual outlets throughout the world.

In this spirit, I call for the "McDonaldization" of our health care delivery system.

It is not within the scope of this book to present the blueprint and operating manual for a "McDonaldized" health care system, but an overview of the concept will suffice to establish its viability. A detailed plan for implementation of such a system is being prepared for publication in the near future.

Let's call this proposed enterprise GHC (for General Health Care). Adequate funding to establish GHC would not even be noticeable in the capital markets. Indeed, the start-up capital required would hardly fund Medicare for a few hours, and such a venture would be highly attractive to investors. Thousands of brilliant brains worry about how to improve the present health care system, which sucks over half a trillion dollars out of the economy every year, a figure that continues to escalate by the minute. Up to 250,000,000 citizens worry about their future. Yet the alternate system that I propose could be initiated for less than $100 million—a mere forty cents per person! After its start-up, this system would be self-sustaining.

GHC would assemble a board of practitioners from every field of health care, and write the book establishing detailed standards of care, specifying the equipment and facilities required to deliver it. Management would then formulate the method of matching the facilities and staff of an GHC "outlet" to the demographic characterisitics of a community or neighborhood in the most efficient manner, based on certain principles.

The first principle would be that the quality of health care must be of the highest standards possible given the state of the art today, with the emphasis in preventive care. This need not adversely affect costs nor reduce profits. In fact, in health care as anything else, I submit that quality is the best economy, and that the long-term profitibility of the enterprise would be enhanced and assured by providing the best care available anywhere in the world.

Aside from the fact that keeping its customers healthy would radically reduce health-care costs in the long run, GHC would profit from plenty of economies that would have only positive effects upon quality while sharply reducing costs.

A GHC outlet would be staffed by a combination of general practitioners and specialists capable of serving the needs of its local market, with the support staff and equipment required to allow these specialists to practice most efficiently. By combining these elements in a single facility, a tremendous savings in overhead expenses results. Other obvious savings result from avoiding senseless duplication of expensive equipment.

By adding weekend and evening hours, the same facility can serve more people, further reducing per-patient overhead costs dramatically.

These simple concepts not only further GHC's second principle of providing quality health care at the lowest possible cost, but they also embody the third principle, that health care should be easily accessible and convenient. In a properly organized milieu, who would have to wait for two hours to get five minutes of a doctor's attention—

and miss work to do it?

A fourth principle of GHC, aimed at improving quality while minimizing costs, would be that doctors as well as all other personnel would be on salary with a profit-sharing bonus plan. This would mean that a doctor would not benefit financially from ordering any unnecessary treatment, so if

it came down to performing a senseless hysterectomy or reading the latest medical journal, there would be every motivation to follow the more productive course of behavior. The profit-sharing plan would reward the employees both for improving quality and reducing costs. By reducing costs in so many ways, GHC could afford to pay the best doctors and health care personnel competitively. In fact, doctors should jump at the chance to earn more money with less worries than they would have in private practice. Reducing needless costs would allow paying nurses and other personnel more than they could earn elsewhere, while offering an environment for the best and brightest to practice their profession in the most pleasant and productive manner possible.

Once prototype GHC outlets had been operated successfully in a variety of demographic circumstances, GHC would offer franchises throughout America. While doctors could own GHC franchises, they would not be allowed to practice in the facilities which they owned. This would avoid any possible conflict of interest.

To begin with, GHC would accept all private health insurance plans as well as Medicare, Medicaid and other subsidized health care financial programs. GHC's reduced costs should be reflected in reduced insurance rates for its members. Ultimately, GHC could offer its own monthly payment plan directly to the consumer and bypass the health insurance companies, further reducing costs.

Malpractice insurance costs would be reduced by purchasing group policies, and further due to improved quality of care due to the organization and motivations of GHC. Ultimately costs would be further reduced by patients agreeing at the time of enrollment to submit any claims to independent arbitration, and to accept prescribed limitations on seeking damages. In the event of an unfortunate mistake, the victim could be justly compensated without having to enrich a bunch of lawyers, and both the victim and society as a whole would benefit from the savings.

GHC would make safe and affordable health care accessible to everyone, drastically reduce costs in the present, and hold them down in the future.

If we wait for the government or the existing health care system to improve things, we will go broke. Yet, the free market could establish the GHC system nationwide within a decade. Once the alternative existed, the free market would revolutionize health-care delivery in America.

The establishment of GHC would engender a new level of competition. With a market as vast as the United States, the success of GHC would encourage the development of competitive systems, and by the turn of the century we could see the Wendy's, Burger King, etc., of health care as well, each striving to offer better care at lower costs than the others. Wouldn't that be a welcome change?

For the present, measures need to be taken to reduce the unsafe health care and malpractice on the part of hospitals. As we have discussed, these problems are usually the result to human error or poor management.

The current shortage of 200,000 nurses will continue to grow, even as the population of our country gets older and requires even more health care services. In the near future, the issue may not be merely the quality of health care in hospitals, but its availability. If we are to improve the existing situation, and prepare for the future needs of our society, we must upgrade the pay, recognition and status of the nursing profession. There are many ways to reduce hospital operating costs without compromising the quality of care; this must not be done at the expense of the nurses. Increasing recognition of the invaluable contribution of nurses to society, and thus improving the status of the profession, requires only a change of attitude, and costs nothing.

It is imperative that the pay scale of the nursing profession be upgraded. However, this should be done based less on length of service and more on quality of performance. In other words, reward good nurses with recognition and better money, by providing incentives for the right kind of people to enter the profession. Improving nurses' pay in this manner would be a cost-effective means of improving the quality of health care, while improving its availability in the future.

Although paying nurses more would cost some money, this could well be offset by improved care. The money spent to defend and settle one stupid malpractice incident could provide a substantial raise for every good nurse on the hospital staff, and would be better spent in that manner.

To protect the patient, hospitals should be required to provide information on prior and pending malpractice complaints, including the nature of the complaint, the personnel involved, and the disposition of the claim. This would allow the patient to make more informed choices of health care facilities, and would provide incentives for hospitals to clean up their acts.

This disclosure requirement would help to offset a hospital's present reluctance to weed out dangerous personnel because it might look bad, and would provide incentives for more comprehensive training and monitoring of personnel. It would also cast light on the administrative personnel of the hospital in the event that incidents ran higher than normal.

For the same reasons mentioned above, doctors should be on salary in hospitals. In the case of hospitals, this would permit the administration to monitor the performance of the doctors. Still, as long as hospitals are paid on a fee-for-service basis, the incentive to eliminate unnecessary surgery and hospitalization will remain nonexistent.

Doctors should not own any part of a hospital where they practice. This would help reduce incentives to order unnecessary hospitalization or surgery, and would reduce malpractice.

Hospital charges should be fixed according to a schedule in the manner recommended above for doctors' fees. There is no excuse for five dollar tissues or razor blades, to say the least.

However successfully such changes might be implemented, the fee-for-service basis of health care delivery under the present system is ultimately at odds with the interests of the individual patient, and thus those of society as a whole. Until a system such as GHC is in place, we can only hope that pressure from the insurance companies will somehow help to reduce hospital charges. But, as we know, the insurance companies have little concern with costs; the more it costs, the more they charge, and the more they make. We will have to rely on the free enterprise system, and an GHC-style approach to save the day—and the country.

Attorneys represent another de facto monopoly that is beyond the influence of the free market. They answer only to themselves. Since they have no incentive to change their enviable situation, we have no choice but to regulate them. Areas requiring immediate attention are: (1) Restructuring the contingency fees charged by plaintiff lawyers; (2) Eliminating incentives for defense lawyers to drag out cases, earning money for the insurance companies and themselves at the expense of the plaintiffs and the rest of us; (3) Discouraging plaintiff lawyers from filing baseless suits and taking advantage of the system to collect money for no good reason; (4) Creating a more just and balanced system of compensation for victims, which would take the speculation out of the tort system and make it more efficient and cost-effective.

If fairness to the victim is the overriding concern in addressing these problems, there is no doubt that things could be improved in the areas of time and expense as well. The contingency fee system makes legal services most accesible to the greatest number of plaintiffs. It would certainly not be fair for a victim to have to come up with thousands and thousands of dollars to seek redress for an incident he didn't ask for in the first place. I do, however, object to the thirty-three to forty percent and more, plus expenses, collected by plaintiff lawyers; this is grossly exploitive. Yet slashing contingency fees would further jeopardize the accessibility of legal services in smaller cases, and that would not be fair to the victims. So a sliding scale of contingecy fees is the logical solution here. The question is, what should the scale be? There have been several suggestions in this regard. The California system has merit. Under that system, the lawyer gets forty percent of the first $50,000 collected, one-third of the next $50,000, one-fourth of the second $100,000, and ten percent of anything over $200,000. This still leaves the poor lawyer about $62,000 out of the first $200,000, which ought to make a few payments on the family Porsche.

Also meritorious is the sliding scale recommended by the U.S. Attorney General's Tort Policy Working Group. This plan calls for a fee of twenty-five percent of the first $100,000, twenty percent of the second $100,000, fifteen percent of the third $100,000, and ten percent of anything over that. This system would cost less than California's, but would be a little hard on the lower end of the scale. This would limit availability of legal services in smaller cases, or encourage lawyers to make a bigger deal out of small cases.

As the table shows, the Attorney General's proposed schedule is most favorable to the victim, and the one-third flat fee most favors the lawyers.

Simply limiting plaintiff lawyers' fees without addressing defense lawyers' is unfair and impractical. One way of reducing defense fees is to require insurance companies to pay interest at one percent over prime rate on awards, calculated from one month after a claim is filed. This would take away much of the incentive to stall cases. It is one thing for an insurance company to pay its lawyers to help it hang onto its money rather than to pay a victim, but paying lawyers on top of giving up whatever interest the insurance company would gain by keeping its money would quickly prove to the insurance companies that the real way to save money is to get rid of the lawyers.

The West Germans have a fee schedule for both plaintiff and defense lawyers which ranges from three to five percent of the jackpot! Still, German lawyers manage to drive Mercedes and Porsches. Similar fees are mandated for matters not directly involving monetary damages. If our own fee schedule resembled that of the Germans, defense lawyers would discover that a lot of their traditional shenanigans were not so profitable, and the wheels of justice would turn much more rapidly.

EXAMPLES OF PROPOSED LAWYERS' FEE SCHEDULES

AWARD AMOUNT	ATTORNEY GENERAL'S PROPOSAL	CALIFORNIA FEE SCHEDULE	FLAT FEE OF 33-1/3%
$ 50,000	$ 12,500	$ 20,000	$ 16,667
100,000	25,000	36,667	33,333
150,000	30,000	49,167	50,000
200,000	45,000	61,667	66,667
500,000	80,000	91,667	166,667
1,000,000	130,000	141,667	333,333

Another means of discouraging groundless lawsuits on the part of plaintiffs, and endless maneuvering on the part of defense lawyers when it is obvious that the defendant is at fault, would be to require that the loser in any case bear the legal expenses of the prevailing party. This system has worked in England for centuries, although in England the amount of the lawyers' fees is set by the judge, not by the whims of the lawyers. Contingency fees already tend to make plaintiff lawyers fairly selective in the cases they accept; knowing that if they lost a case they would have to pay the defense costs would clear a lot of groundless but expensive cases from the docket. This would also take away the incentive for defendants to pay defense lawyers to drag out cases; it would be cheaper to settle than to pay one's own lawyers and the plaintiff's.

Prescribing lawyers' fees and forcing the loser to pay the legal costs of the prevailing party would also help solve another frustrating aspect of the legal system. Often a business or individual will simply pay a claim because settling with the claimant is cheaper than hiring a lawyer to defend against the claim. Sometimes this works to speed up justice, but all too often such a situation is merely a form of legal blackmail.

In the interest of fairness to victims and to society as a whole, a more rational and structured system of compensation of victims must be established.

Victims of injuries or malpractice should have all related medical expenses, present and future, paid as they are incurred. Medical expenses should not be part of a lump-sum settlement.

Victims' lost income should be paid over the period of the loss, rather than as a lump sum. The amount of compensation should be determined not only by past income, as documented by pay-stubs and tax forms, but by consideration of other factors as well. People in many occupations do not receive weekly paychecks, but invest their time and efforts today for gains in the future. Salespeople's, writers', artists', and entrepreneurs' value to society, and to themselves and their families, are not always reflected on their current income tax returns. Thus, it would be unfair to base their compensation on current earnings.

There should be standards of compensation for the loss or

incapacity of each part of the body, so much for an eye, finger, leg, etc. However, when the loss or injury affects the potential earnings of a victim, this must be taken into account. For example, the loss of a finger would not impair the earning capacity of a lawyer, but could be devastating to a professional pianist. If a victim requires retraining in another field to regain the ability to earn a living, his compensation should reflect not only the unusual value of the loss, but the cost of retraining for a new profession. Lawyers argue that, for example, the loss of a finger deserves extra compensation in the case of a person who plays the piano for his own pleasure. This is unreasonably vague. Unfortunately, any loss is accompanied by a loss of pleasure to some extent. It is impossible to quantify the value of subjective factors such as pleasure, feelings or companionship, etc., and we have to draw the line here. Otherwise, the system cannot hope to be rational or efficient for anyone.

Non-economic losses, such as "pain and suffering", require compensation. I agree with those who propose that a rational limit should be imposed on such awards, and in most cases I would favor a limit of $250,000. However, in some cases such a sum is plainly inadequate. For example, the parents of a healthy child whose injuries leave him paralyzed or brain-damaged will suffer the effects of the injury daily for the rest of their lives. In such extreme cases, awards for non-economic damages should be permitted to exceed the limit, up to $1,000,000.

To further shorten the litigation process, and to bring both parties to a fast, realistic settlement, in order for a claimant to collect his legal costs from a defendant, he would have to win an award at least twenty-five percent greater than a settlement offered him prior to litigation. Conversely, if the court-ordered award should turn out to be one-fourth less than the pre-litigation settlement offer, the claimant would have to pay the legal expenses of the defendant, as well as his own.

Implementation of these changes would help to discourage plaintiffs from filing unreasonable lawsuits, and defendants (notably insurance companies) from such aggravating practices as dragging the least little case out for years to avoid payment to the victim, while feeding their fellow Vultures.

In addition to those changes outlined above which would indirectly affect the insurance companies, direct attention is required in five specific areas:

1. Insurance companies should be prohibited from investing in "junk bonds" in cases where the bonds are used to partially finance leveraged buyouts. I have no objection to an insurance company investing in profitable instruments, including bonds, which are less than A-rated, but I believe that the cost to the economy of leveraged buyout deals far outweighs the benefits enjoyed by vested interests such as the insurance companies. If the insurance companies have cash to burn, they should reduce insurance premiums and give some relief to the consumer, rather than engage in risky activities which, if they fail, will only cost all of us more money. After all, insurance companies' investments are supposed to offset underwriting losses and assure the stability of the company so that it can meet its future obligations. Just as the multiplicator effect of increasing insurance premiums ripples through the economy, adversely affecting the cost of every product and service, a rollback of insurance premiums would benefit everyone, and make American products more competitive in the domestic and foreign markets.

2. Until the changes outlined above are affected, which would eliminate much of the incentives for stalling and dragging out claims, the insurance companies should reduce their costs and improve their profits by taking control of their lawyers. If it is true, as the insurance companies say it is, that high tort verdicts are killing them, the first place they can look for relief is to the thirty-six percent of those costs, half of which goes directly to their lawyers, which is spent by the insurance companies to defend themselves against paying what they owe. If they could not rely on us to make up their losses, they would not be so inclined to throw good money after bad by feeding their fellow Vultures—the defense lawyers—at what is ultimately our expense.

3. Insurance companies could save themselves, and all of us, a lot of money and time by instructing their claims adjustors to be fair and reasonable in their settlement offers. Macho claims adjustors, in attempting to gain favor with the insurance companies by hardballing claimants, bring about a lot of needless, expensive litigation which costs the insurance companies far more than reasonable settlements

would.

4. Insurance companies should be no more eager to insure bad doctors than they are to insure bad drivers. This should also apply to private insurance groups established by doctors. If uninsured doctors were not allowed to practice, and insurance companies did not insure bad doctors, there would be a lot less bad doctors practicing and a lot less malpractice to begin with.

5. Insurance companies should refuse to do business with doctors and hospitals who are found to overcharge for services, or to charge for treatments not performed. It must be the responsibility of the insurance companies themselves to monitor the billings of hospitals and doctors and investigate unusual charges. Further, if insurance companies investigated random cases to verify that treatments were medically necessary, or were actually performed at all, this would discourage fraudulent or excessive practices that cost all of us money, and contribute to the Vulture Crisis. Insurance companies should take advantage of the fact that they are not subject to antitrust law, and share findings of excessive or fraudulent billings with all other insurance companies, so that crooked or greedy doctors and hospitals will be put out of business.

With regard to automobile insurance, and liability insurance in particular, if the insurance companies don't get their act together, we may need an alternative system. Automatic universal coverage funded by a surcharge on auto fuel may be a viable possibility. In this system, strict enforcement of drivers' license suspensions and revocations would be required. Under this system, simple liability claims could be settled impartially, without litigation, within reasonable limits. This system would also be fairer to people who drive less than others.

Just as the Vulture Crisis is the result of many factors interacting synergistically, the recommendations set forth in this chapter would act in concert to defuse the Vulture Crisis. While piecemeal remedies can bring temporary relief in some areas, until the problem is recognized in its totality, and all of these measures are implemented, the Vultures will continue to feed and prey on us all.

None of us will be safe until these Vultures are Endangered Species. Even the most kind-hearted animal-lover would welcome their extinction.

Epilogue

Now you know the problems that confront us, and that piecemeal solutions will not resolve them. You also have a real idea of what must be done.

We have been told that the biggest threat to our nation is external: Russian missiles and competition from Japan. So we spend half a trillion dollars every year to defend ourselves. Yet who kills more of us, the Russians, or our own doctors and hospitals?

We have been told that Japanese automobiles and foreign oil are destroying the economic well-being of our nation. What about the $75 billion we spend each year on lawyers, who will send us to the poorhouse if health care bills don't send us there first? At least with our Japanese cars and Middle Eastern oil we won't have to walk, if we can afford insurance!

We have been told that the Federal Budget Deficit and the Savings and Loan "crisis" will destroy our economy if we don't do something about them right away. We won't have an economy left to worry about if the insurance companies continue to drive up the prices of everything until America is completely broke and out of business.

The fact is that the excesses of the Vultures gobble up more than enough to cover the Federal Deficit every year, with enough left over to take care of a little Savings and Loan fiasco besides.

Certainly no one can be indifferent to a situation which steals $1,000 a year from each of us, however elegantly and cleverly it is done. But what can you do?

Part of the solution can come from the private sector, but implementation of many of the remedies proposed in this book will require comprehensive legislation. Until the next election, demand that your Congressperson and Senators stand up to the American Medical Association, the American Bar Association, the American Hospital Association and the Insurance lobbyists and enact the appropriate measures outlined here.

If you don't see any results, don't be surprised. The majority of legislators are lawyers. If we expect things to change, we must replace them with farmers, engineers, accountants, teachers—anyone but lawyers. Let the political party of your choice know that you won't vote to put a lawyer in the dog-catcher's office, much less the Statehouse or Congress.

Our political system still offers us the opportunity to make things right. But we had better hurry, before the Vultures outnumber us.

BIBLIOGRAPHY

BOOKS

BRAGO, *Bundesgebuehrenordnung fuer Rechtsanwaelte,Gesetzestextmit Gebuehrentabelle und Berechnungsbeispiel.* Munich,Muenster: Verlag Franz Rehm, 1987.

Christoffel, Tom, *Health and the Law, A Handbook for the Health Professional.* New York: The Free Press, 1982.

Current Award Trends, 1988 Edition. Cleveland: Jury Verdict Research, Inc.,1988.

Gebuehrenordnung fuer Aerzte (GOA), 3rd Edition. Bonn, Berlin, Munich, Cologne: Carl Heymanns Verlag KG, 1988.

Grossman, Howard H., *For Health's Sake, A Critical Analysis of Medical Care in the United States.* Palo Alto, CA: Pacific Books, 1977.

Hackenthal, Julius, *Auf Messers Schneide, Kunst und Fehler der Chirurgen.* Hamburg: Rowohlt Verlag GmbH, 1976.

McCormack, Mark H., *The Terrible Truth About Lawyers, What I Should Have Learned at Yale Law School.* New York: Avon Books, 1987.

Mendelsohn, Robert S., *Confessions of a Medical Heretic.* Chicago: Contemporary Books, 1979.

Rosenblatt, Stanley M., *Malpractice and Other Malfeasances, The Great Cases of a Successful Trial Lawyer.* Secaucus, NJ: Lyle Stuart, Inc., 1977.

Rosenblatt, Stanley M., *Trial Lawyer.* Secaucus, NJ: Lyle Stuart,Inc., 1984. Rukeyser, Louis, and John Cooney and George Winslow, *Louis Rukeyser's Business Almanac.* New York: Simon and Schuster, 1988.

Treating Malpractice: Report of the Twentieth Century Fund Task Force on Medical Malpractice Insurance. New York: Priority Press Publications, 1986.

U.S. Department of Commerce, Bureau of the Census, *Statistical Abstract of the United States 1988, 108th Edition.* Washington, D.C.: U.S. Government Printing Office, 1987.

Wilk, Chester A., *Chiropractic Speaks Out, A Reply to Medical Propaganda, Bigotry and Ignorance.* Park Ridge, IL: Wilk Publishing Co., 1976.

REPORTS AND STUDIES

Academic Task Force for Review of the Insurance and Trust Systems, "Preliminary Fact-Finding Report on Medical Malpractice." Gainsevill, FL, August 14, 1987.

Academic Task Force for Review of the Insurance and Tort Systems, "Medical Malpractice Recommendations." Gainesville, Fl, November 6, 1987.

Cooper, Mary H., "The Liability Crisis: Is It Over?" *Editorial Research Reports.* Washington, D.C., June 24, 1988.

Danzon, Patricia M., "Contingency Fees for Personal Injury Litigation, Prepared for the Health Care Financing Administration, U.S. Department of Health, Education and Welfare." Santa Monica, CA: The Rand Corp. Institute for Civil Justice, 1980.

Danzon, Patricia M., "New Evidence on the Frequency and Severity of Medical Malpractice Claims." Santa Monica, CA: The Rand Corp. Institute for Civil Justice, 1986.

Hammitt, James K. And John E. Ralph, "Limiting Liability for Automobile Accidents: Are No-Fault Tort Thresholds Effective?" Santa Monica, CA: The Rand Corp. Institute for Civil Justice, 1985.

Hensler, Deborah R., Mary E. Vaiana, James S. Kakalik, and Mark A. Peterson, "Trends in Tort Litigation, The Story Behind the Statistics." Santa Monica, CA: The Rand Corp. Institute for Civil Justice, 1987.

Kakalik, James S. and Robyn A Eisenshtat, "Costs of the Civil Justice System, Court Expenitures for Processing Tort Cases." Santa Monica, CA: The Rand Corp. Institute for Civil Justice, 1982.

Kakalik, James S. and Nicholas M. Pace, "Costs and Compensation Paid in Tort Litigation: Testimony Before the Joint Economic Committee of the U.S. Congress." Santa Monica, CA: The Rand Corp. Institute for Civil Justice, 1986.

Peterson, Mark, Syam Sarma and Michael Shanley, "Punitive Damages, Empirical Findings." Santa Monica, CA: The Rand Corp. Institute for Civil Justice, 1987.

Schroeter, Leonard W. And William J. Rutzick, "Tort Reform: Being an Insurance Company Means Never Having to Say You're Sorry." *Gonzaga Law Review*, Vol. 22, No. 1, 1986-87.

Taylor, Humphrey, Michael R. Kegay and Stuart Leichenko, "Public Attitudes Toward the Civil Justice System and Tort Law Reform, Conducted for Aetna Life and Casualty Co." New York: Louis Harris and Assoc., March, 1987.

Tipton, S. Victor, "Cases and Commentaries." *Academy of Florida Trial Lawyers Journal, No. 307.Tallahassee, FL, 1988.*

United States General Accounting Office, "Report to Congressional Requesters: Medical Malpractice, Characteristics of Claims Closed in 1984, GAO/HRD-87-55." Washington, D.C., April, 1987.

United States General Accounting Office, "Fact Sheet for the Chairman, House Committee on Ways and Means, Tax Policy: Financial Cycles in the Property/Casualty Industry, GAO/GGD-86-56FS." Washington, D.C., April, 1986.

United States General Accounting Office, "Report to Congressional Requesters: Medical Malpractice, Six State Case Studies Show Claims and Insurance Costs Still Rise Despite Reforms, GAO/HRD-87-21." Washington, D.C., December, 1986.

United States General Accounting Office, "Report to Congressional Requesters: Medical Malpractice, Insurance Costs Increased but Varied Among Physicians and Hospitals, GAO/HRD-86-112." Washington, D.C., September, 1986.

United States General Accounting Office, "Report to the Administrator, Health Care Financing Administration: Medicare, Reviews of Quality of Care at Participating Hospitals, GAO/HRD-86-139." Washington, D.C., September, 1986.

United States General Accounting Office, Comptroller General, "Report to the Chairman, Committee on Finance, United States Senate, Congress Should Consider Changing Federal Income Taxation of the Property/Casualty Insurance Industry, GAO/GGD-85-10." Washington, D.C., March 25, 1985.

United States General Accounting Office, "Report to Congressional Requesters: Medical Malpractice, No Agreement on 86-50." Washington, D.C., Feb. 1986.

United States General Accounting Office, "Report to Congressional Requesters: Insurance Profitability of the Medical Malpractice and General Liability Lines, GAO/GGD-87-67." Washington, D.C., July, 1987.

United States General Accounting Office, "Testimony, Profitability of the Medical Malpractice and General Liability Lines of Insurance, Statement of William J. Anderson, Assistant Comptroller General, General Government Programs, Before the Subcommittee on Commerce, Consumer Protection, and Competitiveness Committee on Energy and Commerce, House of Representatives, GAO/T-GGD-87-13." Washington, D.C., April 21, 1987.

United States General Accounting Office, "Report to the Secretary of Health and Human Services, Expanded Federal Authority Needed to Protect Medicare and Medicaid Patients from Health Practitioners Who Lose Their Licenses, GAO/HRD-84-53." Washington, D.C., May 1, 1984.

United States General Accounting Office, "Report to Congressional Requesters: Medical Malpractice, A Framework for Action, GAO/HRD-87-73." Washington, D.C., May, 1987.

Wilk, Chester A., "The Justice Department and Federal Trade Commission Must Do Their Job Now." Press Release, Chicago, IL, August 26, 1988.

ARTICLES

Reske, Henry J. "Was There a Liability Crisis?" *American Bar Association Journal*, January, 1989.

McGinn, Paul R. "M.D.-Owned Insurers Calling for Broad Reforms." *American Medical News*, June 10, 1988.

Farrell, Christopher. "Let the Free Market End Malpractice Warfare." *Business Week*, August 8, 1987.

Farrell, Christopher. "California Takes A Wrong Turn On Auto Insurance." *Business Week*, November 28, 1988.

Garland, Susan B., "Congress Puts Doctor-Owned Labs on the Examining Table." *Business Week*, August 29, 1988.

Garland, Susan B., "Health Insurance: AnyWay You Look At It Business Will Pay." *Business Week*, February 13, 1989.

Hamilton, Joan O'C., "Health Care Costs Take A Turn For The Worst." *Business Week*, October 31, 1988.

Hamilton, Joan O'C., "The Prognosis in Health Care: Critical and Getting Worse." *Business Week*, January 9, 1989.

Hamilton, Joan O'C., "High-Tech Health Care: Who Will Pay?" *Business Week*, February 6, 1989.

Tell, Lawrence J., "United They Stand—At the Defense Table." *Business Week*, May 30, 1988.

"The Manufactured Crisis: Liability Insurance Companies Have Created a Crisis and Dumped it on You." *Consumer Reports*, August, 1986.

Brownstein, Vivian. "Where All the Money Comes From." *Fortune*, January 2, 1989.

Hutton, Cynthia. "Greed Really Turns Me Off." *Fortune*, January 2, 1989.

Kirsch, Sandra L. "They Cleaned Our Clock." *Fortune*, January 2, 1989.

Newport, John Paul. "LBO's: Greed, Good Business—or Both?" *Fortune*,

January 2, 1989.

Kleinmann, Leanne. "Code Blue." *Health*, February, 1989.

"D.C. Bar May Relax Law Partnership Rules." *Insight on the News*, January 16, 1989.

Holzman, David. "Malpractice Crisis Therapies Vary." *Insight on the News*, December 12, 1988.

Holzman, David. "Medicine Minus a Cost Tourniquet." *Insight on the News*, August 8, 1988.

Holzman, David. "Rising Cost of Insuring Workers." *Insight on the News*, January 16, 1989.

Holzman, David. "Strong Medicine for Bad Doctors." *Insight on the News*, April 11, 1988.

Holzman, David. "When Profit is a Hospital's Lifeline." *Insight on the News*, November 21, 1988.

Hudson, Kathryn. "Breaking Down a Bar to Discipline." *Insight on the News*, January 9, 1989.

"Lawyers' PACs Boost Political Donations." *Insight on the News*, December 12, 1988.

"Lawyers' Starting Pay Biggest in Big Apple." *Insight on the News*, November 21, 1988.

Shear, Jeff. "Testing Whether Medicine is Right." *Insight on the News*, October 17, 1988.

Crane, Mark. "How Lawyers Pick the Doctors They'll Sue." *Medical Economics*, September 7, 1987.

Stevens, Carol. "Can the AMA Sell its Own Brand of Malpractice Reform?" *Medical Economics*, March 7, 1988.

Cebrabino, Frank. "Judge Hears Arguments in Bar's Gag Rule." *Miami Herald*, February 11, 1989.

Goudreau, Rosemary. "M.D.s Rejoice, Lawyers Seethe Over New Malpractice Statute." *Miami Herald*, February 6, 1988.

Schwedock, Peter S. "Insurance Firms Share Blame on Marks." *Miami Herald*, October 9, 1988.

Starita, Joe. "Insurance Mill Enriches Lawyers, Doctors; Public Ultimately Pays the Bill, Insurance Companies Say." *Miami Herald*, October 9, 1988.

Starita, Joe. "One Problem: Plaintiff Wasn't In Accident." *Miami Herald*, October 9, 1988.

Starita, Joe. "Back Treatment Was Wrong, Expert Says." *Miami Herald*, October 9, 1988.

Starita, Joe. "Memo to Marks Staff: Confusion to the Enemy." *Miami Herald*, October 9, 1988.

Starita, Joe. "Ex-Workers Disclose Lawyer's Practices." *Miami Herald*, October 17, 1988.

Starita, Joe. "Doctor Takes the Fifth in Accident Inquiry Suit." *Miami Herald*, November 13, 1988.

"Malpractice Suits: Doctors Under Siege." *Newsweek*, January 26, 1987.

Miller, Annetta, Elizabeth Bradburn and others, "Can You Afford to Get Sick?" *Newsweek*, January 30, 1989.

"Are Insurers Caught in a Squeeze or Putting it On?" New York *Times*, May 25, 1986.

Warshofsky, Fred. "A Cure for Doctors Who Are Hazardous to Your Health." *Reader's Digest*, January, 1987.

"Doctors Need Protection From Suit Happy Patients." *Rocky Mountain News*, April 18, 1988.

Chiang, Harriet. "State Bar Acts Against Head of Lawyer Group." *San Francisco Chronicle*, July 15, 1987.

"Amendment 10: Don't Cap Damages." *South Florida Business Journal*, October 17, 1988.

Myers, Laura. "Can Amendment 10 Cap Anguish of Physicians, Lawyers?" *South Florida Business Journal*, October 3, 1988.

Morrison, Michael. "Health Care—Why the Crisis?" *The Plain Truth*, March 1989.

Church, George J. "Sorry, Your Policy is Cancelled." *Time*, March 24, 1986.

Greenwald, John. "A Head-On Collision." *Time*, November 28, 1988.

Gup, Ted. "Health Care: Beyond Bromides." *Time*, October 31, 1988.

Lacayo, Richard. "The Malpractice Blues, Physicians and Attorneys Argue Over Who is to Blame." *Time*, February 24, 1986.

Rudolph, Barbara. "Where's the Limit? The Biggest Takeover Battle in History Raises Questions About Greed, Debt and the Well-being of American Industry." *Time*, December 5, 1988.

"The Debate: Swamped by Suits." *U.S.A. Today*, January 21, 1988.

Findlay, Steven. "Looking Over Doctors' Shoulder." *U.S. News and World Report*, January 30, 1989.

Silberner, Joanne. "When to Sue Your Doctor, Minimizing the Headaches of Malpractice Malaise." *U.S. News and World Report*, December 14, 1987.

Wiener, Leonard. "Will Your Car Coverage Vanish?" *U.S. News and World Report*, January 9, 1989.

Sandroff, Ronni. "How Safe Are Our Hospitals? We Rely on Hospitals for Quality Health Care, But Who Checks up on Our Doctors and Nurses?" *Vogue*, April, 1988.

"Talking to People in Coma." *Vogue*, April, 1988.

Hermann, Philip J. "Million-Dollar Verdicts and Other Rarities." *Wall Street Journal*, April 8, 1987.

Schmitt, Richard B. "Lawyers Face Major Push to Cap Fees, Insurers Lead California Effort on Restrictions." *Wall Street Journal*, August 26, 1988.

Shuchman, Miriam, and Michael Wiles. "Malpractice: The Doctors Blame the Lawyers, The Lawyers Blame the Doctors, and the Insurance Companies Say They're Losing Their Shirt." *Washington Post Magazine*, March 2, 1986.